VALUI

A
50
5/21

VALUING PEOPLE
Human Value in a World of
Medical Technology

D. Gareth Jones

paternoster
press

Copyright © 1999

First published in 1999 by Paternoster Press

05 04 03 02 01 00 99   7 6 5 4 3 2 1

Paternoster Press is an imprint of Paternoster Publishing,
P. O. Box 300, Carlisle, Cumbria, CA3 0QS, UK
www.paternoster-publishing.com

British Library Cataloguing in Publication Data
A catalogue for this book is available from the British Library

ISBN 0-85364-991-X

Cover Design by Mainstream, Lancaster
Typeset by WestKey Limited, Falmouth, Cornwall
Printed and Bound by MPG Books Ltd, Bodmin, Cornwall

Contents

Preface

Why write a book about the value we place on human beings? In these days when family values are emphasized on many fronts, the answer may appear obvious. But this is not the topic with which I am concerned. My starting point is biomedical technology and the many accomplishments of this form of technology, accomplishments that have revolutionized our daily lives, as well as our views of ourselves. However, before stating what this book is, it may be easier to state what it is not.

First, having co-authored *Medical Ethics* (Oxford University Press, 1997) I realized the need for a book that goes beyond that type of information, so this is not a textbook.

Second, it is not intended to be exhaustive in its coverage. I have felt able to concentrate more on issues at the beginning and end of human life, and I have said relatively little about clinical ethics.

Third, it is not a theological treatise, and it makes no attempt to provide a comprehensive analysis of biblical and theological contributions to thinking on the human person.

What then is it? It is a reflection of where I stand on a number of crucial matters dependent upon biomedical technology. This informs much of the debate, and my acceptance of many forms of technology also informs my whole approach.

I write as an evangelical Christian and as a scientist. More specifically, I am an anatomist, with interests in neurobiology, the human body and bioethics. In other words, I am both a scientist and a Christian, and my position and interests as a scientist influence where I come from. For this I make no apologies. Nevertheless, I also write firmly as one who is committed to the Bible as God's revelation of himself and his purposes.

My training as a scientist means that I take a polemic stance. I want people to think and be challenged. I am not out to alter people's thinking, unless they themselves become convinced that my position is more adequate than the one they hold. Above all I want people to take the Bible seriously, and to use it to inform their thinking on very difficult and complex issues. Although the Bible does not provide detailed answers in many of the areas with which I deal, it has exceedingly helpful insights for those who seek to follow Christ. This viewpoint will be discussed in detail.

This book is for *ordinary* people, not just for scientists, doctors, health care workers, pastors or counsellors. It is for all who want to think long and hard about the world around them, in this case the many forms of technology that affect our health, expectations, aspirations, and even our place in the world.

In some respects this book is a follow-up to two of my previous books *Brave New People* (IVP, 1984), and *Manufacturing Humans* (IVP, 1987). While those were about the artificial reproductive technologies, this one has a broader sweep. It deals only incidentally with those issues. Nevertheless, the status of the embryo cannot be overlooked, but neither can the status of the aged and demented, nor can genetic issues be bypassed. All are relevant to our experiences, and are part and parcel of our humanness.

The early material for this book was given as lectures; at New College Berkeley in the United States, and at a Hospital Chaplains Conference in New Zealand. Individual lectures have been given to a number of Christian Medical Fellowship meetings in various countries. Some parts of the book have appeared as articles in journals such as *Perspectives on Science and Christian Faith, Science and Christian Belief, Journal of the Christian Medical Fellowship, Triple Helix*, and *Freedom and Faith*; while parts of chapters 3 and 4 appeared in fuller form in *Manufacturing Humans*. To all who have provided feedback, I am very grateful. At many points I make my way through dangerous territory, and constructive feedback is always helpful.

A number of people have helped with various drafts of the book. Barbara Telfer helped enormously with editing and with numerous creative suggestions. To her I am especially grateful. I am also grateful to Carolyn Armstrong and Carolyn Jones for their help at various points.

The latter stages of the book were put together on the delightful Pacific island of Rarotonga in the Cook Islands, surrounded by enchanting and relaxing tropical scenery, and by the gurgling of my young granddaughter. Both parts of this scene bring to mind the wonder and joy of God's creation, the inestimable benefits of good health care, and the love and concern of young parents. All are essential if we are to accept that human life is a gift from God, a gift for each one of us, and a gift to be cherished and developed. Sadly, there is much around us to mar this gift, to demean and impoverish human life, and to devalue what should be of greatest value. This book is an attempt to open up just a few of these vistas, and to throw light on ways in which human life may be valued more.

Gareth Jones

One

Problems at the Edges of Life

Inconsistency

Louise and Brent are a young executive couple, who do their best to live consistent and helpful lives as Christians. They place a high priority on moral values, and take seriously the needs of those less fortunate than themselves. If asked, they would answer that they place a high value on human life. They treat their children in an exemplary fashion, and go out of their way to assist those in need; such as school children from a deprived suburb, or lonely neighbours requiring company and encouragement. Despite sympathizing with the suffering caused by famine they refuse to support aid agencies, their argument being that those in countries with endemic famine do not do enough to support themselves. Also, they are overwhelmed by the numbers involved and by what they see as the false religious priorities of such countries.

Another couple, Margaret and Bruce, a little older than Louise and Brent, also go out of their way to help those around them. A couple of years ago Margaret gave birth to a premature baby at 25 weeks gestation. Enormous efforts were made in a specialist unit to save the baby's life. These were successful, and four months later the baby came home to much rejoicing. The cost of £500,000 caused them no problems since they were so delighted with their child. Recently, they have become involved in the running of a nursing home for geriatrics, and are appalled by the costs involved in maintaining some of the patients with multiple catastrophic illnesses. They cannot justify these costs, and feel that less 'heroic' treatment should be made available to many of these patients.

These two scenarios take us into the lives and attitudes of two couples, both of whom take seriously their moral responsibilities. Neither couple dismisses any human being as unimportant, but at the same time they place different values on different human beings. Actually they are placing greater value on some individuals than on others. Louise and Brent place greater value on people in their neighbourhood than on those in developing countries. Margaret and Bruce think that the life of a premature baby (especially theirs) is worth more than the lives of the old and demented. They probably do not intend to do this, and if challenged may well deny that this is the case. They have probably not thought this matter through, and they may not be deliberately distinguishing between different groups of human beings; but their actions demonstrate their priorities.

As individuals, we tend to place a higher value on people close to us when compared to people distant from us – for instance, the members of our family or close friends, as opposed to those we hardly know. We also seem to place a greater value on people with lifestyles and aspirations similar to our own than on people with very different philosophies: we place a higher value on those who are like us rather than on those who are not like us. People who are healthy and contribute to society tend to be held in higher esteem and considered of more worth than people who are unhealthy, mentally retarded or senile. In the world at large, a consistently higher value is bestowed on those of one's own society or of similar societies than on those belonging to societies with fundamentally different religious or political philosophies, or even standards of living.

We live with paradoxes. We, in western societies, are able to live relatively comfortable lives while innumerable children in other parts of the world die each day of malnutrition. Vast sums of money are devoted to saving or prolonging the life of a single individual using sophisticated technological medicine, when other individuals in that same society are dying due to the lack of basic medical resources. Large numbers of prenatal deaths occur through induced abortion and yet the lives of a few very premature infants are salvaged by expending considerable medical and financial resources. Many societies are prepared to kill large numbers of citizens belonging to countries with different political philosophies, because maintenance of a particular way of life is thought more important than the lives of other human beings.

It is notoriously difficult to treat equivalently, people, or groups of people, who are different. Is there any way out of this predicament?

Who should be rescued?

Let's play a macabre game, unlikely and tantalizing perhaps, but surprisingly instructive. In this game, a fire has started in a building, various occupants are trapped inside, and we (as the rescuers) are only able to take out one occupant at a time. All are equally accessible, and it will take the same amount of time to rescue each occupant. Who are the occupants?

Occupant one – A middle-aged man who has a successful business employing 90 people. He is in good health and under normal circumstances would be expected to live for at least another 20 years.

Occupant two – An 85-year-old man suffering from Alzheimer dementia. He can no longer look after himself and is entirely dependent on his aging wife, whose health is beginning to suffer under the strain.

Occupant three – A healthy thirty-year-old pregnant woman into her sixth month of pregnancy, married and a lecturer in computer studies.

Occupant four – A healthy 38-year-old pregnant woman into her eighth month of pregnancy, living with a common-law husband and suspected of having links with an underground terrorist organization known for its bombing of civilian targets.

Occupant five – A fifteen-year-old girl who is a very gifted high school student.

Occupant six – A two-year-old boy who is severely mentally retarded and is being looked after by the fifteen-year-old girl.

In an ideal world everyone would be rescued, but in the situation facing us in this game this is not the case. We know that some will, in all probability, perish and we have to decide in what order we will rescue the occupants. This confronts the rescuers (which is us) with real choices. What approach will various rescuers take when confronted with these hideous possibilities?

Rescuer A thinks that all who are in danger should, if at all possible, be saved. For her, all human life is sacred and the lives of all human beings have absolute value. Choices between different lives should not be made, and every effort is to be expended to salvage every life in danger. In practice, all may not be saved but no one life is more important than any of the other lives. Under no circumstances will preference be shown to any of the occupants.

Rescuer B considers that every *innocent* human life is to be saved. Using this criterion, he has a problem with the pregnant woman who is a suspected insurgent. Since she has set out to jeopardize the welfare of the country, and since she has already been responsible for killing a number of ordinary citizens, he does not consider her to be innocent. If a choice has to be made between those who can and those who cannot be rescued, occupant four will be left till last. This rescuer still considers that all human life is of absolute value, but other factors have to be taken into account.

Rescuer C would like to be able to save all. However, she is well aware that this will not be possible in this situation, and is prepared to make choices. She accords the middle-aged man greater value than the aged man with Alzheimer's disease, she values more highly the fifteen-year-old girl than the two-year-old boy with severe mental retardation. She does not want to choose between the two pregnant women since two foetuses are dependent upon them, but if she has to choose she will make greater efforts to save the good citizen. These are intuitive decisions and do not provide an order of rescue from first to last. Her preference is to rescue occupants one, three, and five first in any order, and occupants two, four and six last (possibly occupant four before occupants two and six who have serious medical problems).

Rescuer D places greater moral value on *human beings* than on human life in general abstract terms, and she weighs up the respective merits of the people whose lives are at stake. For her occupants two and six are of less value than the others, as they are not whole persons in terms of their mental faculties. She views occupants three and four as one person each, since their foetuses are not persons with equal status to the adults. However, she also uses a second principle, one which places greater value on those who benefit the community. Hence, occupant one is rescued first, occupant three second, occupant five next, and then occupant four.

However we respond to the decisions of these would-be rescuers, they are all assessing the value of human beings in a serious manner. In an ideal world there may be no problems, but that is not the world we inhabit. On many occasions, all cannot be rescued and all humans cannot be treated equally. The rescuers in this instance want to do their best; they want to rescue everyone, but this is not always a viable option. None of the rescuers has any intention of downgrading human value, although their responses vary. Are all these responses Christian, or are only some acceptable to Christians?

How should Christians respond?

Should there be a fifth position, one that uses biblical language and employs biblical texts in support of it? A position based on biblical verses suggests that the writers of the Bible set out to solve the specific ethical dilemmas we encounter today. But was this their purpose, and if it was could they possibly have provided solutions to problems they had neither met nor thought about?

For some Christians, only two of the rescuers provide models for us today, namely, rescuers A and B, since these positions alone appear to place the greatest value on human life. They, therefore, enshrine *the* Christian stance. They represent the ideal in a world where the ideal is rarely encountered; for Christians who think like this, there is no room for the pragmatism of rescuers C and D. Yet other Christians find merit in the attitudes shown by rescuers C and D, finding in them important elements of realism and pragmatism. While these rescuers did not set out to devalue the worth of any of the occupants, they weighed up what to them were important factors and then set about to rescue those with the greatest potential contribution to human society.

Unfortunately, ethical debate is frequently polarized; the ideal and the pragmatic are seen as opposites. They represent 'rules' as against 'compromise', the 'what ought to be' against the 'what is'. The rules or 'what ought to be' approach emphasizes the ideal; that which should occur in a perfect world. This underlines absolute values, and looks to the theological truth that God has perfect standards for his creation, standards enshrined in the Ten Commandments. As a result, this approach frequently leads to rejection of many practices and lifestyles common within society. The alternative approach, the 'what is' approach, emphasizes the pragmatic, and recognizes that in a pluralist society many different ethical standards exist. This approach is an intensely practical one, its realism recognizing that on many occasions there are exceptions to the ideal and compromises have to be made. These have to be coped with by Christians living in a pluralist society. This second approach emphasizes the theological truth that we live in a fallen world and that we fail to live up to God's standards. It underlines the need for grace, mercy and compassion, when confronted by failure and sin. Both approaches have their dangers as well as their advantages, the danger of the 'what ought to be' approach being legalism; that of the 'what is' approach uncontrolled excess. Their respective emphases are absolute rules on the one hand, and no rules on the other.

This tension will emerge time and again within the biomedical arena, and it will repeatedly force us to face up to the value we place on human life. This may be the value we place on foetuses, or on badly damaged adults; or it may take the form of the costs of valuing human life. As in the rescue scenario, choices frequently have to be made. These may be choices between a foetus and its mother, between the treatment given to one patient against the needs of another patient, or between sacrificing some embryos in order to save other embryos in the future.

It is easy to limit discussion about the nature of a Christian contribution to the general level, that of placing absolute value on human life. This is the level of most sermons, where principles are sketched in outline but are not worked through and analysed in detail. This is no criticism of sermons, but it reminds us that ethical issues demand detailed answers, even when it is safer to avoid definitive conclusions. I am not pre-judging any answers at this early stage of the book, but am simply making the point that we shall have to tackle detailed issues in detailed ways. This, in turn, will demand a close look at how we work out appropriate Christian answers.

Before moving in that direction, let me make two observations. The first is that the responses of all four rescuers will be supported by Christians. Of course, different Christians will support different rescuers, but none of the responses is outside the boundaries of a Christian response. This observation by itself does not justify any of the responses; that will come later in the book. Consider this question: Are those Christians who adopt the positions of rescuers A or B being more faithful to the biblical revelation than those who adopt the positions of rescuers C or D? My answer will be that they are not, but my reasons for this will only become evident in due course.

The second observation is that many non-Christians occupy these same positions, in that they are found all the way from rescuer A's position to rescuer D's position. The overlap between Christians and others is considerable, and while there may be far more Christians who adopt an absolute stance against the taking of human life in some areas (for example, on abortion and euthanasia), the responses may be far more mixed in other areas (for example, concerning the amount of money to be spent on adopting preventive health policies, or in the design of roads or cars). What this suggests is that Christian positions are not nearly as predictable or homogeneous as sometimes thought. Does this mean that Christians have nothing significant or special to contribute to ethical debate within society? My reply to this question will be worked out in subsequent chapters. My contention will be that Christians have an enormous contribution to make to ethical debate within a pluralist society, but it may not always be the type of contribution some Christians expect.

Complexity and uncertainty

For some people the rescue scenario I have used is a distraction; it is only a game. This is not how things are in real life, which is not a game. I agree, we are not usually confronted by burning buildings, where we can make choices about who is and is not to be rescued. Nevertheless, an increasing number of public health systems throughout the world force on us precisely these choices. The details vary, but in societies where all cannot receive the treatment to which they are entitled or from which they could benefit, choices are being made every day. My game could easily be recast as a daily occurrence in public hospitals. We would like to treat everyone who might benefit, but there are not sufficient resources to go around. What then? Choices of one sort or another have to be made.

Alternatively, think of a scenario where those in danger include your seventeen-year-old child, a seven-month-old grandchild, and your spouse. Three other people are also at risk, very similar in status to those related to you but these people are strangers. How do you respond? Do you place those close to you at the top of your list of priorities, even though you know you are biased, and even though this is placing different values on people. In reality, you should not be in a position to choose, precisely because you are biased, but does this not leave us with an uneasy feeling? If all humans are of absolute value, and if all cannot be rescued or treated, how do we respond?

All I am saying at this point is that we have to have guidelines to assist us. If we reject the necessity for these, we are simply putting our heads in the sand, and hoping that the unpalatable problem will have disappeared when we next emerge from the sand. Unfortunately, it will still be there, still crying out for an answer.

The complex nature of bioethical issues poses a problem for Christians, who are used to looking to the Bible for answers to moral and spiritual questions. What sort of answers do we expect the Bible to provide with regard to bioethical issues? We may expect *precise answers* telling us exactly how to act in relation to individual patients. Or, we may expect *general pointers*, providing us with an overall framework within which to assess the situation of individual patients. In other words, different answers may lead in different directions.

I favour the latter position, with its goal of providing broader directions, within which the thinking and attitudes of Christian doctors, nurses, scientists, sociologists and counsellors can be developed. I become very wary when general principles are put forward as though they are specific directives of relevance to every individual in every situation. For instance, there is a major difference between the general principle that 'I am in favour of preserving human life', and the decision about 'what I should do in *this specific* situation *now*'.

Many long for certainty and for unequivocal guidance over what to believe and how to act. They also expect this guidance to remain unchanged from one year to the next. Our major beliefs about God and Christ have been worked out over many hundreds of years and we cannot expect similar firm guidance on matters that have only been debated for 20 to 30 years or hardly at all. In these instances, uncertainty or even a change of viewpoint on some detailed bioethical matter may be quite acceptable; it may not be a mark of unfaithfulness, but rather of openness to a growing understanding and maturity within the Christian community. We are all learning, and we must be prepared to admit this.

These are crucial matters for Christians, since they can so easily lead to division within the body of Christ. They also need to be seen in perspective. The broad principles, on which there is little if any division of opinion, are the truly crucial ones. And for me, one of the most significant ones is the realization that each individual person and patient is an icon (or image) of God. This does not solve all medical (or any other) ethical problems, but it is a salutary reminder that we are treading on holy ground as we interact with people, and especially with people in need.

General as this icon perspective is, it introduces an equality between health professional and patient, that undergirds all forms of treatment and clinical relationships. It also questions important facets of the hierarchical structure of clinical practice in hospitals. From a Christian point of view it is perhaps the major undergirding of ethical practice, and one to which I shall return.

Writing as a scientist and a Christian

In the preface I stated that my approach is that of an evangelical Christian and a scientist. This is an important statement, since it has a major influence on my approach to the issues in this book. But should I admit to this? Does being a scientist affect what I believe and how I act as a Christian? Does it influence my attitudes in secular ways? These are important questions, since my approach to the crucial issues encountered at the beginning and end of human life may have been affected detrimentally by living year after year in a scientific environment. Functioning as I do each day with secular thought forms rather than theological ones, may have exposed me to unhealthy secular influences and therefore may have blighted my approach to embryos and people with severely damaged brains. In addressing these possibilities, I shall first consider some of the important characteristics of my approach as a scientist.

A *first* characteristic is that I am always enquiring and searching, and this inevitably influences my Christianity. I am prepared to ask awkward questions, and to think the unthinkable. I do this repeatedly as a scientist, and inevitably I do it as a Christian. For some people this is dangerous in the extreme, because they see it as placing the whole of the Christian faith in jeopardy, but for me it is nothing of the sort. Nothing is above analysis and assessment, just as nothing is above questioning in any true scientific realm. I have done this ever since I became a Christian, and I can see no reason why I will not continue to do it. It is basic to what I am as a Christian. But this does not mean I have ended up with a watered-down faith. Faith grows as it is exposed to challenges, whether these be in the form of suffering or hardships, or by being challenged intellectually.

From this follows a *second* characteristic, and this is that I consider it a privilege to spend my working days in the midst of people who are also scientists and academics. Most of these do not accept the basic tenets of the Christian faith, and some will argue cogently against it. The importance of this is that I should understand my Christianity as well as I understand my science. Since my scientific interests include the organization of the brain from its very first glimmerings in early development through to maturity, old age and dementia, as well as a range of issues surrounding the dead human body, it is imperative that I attempt to view these areas from a Christian perspective. In doing this, I am both fascinated by these issues and committed to the worthwhileness of science as a means of providing an understanding of them. My science is not an optional extra but a God-given opportunity to probe the secrets of the human body and brain.

A *third* characteristic of science is its search for truth, and the importance of honesty and openness in this search. Unfortunately, this has taken a battering over recent years as increasing instances of fraud and deception in science have come to the fore. Nevertheless, there is no getting away from these prime requirements of the scientific endeavour. When I embark on a scientific project I do not know precisely where I will end up, and this is something I bring with me into ethical debate. I operate within well-defined parameters, but the details may well be unknown.

This leads to a *fourth* characteristic: the importance of change. Scientists are always on the lookout for new ideas, for new ways of doing things, and for new ways of expressing what they think or believe. I find that I am not content with what sufficed 20 or 30 years ago, although this does not mean I throw every central truth overboard. I have not done this, and I have no intention of doing so, but it does force me to assess what is of lasting value as opposed to what is transient and ephemeral. Are some ways of behaving more dependent on cultural attitudes than on biblical teaching? Why do we believe *this* rather than *that*, and is *this* as biblical as we might fondly have imagined? If not, dispense with it, whatever former generations may have thought. The biblical Christian should rely only on serious Bible study, rather than readily accept the views of the local pastor or the international Christian guru. See how far Scripture takes us, and admit that this may not answer some of our very specific questions in biology or medicine. Then act as a person of integrity, dealing honestly with the limited data, speculating if need be, but always acknowledging when you are speculating.

Any decent scientist will demonstrate a free spirit of enquiry, which surely should be a characteristic of all Christians, but especially those who are scientists by training. Christians should love the truth, and should do everything to ensure that both their beliefs and lifestyles are based on it. We should be ready to admit when we are wrong and ready to correct error (especially in ourselves). Scientists who are true to their craft have an aversion to dogmatism, and this is an important feature of the Christian character as well.

Implicit in all these characteristics is yet another one, and this is that scientists are not content with being vague and waffly. They want precision and detail. After all, they formulate hypotheses or ideas which they then set about testing and disproving. While it would be unrealistic to think that scientists act like this in every area of their lives, if they are consistent in their thinking they will tend to be logical and precise. This has enormous implications in the inevitably murky areas at both ends of human life, where it is all too easy to be vague. Scientific precision abhors such vagueness. It should come as no surprise then that I aim for precision, no matter how tentative that precision may sometimes have to be.

No scientists worthy of their salt set themselves up as infallible authorities. All ideas and views are open to being tested and revised. Neither should I as a Christian set myself up as an infallible authority. There is only one authority and that is Christ, to whom I am always to be subject and from whom I am always to learn. When Christians disagree, we have to admit that our interpretation of Scripture may be wrong and our dependence on the Holy Spirit may be inadequate. As a scientist I have little difficulty with this crucial concept.

Scientists like myself have a legitimate contribution to make to debate at the interface of science and theology, and the realm of the embryo is no exception; neither is the realm of the brain-dead individual or of the patient with severe Alzheimer's disease. The Christian church should welcome such contributions even if it sometimes finds them difficult to handle. All I am doing here is raising what I consider to be important areas for discussion, thought and prayer.

The perilous contribution of scientists

Scientists tend to refuse to accept superficial answers, and people like me spend much time in intellectual territory where many Christians are not prepared to go. Why don't I give simple, uncontroversial answers with which no conservative Christian would disagree? The answer is simple. I believe I have been called into these realms of intense cultural disquiet, where I am to integrate my faith and learning. As a human anatomist, with a particular interest in the brain, as well as in human development and aging, these are the areas where I am to spend most of my efforts at integration. I am to be prepared to give an answer to anyone who asks me how I live as a biomedical scientist and a Christian.

I have never been satisfied by those who appear to keep their science and their faith in watertight compartments. Far too many in my experience are first-rate scientists and sincere Christians, but appear to be able to live with a vast chasm between the two. Then there are others who are interested in the relationship between Christianity and science, but the debate in which they are interested is one that does not involve their own area of science. The trouble here is that their scientific expertise does not inform the faith/learning dialogue. It also allows them to be highly critical of scientists in branches of science other than their own, as though they themselves are not scientists at all. It also means they are able to function in their own scientific areas in secular ways.

What is required is that our faith influences our science and our science influences our faith, as long as our faith is firmly controlled by a biblical ethos. Some will be alarmed at a statement like this, since it smacks of a relativistic faith. However, I would make a similar statement about accountants, shop assistants, school teachers, or counsellors. Integration of our faith with any aspect of human existence and experience has its dangers. On the other hand, lack of integration leaves our Christianity isolated from ordinary life; its purity may go unchallenged, but its ability to inform and transform daily existence is limited. And surely, Jesus was striving for integration when he recounted his parables of the light and salt, the wheat and tares, the talents, and the unscrupulous servant, and when he urged his followers to be in the world but not of it. This is how he himself lived when he mingled unashamedly with the outcasts of respectable society.

Christians who are in science and who take both their science and faith very seriously, are not the most comfortable people to have around in the church. To some they appear like the outcasts of respectable religious society, not because they are any less faithful than others, but because they are (or should be) the questioning and prodding members of the church. To some this appears dangerous. For me, this is a mark of health and vitality.

The remaining chapters of this book will question and prod, not because I like doing so but because there is no escape from questioning and prodding in the uncertain areas at the start and end of human existence. Some might interpret some of my suggestions as perilous and dangerous. Bear with me; I long as much as anyone to get to the bottom of the mysteries and perplexities represented by brain birth, the early embryo, the persistent vegetative state, the significance of fertilization, and the potential of gene therapy. My Christianity as much as my science pushes me to take these realms seriously.

Two

Biomedical Technology:
Help or Hindrance?

Setting the scene

An epitaph

Sacred to the memory of Anne, only daughter of George Finch Esq of Valentines in Essex. An excellent person, well natured, discreet and vertuous, most affectionately beloved by her relations and most justly esteemed by all that knew her. It pleased God to visit her with a tedious and severe illness, which (though in the flower of her age and blessed with a plentiful fortune) she bore with great evenness and constancy. She prepared herself by frequent and fervent devotion for her dissolution which she waited for with such pious resignation as manifested her heart to be affected with the power of religion and the well-grounded hopes of a blessed eternity. Her life being the more desirable. In that the first real occasion of grief she gave her sorrowful mother was her death.

These words written in 1713 on a headstone in Bath Abbey in England undoubtedly reflect very genuine, pious feelings. The question is, do they reflect a more virtuous and godly approach than ours, or has medicine opened up a new world which demonstrates more of what it means to be created in the image of God? Could present-day medicine have been Anne Finch's saviour?

Directly relevant to modern medicine is the following quotation from Oliver O'Donovan's book *Begotten or Made?*

Medical technique has been shaped and developed with the intention of fulfilling aspirations for freedom, freedom in this case from the necessities imposed upon us by our bodily nature. But not until recently . . . has society ventured to think that medical technique ought to be used to overcome not only the necessities of disease but also the necessities of health . . . The old conception of medicine as a collaborative enterprise, in which doctor and patient each have freedoms and responsibilities, can no longer be sustained . . . Christians should . . . acknowledge that there are limits to the appropriateness of our 'making'. These limits will not be taught us by compassion, but only by the understanding of what God has made, and by a discovery that it is complete, whole and satisfying . . . Technique must have its sabbath rest. (pp. 6, 10 & 12)

These words, written in 1984, are part of a severe critique of modern medicine. Condemnation of modern medicine, in this instance, stems from an assumption that it has become part of an inevitable process of social change that holds out great dangers for humanity. O'Donovan considers that medical technology has betrayed its heritage of humility and has been transformed into a means of manipulating human nature. This is *medicine as destroyer*.

These two pictures, those of saviour and destroyer, represent two extremes. In spite of this, they have one feature in common, and this is *control*. Any effective medical procedure, just like any effective scientific development, will only be effective if it is capable of exerting control over previously uncontrolled forces. There is no medicine worthy of the name without control. The tragedy of Anne Finch in 1713 could only have been averted by understanding and subsequent control. Medicine as saviour is medicine the controller.

The opposite end of the spectrum also centres on control, this time the perception that medicine is exerting too much control. The control of individuals' health, social aspirations or self-determination is regarded by some as excessive; it is misdirected control. Such misdirected control is viewed as manipulation, since implicit within it is the quest for freedom from natural limits. Sometimes even such aspirations as the freedom not to suffer are condemned, since they are regarded as aberrant control.

The question of control cannot be avoided, which is hardly surprising since control is a manifestation of what we are as human beings made in the image and likeness of God. I want to consider a number of illustrations of control from medical practice, remembering that the crucial question is 'Does the control exerted by today's medicine and medical technology make it a saviour or destroyer?'

A hierarchy of control

A general practitioner prescribes antibiotics for a patient with a respiratory tract infection. The patient is restored to health due to administration of a short course of drugs to combat the infection and the body returns to its original healthy condition.

A general surgeon treats a patient with appendicitis. The patient presents with an inflamed appendix, and the doctor removes the appendix. All proceeds smoothly, and the patient is discharged minus her appendix. Although the change is a simple one, the patient has been modified by utilizing the doctor's expertise. Without such interventionary control the patient would have died; instead she resumes life to its full capacity.

An orthopaedic surgeon is confronted by a patient with arthritis affecting a hip joint. It is chronic and serious, the patient is in pain, and her mobility is being seriously affected. A decision is taken to replace the hip joint with a prosthesis; the patient has an artificial joint inserted. This functions well, the patient is satisfied, and the surgery is considered successful. This has been accomplished, not only by removing something diseased but by replacing it with something artificial, the aim of which is to mimic the functioning of a healthy joint. This has only been made possible by an array of technological achievements, all of which point to human control of a highly technological nature.

An oncologist confronted by a patient with a carcinoma of the descending colon, decides to remove the colon and rectum and provide the patient with a colostomy. In this instance, not only has the doctor removed something, but she has also created a means of functioning that does not exist under normal circumstances. From now on the patient will function in an 'unnatural' manner; and this has only been made possible by considerable understanding of the physiology of the gastrointestinal tract and by a wide range of surgical and allied abilities. This is control of a high order.

All these illustrations point to the legitimate use of the powerful abilities of medical technology to restore health. It demonstrates how fortunate we are in terms of what can be done by medical professionals. In spite of the high degree of control underlying these particular operations and in spite of the considerable modification and manipulation inherent within a couple of them, we are grateful for the doctors' expertise. These responses are valid ones and, in principle, are exemplary in both Christian and ethical terms. These operations are to be commended rather than condemned, because they are good examples of ways in which human responsibility and control are to be exercised. In Christian terms, our emphasis is on health professionals acting as God's agents, as they make use of God-like abilities. I doubt whether we ever depict these operations as examples of doctors acting in rebellion against God.

But have we got it all wrong? The potential benefits to the individuals may have been gained at too great a cost. It may be that developments like these will have a negative impact on society in the future; they may be detrimental. Let us, therefore, look at some additional illustrations as we explore possible dangers of medical control, and as we move into less-clear territory.

The entry of ambivalence

A vascular surgeon operates on a frail elderly patient to repair an aortic aneurysm. A few days later it is necessary to operate for the second time as adhesions have formed. Following this the patient is placed in intensive care; he is very fragile. Added to this there is disagreement between the surgical and intensive care teams on appropriate treatment. On the other hand, the patient's wife wants no further 'heroic' measures to be undertaken. In spite of this, the surgeon undertakes a third operation for further adhesions. The patient dies shortly after surgery.

Is the vascular surgeon manifesting God-like characteristics or exhibiting unwarranted control? It is easy to appreciate that there will be differences of opinion at a professional level, but we also have to ask something more fundamental. In undertaking a further operation, was the vascular surgeon acting in his or her own interests and not in the interests of the patient? We do not know, although it is probably a mixture of both: partly God-likeness and partly unwarranted (or at least ambivalent) dominion. For finite and sinful beings, it is impossible to extricate the one completely from the other; hence, the existence of ethical dilemmas where we are at a loss to know which course of action is for the best.

What this last illustration demonstrates is that biomedical technology does not have the simplistic moral facade sometimes attributed to it. Its accomplishments stem from the power it bestows on humans to alter the course of nature, a course that in the examples given so far is a pathological one. The natural course of events is frequently supplanted by an artificial course, one that breaks the patient free from a natural limit, albeit the limit of disease. There may well be no problem here, since the triumph of medical technique up to this point has been a triumph over disease, and over the evils and suffering of disease. This is generally recognized as a good, fitting as it does within traditional Christian expectations of medical practice. It is a part of God's general providence, and his desire that the whole of creation should be redeemed from the turmoil and despair of evil – even if temporarily in these instances.

And yet, this illustration provides us with uncertainty. Even the mission of healing has limits, and biomedical technology as saviour has to be treated with immense caution. But who or what are we talking about? Is it the vascular surgeon who is saviour, or is it the technology that is saviour? There seems little doubt it must be the surgeon, the human being with all the technological gadgetry at his or her disposal. Whatever problems we encounter with technology are human problems about the ways in which ordinary people wish to utilize the technology.

This illustration is also a very unclear one, with its tension between what surgery might have accomplished (if the patient had lived for a few weeks or months longer), and the actual failure of the surgery in this particular instance. In other words, the outcome was an uncertain one, and doctors with different perspectives disagreed. Even had it been successful in the short-term, the long-term prospects for the patient would still have been dubious. And this introduces what I shall call a 'time dimension'. A few years ago, no one would have contemplated this series of operations, and some years into the future the short-term success rate will probably be much higher than today. In other words, technology is changing, and the technological changes are inevitably accompanied by changing ethical, social, and perhaps even theological, perspectives. Frequently, it is not a question of saviour *or* destroyer, but saviour *and* destroyer with the balance between the two sides of the equation in continuous flux. At one point in time the destroyer element may outweigh the saviour element, whereas later on the reverse may hold. Not only this, the destroyer element usually predates the saviour element.

Two forms of control

A patient is in a persistent vegetative state. It is now six months since the automobile accident, that resulted in

*severe damage to the higher centres of her brain. In normal
clinical terms the chances of recovery to any sort of meaningful human existence are nil. She is in her present state
because of a high degree of biomedical control when she
was first brought into hospital, in that her life was saved at
that time by intensive resuscitation. Enormous efforts were
employed to sustain her life and combat illness, and they
were partially successful. Since then she has been sustained
by excellent nursing, by artificial feeding, and by treating
infections as they arise. She could continue in this state for
some years. There is ethical ambivalence on the merits of the
short-term treatment that saved her life in the first place,
and on continuing to keep her alive in the knowledge that
she will never again manifest any of the marks of human
personhood. The medical and nursing staff want all forms
of artificial assistance discontinued; her parents wish it to be
continued indefinitely.*

One of the crucial questions here is whether the medical profession acted as God's agent in sustaining this life initially,
and whether it is continuing to do so through artificial feeding. Is human control being exerted by *continuing* to use the
technology (including artificial feeding), or by *discontinuing*
it?

The reality here is that there is no way of avoiding some
form of control. To have refrained from investigating emergency treatment in the first instance would itself have been an
example of control – deciding against using the technology at
one's disposal, on the ground that it would not be in the
patient's long-term interests. Alternatively, to commence
treatment and then later decide that existence in a persistent
vegetative state is meaningless in human terms, and therefore
discontinue treatment, is yet another form of control. One
way or another, there is no escape from serious decision-
making.

What are we to make of the role of technology in this
instance? Could an initial decision to refrain from using the
technology be described as saving the patient, when it would
have led to her early death? It may have saved her parents from

future distress, but it is difficult to describe this as serving her. A non-technological response in this instance, therefore, would not have constituted a saviour-like function, although it may equally not have been serving a destroyer-like function.

Let us ask a different question then. Can we talk about 'natural limits' in this case? It would be easy to argue that the limits of nature would have been death shortly after the accident: nothing should have been attempted; no technology should have been used, and no ethical problems would have arisen later. This is fine, but it does not sit easily alongside other perceptions we have of the medical enterprise. To refrain from using the technology at one's disposal is not an ethically neutral stance; it is a definitive ethical statement that almost certain death is preferable to life, especially if the life may be compromised. The essence of the ethical decision is to determine how compromised the future life is likely to be, and then in the light of that judgement to decide what technology – if any – should be used. The technology itself is not dismissed out of hand, but its usefulness or otherwise is assessed in the light of the patient's condition and bearing in mind the known efficacy of the technology in similar situations. The ambivalence of the technology stems from its limitations, and not from its terrifying power.

If the patient lapses into a persistent vegetative state, the technology and the human judgement have proved inadequate. Any decisions that must now be taken stem from this inadequacy. Let us remember, though, that this is far more the inadequacy of human finiteness than it is of human sin, as long as basic ethical principles have been followed. The medical staff have failed to combat the extent and nature of nervous system damage; they have been beaten, and the technology at their disposal has not proved sufficiently powerful.

What are we to make of this? Is it arrogant to work towards attaining a level of technology sufficient to overcome extensive brain damage? Or is the longing to do this part of a legitimate desire to overcome the evil of accidents and illness, themselves part of the greater desire to subdue destructive forces within the environment? Humans, as those who image God, are creative, rational beings, who long to go beyond that which they have previously achieved, especially when this involves overcoming that which is evil and destructive. They are thus like their creator, and it is in this capacity that they long to do that which they have never previously accomplished. In this spirit, technology occupies a rightful place within a Christian perspective. The danger lies in expecting too much of it, in not knowing when to accept its limitations and inadequacies, and in failing to realize when we are transgressing the boundaries of legitimate human endeavour.

Underlying all these illustrations is an immense degree of human control, without which there would be no modern medicine as we know it. It is control that can be used to good effect; it is control that can go abysmally wrong. However, this is integral to what we are as human beings, and to the mistakes we make and the errors of judgement to which we are prone. It also stems from the ease with which we sometimes put arrogance ahead of the good of others, including the good of patients and of the weak and disadvantaged. And, inevitably, there are genuine ethical conundrums where we do not know which course of action is the most consistent with established ethical principles.

Dubious control

A couple is healthy in every respect, except for their infertility caused by blockage of the wife's uterine tubes. Microsurgery has been carried out to correct the blockage, but this proved unsuccessful. They enter an in vitro fertilization (IVF) program where eight embryos were produced, and six have been used. Those six have resulted in two children. The couple do not want any more children and so a decision has been mutually agreed upon concerning the disposal of the two remaining embryos.

Here, medicine's control has moved beyond that concerned solely with bypassing the infertility, since it has resulted in the production of additional human embryos that are not required by the couple concerned. Is this an example of straying beyond medicine's traditional role of dealing only with ill health, or can infertility be classed as ill health? And what about the unwanted embryos? Was their production an example of medical technology as a destroyer of human integrity, or were they an inevitable end result of a legitimate technological process?

We are being presented with the problems of medical technology as usually depicted. It is claimed by some that correction of a physical defect, blocked uterine tubes in this case, is acceptable, but bypassing that same defect via IVF and the production of human embryos in the laboratory is not acceptable, or at least is tinged with profound ambiguities. It is not my intention to minimize the differences between these two positions; what I am concerned with is to ask whether the differences throw any light on the role of medical technology in these matters. Whatever the differences are, they are not technological differences.

Both microsurgery and IVF require technological expertise, since without such expertise, neither would be feasible. At present both approaches are relatively unsuccessful, and both place human embryos at risk. Not only this, but the success rate of both will be increased by better technology. It is difficult to argue, then, that in one of them technology poses no moral peril, whereas in the other it is morally dangerous and an unnerving form of illicit human control. That conclusion can only be arrived at by introducing many other viewpoints, such as the inseparability of procreation and sexual intercourse, and the full humanity of human embryos. Whatever they do or do not mean, these ideas have nothing to do with technology.

Some argue that the ability of technology to interfere with embryonic development and to manipulate embryos goes beyond the legitimate bounds of human control. For them, this is dangerous territory we should not be exploring, opening up as it does innumerable avenues in gene therapy, genetic manipulation, and even eugenics (see Chapter 8). It is said that we lack the wisdom to deal morally with such areas, even if we develop the scientific expertise to change and control future life forms. As sinful beings, we misuse such developments far more readily than we wisely use them; we destroy others rather than build them up and provide for their legitimate needs.

These criticisms are based on the assumption that no form of embryonic manipulation should ever be undertaken, and yet reasons are not usually given for drawing a line at this point (see Chapter 7). After all, if it could be demonstrated that a particular form of manipulation will benefit the embryo in question (gene therapy, say), why proscribe it? I am not underestimating the many possible dangers with gene therapy (see Chapter 8), but it does show that drawing lines like this is very arbitrary. Placing the embryo off-limits to manipulation cannot be justified in terms of excessive human control. Opposition to manipulating embryos stems from arguments such as the lack of consent, the unacceptability of destroying embryos non-therapeutically, or dangers inherent in the techniques themselves. Any proposal for a moratorium on research (or even therapy) using human embryos stands or falls on the nature of these arguments and not on the unacceptability of technological procedures.

A different area of medical technology is that of contraception and abortion. First, consider a healthy woman using a contraceptive pill (a hormonal preparation which prevents the occurrence of fertilization) which can only be obtained by a doctor's prescription. It seems that here medicine is serving a purely social role. Is this an instance of medicine as saviour or medicine as destroyer? Even if it is acting as saviour where *fertility* is a problem, its use is unrelated to moral considerations. This is medicine as technique; it is medicine divorced from any moral framework.

What, then, about abortion in which medical procedures are employed to destroy foetal life? For many commentators this is medicine in its most obvious guise as destroyer; in part, this is true – foetal life is destroyed. But the mother's life may be saved, or enormous problems may be alleviated, or a tragic, painful and short-lived infant's life may be averted. Even in this very extreme situation the balance between destruction and salvation may not be as clear-cut as sometimes thought. The balance becomes even more unclear when tissues from the aborted foetus are transplanted into severely ill children or adults (see Chapter 11). The transplantation is an example of medicine as saviour, even if the abortion is viewed as medicine as destroyer. Enormous care has to be exercised to ensure that the destructive function is not carried out *in order* to facilitate the saviour-like function.

Both contraception and abortion demonstrate how medicine may serve a social role, destroying one form of human life in order to save, or at least assist, another human; or using the end result of destruction in order to help another. Here we walk a tightrope between the alleviation of disease and social engineering. However, this is not a clear-cut choice generally – elements of both are involved. Is there any escape from this? Is it possible to place medical technology in a 'disease' compartment, and isolate it completely from the rest of life?

If this were possible, it would solve many of the increasingly severe problems encountered by medicine that has at its disposal very sophisticated technology. However, this in turn, assumes that disease and health can be separated into watertight boxes, something that is only possible when medicine is viewed as a technologically based discipline. In reality, disease and health overlap far more than this rigidly circumscribed model suggests, and human well-being is far more than a mere absence of overt pathology. Surely, this is what any Christian perspective would lead us to, with its emphasis on wholeness, on right relationships with others and with God, and on appropriate priorities in every area of life.

How, then, are we to view practices such as hormonally based contraception and abortion? The temptation of a non-technological world in which these were not possible with the efficiency known today is to say, 'Look what medical technology has to answer for'. Apart from the appalling one-sidedness of such an analysis, it demonstrates a longing for a primitive, uncontrolled state of pseudo-bliss, in which the forces of nature are elevated and human responsibility is denigrated. This is the antithesis of a Christian response with its emphasis on human control and human responsibility, and an awareness of human finiteness and human sinfulness.

There is no means of averting the ethical problems posed by high technology contraception and abortion. While they should never be approached as technological issues alone, the only decision-making of consequence is to determine how to use the technology in a way that affirms human value and human dignity. To decry the availability of the technology is neither especially ethical nor especially Christian.

As human beings created in God's image we have to guide and direct all forms of technology, and we also have to argue for its rightful place within our societies. However, the problems surrounding modern medicine are immense, and some of them are shaking the foundations of our societies.

A community in transition: from hope to despair

Here are three word-pictures that provide a rough glimpse into an imaginary community and its dependence upon medical services. The details are not important; what is important is their thrust.

Picture one
Consider a community in which there is no sophisticated medicine of any description, and not much knowledge of public health measures. Most people die by the age of 40, and two out of three infants die before they are one-year-old. The community survives at a fairly basic level, and is very much in touch with nature, the elements, and religious forces. Much of the ill health is ascribed to the actions of local gods, and any good health and survival are put down to propitious forces around them.

Picture two
This is the same community some 30 years later. Western influences are now being felt, various medical and surgical procedures are available to the people, and public health measures are being instigated. Life expectancy has now risen to around 60 years, and one out of three infants die before they are one. The people are grateful for these very definite changes, and those who are Christian (due to the presence of Christian missionaries) are grateful to God for what has happened. Life is no longer mere subsistence; it can be enjoyed and the skills of the people can begin to

flourish. The community has been transformed beyond recognition.

Picture three
It is another 50 years further into the future, and the same community is now a far larger one. It has numerous contacts with other similar communities and with the world at large. High technology medicine is now widely available and practised within it. Most people expect to live to about seventy-five years, and only 1 in 50 infants die in their first year of life. The people are healthy, although they are afflicted by typical western disease patterns. They now look to medicine for health and vigour, and relatively few of them see any relevance of God, or indeed of any religious ideals at all. They have become dependent upon medical (and many other forms of) technology, so much so that their horizons have become restricted by the prowess and limitations of biomedical technology. In materialistic ways, the community has a great deal, but in spiritual matters it gives the impression of being impoverished. It is somewhat lost, and ill at ease.

These word-pictures point out a few salutary lessons about our own societies – where they have come from, and where they are going. And in doing this, they also begin to show how close is the relationship between medical abilities and our view of both ourselves and the human enterprise. Medicine never operates in a vacuum; it is the product of its society which, in turn, it helps to mould.

Would it have been better had these developments not occurred, or if only some of them had taken place? I accept that the numerous revolutionary changes brought about by medicine have, on the whole, served human welfare. I have no doubt that the situation depicted in picture two is far preferable to that depicted in picture one. However, scientific and medical advances are capable of destroying as well as benefiting human aspirations, and this is where the problems highlighted by picture three come into focus. What this tells us is that, in order to serve human welfare, medical advances require direction and wise control. If these are not provided, medical technology may reach a stage where it could cause more problems than it solves. Of course, the advantages and disadvantages affect different aspects of life, and so finding a balance is not easy.

To what extent are the dignity and worth of human beings elevated or destroyed by technology? Do we inevitably become subservient to technology, so that the loss of human and spiritual values is inevitable within a technological society? The emphasis of this chapter has been on the central role of responsible control, without which technology may assume a dynamism and rationale of its own. Is responsible control possible by beings who are self-centred and who so often seek to manipulate technology for their own sinful ends? Is there a point at which technology works against Christian goals?

It is in response to questions of this type that Christians with differing perspectives come into conflict. For some, there is no hope in a technological world (especially one dependent on biomedical technology), which is viewed as standing in fundamental opposition to the Christian world-view. This is a position of *theological despair*, since Christians are to despair at the direction already taken and likely to be taken in the future in the biological and medical areas. Developments in these spheres will lead to the manipulation of humans in ways that will detract from their God-likeness. Generally, those with this position view technology inconsistently, since they accept its validity in non-medical spheres. These include spheres where the implications for human value are considerable, as in dependence upon weapons with immense destructive power, or in automobiles that lead to death and injury of untold numbers worldwide.

An alternative position is that of *theological caution*. This stance does not pretend that technology will lead to an idealistic, brave new world, but it accepts that technology can be harnessed for good as much as anything else in society can be harnessed for good. People with this position are also aware that technology can be harnessed for evil, and that the good and evil emanating from any technological application are always intertwined. Nevertheless, technology is no more misleading than any other facet of the human endeavour. They are all components of a world in conflict.

Such a position is far removed from a third position, that of *theological optimism*, according to which technological achievements play an integral role in achieving some form of new world order. This is best illustrated by referring to the potential in some forms of genetic technological advances where emphasis is on creating more intelligent, more attractive, and stronger human beings. For me, this is idealism out of control, and of little interest for Christians.

Theological caution refuses to lose sight of the crucial importance of human value. Under no circumstances are the dignity, worth and autonomy of human beings to be sacrificed to technological imperialism; rather, all technology is to be directed towards upholding the value of humans as people created by God for his purposes. The direction taken by technology is totally dependent on either the responsibility or irresponsibility of people. Christians are to ensure, as far as they are able, that it is used to help people to improve their health and living standards and so make them better able to develop their potential as people created in the image and likeness of God.

Technology at the ends of human life

The position of theological caution is very much the position of the scientist/Christian, with the optimism of the scientific endeavour tempered by the Christian's far more pessimistic assessment of human nature as being in opposition to God. It is the scientist in me that leads me to question a theologian's stance in the guise of Oliver O'Donovan's critique. But by the same token it is the theologian in me that leaves me very uneasy by the bland allurements of rampant technological imperialism.

As a Christian I am immensely grateful for so many of the scientific advances in the medical arena; this is technology at its best. Nevertheless, both basic biomedical science and its many technological applications in medicine do not exist in a spiritual and moral vacuum. Neither do they only exist in situations where the advances are going to be welcomed by everybody. Technological advances will occur in every domain, including those at the beginning and end of human life, and it is to these that we have to turn. However, before we do this it is essential to investigate some biblical foundations, because these constitute my starting point as a Christian.

Three

Biblical Foundations

Unhelpful approaches

It is relatively easy to expect simple 'yes/no' answers to ethical conundrums. I am not suggesting there are never clear 'rights' and 'wrongs'. There are. For instance, God says 'no' to killing. But this raises the question of what we mean by killing when immersed in some of the contemporary bioethical quandaries. It is easy to apply this 'no' to some procedures (for example, opposition to induced abortion), but refuse to discuss what 'no' might amount to in other procedures (for example, extent of the effort and resources to be expended on saving 23-week-old premature babies). Our assurance that killing (and perhaps letting die) is always wrong varies considerably from one medical area to another, but many people find it difficult to admit this and concentrate instead on selected areas, such as abortion and euthanasia. This leaves many other areas where it may be exceedingly unclear what actions constitute the best treatment, and where we are hard pressed to know what God's 'no' to killing may entail. The temptation is to downplay the moral and spiritual dilemmas in these realms, and keep in the public eye those issues that lend themselves to what we think are clear black-and-white answers.

In other words, we all too often fail to accept that answers in the bioethical realm may not always be clear-cut. We are accustomed to black-and-white answers on major theological questions, so that grey answers to other sorts of questions appear unsatisfactory and may even be interpreted as a mark of unfaithfulness. This confuses the ethical with the spiritual.

A second area is our failure to be consistent both in the ethical principles we employ and in their application. We may be vehemently opposed to the taking of human life in some circumstances, on the ground that all human life is to be accorded absolute value. However, in other areas we find reasons why human life can be taken. For example, we may consider that the taking of human life on an extensive scale in war is acceptable, even though it is extremely difficult to know whether most modern wars are 'just'. At the same time we may be horrified by the taking of foetal human life in abortion, even when the circumstances are extreme ones. I am not of necessity condemning these stances; it may be legitimate to take human life in some circumstances but not in others. The point I am making is that we have to be exceedingly careful about the reasons we use. If we argue that human life is of absolute value in one circumstance, it cannot become less than absolute in another.

A third problem area concerns the ease with which we allow already formulated answers to take precedence over biblical data. In some areas we appear to know with unnerving certainty what is right and wrong, but sometimes these stances are based on a paucity of biblical information. Are we, therefore, guilty in some situations of forcing biblical data into a predetermined mould? No one is immune from this possibility on any side of any debate. Do we actually know what value the biblical writers place on human life *per se*? So often we fail to ask this question, because we seem to know the answer on some bioethical questions. But do we, or are we mirroring particular cultural and social attitudes? All of us are subject to the multi-dimensional pressures of our culture (both Christian and secular). What is important is that we are aware of these pressures and, as far as we are able, take them into account when assessing issues theologically and ethically.

Fourth, a constant temptation is to fail to ask precisely what it is that biblical data contribute to ethical perspectives. Should we expect a Christian perspective to be diametrically opposed to one formulated on some other basis? Is there a distinctively biblical perspective for some of the detailed ethical issues that confront us today? There are no texts or verses to cover a range of ethical issues within contemporary biomedicine (although some may disagree with this statement). It may even be that there is no biblical position at some points. For instance, is there a specific Christian position on which definition of 'brain death' one should employ (a 'whole brain' as opposed to a 'higher brain' definition)? Is one more amenable to Christian presuppositions and aspirations than the other? It is interesting that such major Christian ethicists as Paul Ramsey and Stanley Hauerwas have both argued that there is nothing in Christian convictions that entail a preference for any one definition of death.

Another problem sometimes encountered is our failure to listen to those with different perspectives from our own: those from outside the Christian faith and those from differing Christian traditions. The complexity of so many of the questions we have to confront when discussing human value within biology and medicine demand that we seek as much assistance as possible from those with value systems overlapping our own at significant points. Rather than being a threat, this should be viewed as a source of strength and support.

Christians sometimes find it difficult to accept that they can benefit from the insights of secular thinkers on ethical matters. I consider we have a great deal to learn from those around us, as long as we assess very carefully what it is we are learning. The ethical thinking of Christians does not take place in some watertight compartment, as though there are distinctly Christian stances on ethical issues. Even when there are clear distinguishing features between Christians and others, the differences may be relative.

Unfortunately, we may on occasions be unwilling to ask difficult questions, because we fear that the answers may upset our faith or some of the certainties to which we have become accustomed. Christians should be the last people to respond in such a way, because the true certainties of their faith are so much firmer than the ephemeral bases others have for their existence. Let us ask the difficult questions, about when human life begins and ends and whether there are any differences between actively and passively taking life, and see where we end up. It is only through the way in which we handle the difficult questions that we can be seen as people of integrity.

Finally, too many Christians are prone to narrow down their ethical interest to one or two specific issues, and ignore the remaining ones. I question whether this is a biblically oriented approach, since it misses the biblical emphasis on people in their wholeness. It has far more in common with the approach of single interest groups with their overtones of political activism, than with Christian approaches.

I have no doubt that Christians have a great deal to contribute to bioethical debate, but the contribution may differ from what some of us expect. My starting point is provided by the Bible, but even here we first have to consider the approach to adopt.

Approaches to the Bible

One approach is to use the Bible as a source of *moral rules*. According to this, moral dilemmas can be sorted out by discovering an appropriate moral rule, such as the rule against killing, or the rule against committing adultery. Such rules are absolute, and to deviate from them is to depart from the Bible as one's sole authority in matters of conduct. However, problems arise when such rules come into conflict. How do we judge which rule is more important than another rule? Is there an infallible ordering of rules?

A *second approach* is to recognize in the Bible sets of *moral principles*. An example of such a principle is the dignity and worth of every individual before God. According to this approach, these principles are applicable for all times. What we have to do is to seek to understand their meaning and relevance, and then apply them to the specific problems confronting us. We are to use our judgement, discernment and intelligence, and then in faith and in obedience to the Holy Spirit, make decisions in the concrete circumstances of which we are a part.

A *third approach* stresses the *response in faith* which the believer is to make to the living presence of God. What is important here is the person's own relationship to God, and the way in which he or she puts this into practice. With this approach, rules or principles assume secondary importance.

The chief concern is with what God is doing now, and therefore with the manner in which he wants us to respond and live, rather than with commands or directives he has given in the past.

My own approach is to acknowledge that the biblical writers do, indeed, lay down certain basic rules, such as those in the Ten Commandments. But these in their stark simplicity will not provide specific direction in many contemporary situations. They need to be fleshed out by more specific moral values. Once we have some idea of what might be the relevant biblical principles for a particular situation, we then have to apply them, and it is at this point that we need the Holy Spirit as our authority. The outworking of all the rules and principles of the Bible must be in the context of our own God-centred relationship with other people. We must convey to others the life of the risen Christ, rather than a harsh unyielding legalism. We are to be firm, and we are not to yield on our standards, but running through our stance must be a deep concern for human life in all its wholeness and completeness. This was something so wonderfully demonstrated by Christ himself.

As a consequence, my approach is to utilize both theological truths I referred to in Chapter 1, the 'what ought to be' and the 'what is' approaches. I regard them as complementary; both are essential if we are to function as Christians in a secular society. I have sympathy, therefore, with all the rescuers in the scenario in Chapter 1, although I find myself closer to rescuers C and D than to A and B. This is because I believe one has to work out the consequences of one's position. There are no grounds for stating that the positions of rescuers C and D are less faithful expressions of Christian commitment or of adherence to the biblical revelation, than those of rescuers A and B, much as I sympathize with these latter two. What is essential is that in everything we do we look to Christ, so that in our relationships with others, we are as Christ to them. At the ethical level, it is essential that we search for moral values that accord with the general thrust of biblical teaching, remembering that the Bible is not a textbook of ethics or anything else.

Looking for ethical guidelines

In the most general of terms one can say that the specific conflict encountered in medical dilemmas is a manifestation of a more fundamental conflict, that between *absolute principles* and *consequentialist principles*. Absolute principles emphasize the inherent rightness or wrongness of actions, whereas consequentialist principles stress the consequences of actions. The difference can be illustrated by the following:

> An absolutist may say that, since killing innocent people is always wrong, it is better to refrain from killing one innocent person even if the end result is the unintended death of three other innocent people. This is preferable to being guilty of the death of the one person. In contrast, a *consequentialist* may contend that one's aim should be to save the three at the expense of the one.

Consider the *sanctity of human life*. An absolutist may argue that we are obliged to try and save every single life no matter what the consequences, whether economic or to the welfare of other patients. On the other hand, a consequentialist may advocate the destruction of handicapped people considering this to be in the best interests of society as a whole. I have no wish to defend either extreme position, since each leads to the neglect of patients: *other* patients in the case of the absolutist position, and *handicapped* patients in the case of the consequentialist.

In practice, the two principles coexist within society, and most – if not all – medical practitioners (including Christians) utilize the two principles. This is simply because each approach has advantages and disadvantages. Consequentialism is realistic, it assumes responsibility for the effects of human actions, and it aims to reduce the lot of human suffering. On the other hand, actions cannot be evaluated solely in terms of their consequences, and this approach may put at risk despised and unpopular minorities within society. For its part, absolutism is valuable because rules provide crucial signposts for ethical decision-making, and some rules may protect exceedingly basic values, such as human dignity. Nonetheless, rule-centered approaches also have limitations: they may obscure fundamental principles underlying the rules, some rules are relative, and on occasion fundamental moral rules come into conflict with one another.

Many seek to find a middle path, balancing the two approaches. It is possible to show very great respect for widely held rules, but at the same time be prepared to deviate from them when confronted by exceedingly difficult circumstances and undesirable consequences. We frequently live with conflict between principles such as these, and we experience the tension that inevitably exists between the two. But we also have to decide whether some principles are actually more important than others, and it is at this point that ethicists disagree, with some making such distinctions but others refusing to do so. I consider that distinctions have to be made, and am prepared to distinguish between different levels of principles, such as first-order and second-order principles.

Of these, it is the first-order principles that are the most crucial. They are all-embracing values like *justice* and *love*. They are absolute, unconditional and unequivocal. Since they are all-embracing commands they cover every conceivable human situation. The second-order principles are more specific and include values such as the following:

- Doing good and not doing harm.
- Respecting people rather than using them.
- Respecting the autonomy of people.
- Preserving life.
- Telling the truth.
- Seeking not to harm innocent people.
- Ensuring that a professional relationship is never exploitative.

A little thought will show that none of these values is straightforward: they all enshrine moral ambiguities. For instance, with regard to preserving human life, existing ethical codes stress the doctor's obligation to respect life, rather than to preserve it at all costs. However, if there is no obligation to preserve life at all costs, a distinction may have to be made between actively killing a patient and letting that patient die, or in different circumstances one person may be allowed to die or be killed indirectly in order to save the life of another person. There is no escape from decision-making, either for those who accept that human life cannot always be preserved, or for those who think otherwise. Moral ambiguity is inevitable. The world in which we live provides us with dilemmas and these are especially problematic in modern biology and contemporary medicine. One could work out a biblical basis for each of the values I have just referred to, thereby giving them a sound Christian context. What we need to understand is that these values assist us in deciding how we are to relate to each other. They tell us nothing about God's plans for us or others. As we do our best for others, we realize just how limited and imperfect we are. We dare not state with assurance, 'Thus says the Lord,' as though our efforts are entirely in line with what God would have done. Christians do their best to please him and do their utmost for fellow human beings, and they seek Christ's direction for all their efforts. But infallibility will always elude us, and humility is to be our greatest virtue.

Suggestions for Christians

Christians must be determined to be scrupulously honest in their use of data. It is all too easy to use biblical data selectively, utilizing those data that support a position we hold on other grounds. Not one of us is immune from criticism at this point. It is essential that we avoid giving the impression that the ethical position we adopt is, without further discussion, based solely on the Bible, and is the only position any faithful Christian can hold. This is very rarely, if ever, the case when confronted by the many specific ethical issues implicit within modern medicine.

There will inevitably be a diversity of responses within the Christian community. There is no one 'correct' or 'orthodox' Christian response to most of the issues raised by the developments of medical technology. One would expect agreement on broad principles among those within the Christian community, but the specific outworking of many of these principles may, quite legitimately, vary. Christians are to be known by their loyalty to Christ, and not by superficial conformity on selected ethical questions. This oneness in Christ should lead to productive discussion of those issues on which there is disagreement.

Christians are to be committed to serious ethical analysis. We may feel content when we have expressed total opposition to the destruction of human embryos, to infanticide, or to withdrawal of fluids from patients in a persistent vegetative state. But is this adequate? However well-meaning such positions may be, they are not always based on detailed ethical analysis. If that is true, they may be ill-equipped to deal with difficult cases. Serious ethical analysis should be viewed as an essential adjunct to biblical insights and to the leading of the Holy Spirit. They are two sides of the same coin, and the witness of Christians is diminished if either side is neglected or downgraded.

We should be ready to interact vigorously with the thought forms and attitudes of those within secular society. If Christianity is to influence secular society, it has to enter the debating chamber of biomedical ethics. It is not sufficient to be confrontational, always objecting to the directions society is taking. While there may be some place for this, it is more important that Christians act as salt and light (Mt. 5:13–16) to that society, seeking to influence its course by informed debate.

Principles and themes from the Bible

In approaching questions concerned with the nature of human existence and the meaning of human life, our starting point is very important since it influences our attitudes towards ethical questions. For me, the launching pad is the revelation of God in the Bible. This is as authoritative for bioethics as it is for any other area of life. But what sort of answers do we expect to find in the Bible?

It has already been noted that the biblical writers lay down certain basic rules, but that these by themselves do not provide ready-made answers for most of the dilemmas facing us. The rules and values of the Bible must be worked out within the framework of our own relationship with God and other people. It is our responsibility to convey to others the life of the risen Christ.

There are two approaches to interpreting the teaching of the biblical writers commonly used by evangelical Christians. The first involves searching the Scriptures for biblical *principles* and theological *themes* relevant to the value we place on human beings and, therefore, relevant for considering biomedical dilemmas. The second depends on searching the biblical narrative for *specific* examples that appear to illustrate the significance placed by God on certain human beings; these examples are then used as the basis for general statements about God's view of all human beings.

The search for general principles and major themes cannot, by itself, solve our moral problems. What it does is establish a moral agenda and define the relevant area within which we need to seek answers. Robert Wennberg (*Life in the Balance*) has argued that we should not look to Scripture as a kind of moral thesaurus with answers to all our ethical questions. On the contrary, what it does provide us with, in his words, is 'a storehouse of theological themes', which we can then use to tackle the awkward queries confronting us.

Examples of such themes might be the general principles of justice and love and, more specifically, the dignity and worth of every individual before God. Against a background provided by these themes, considerable care will be taken to protect the weak within society, from the unborn to the mentally retarded, to those with dementia. We will aim to ensure that justice applies to these groups as much as to groups able to defend themselves, and efforts will be made to work out what are the practical consequences of just dealings.

In contrast to this approach, the 'specific examples' approach considers that the Bible's major contribution to ethical decision-making is as a source of moral rules, such as the rule against the taking of human life. And so an action like abortion is viewed as breaking this rule. Hence the categorical assertion by some that 'abortion is murder', and the claim that it is contrary to the will of God. In an attempt to demonstrate that the whole tenor of the biblical teaching is opposed to abortion, appeal is made to specific biblical passages (e.g. Ps. 139:13–16; Lk. 1:41–4). Since these do not deal explicitly with abortion, they are used to demonstrate that human life commences at the moment of conception (and that foetal life has absolute value). The problem here is that these ideas are far removed from the general moral rule against the taking of human life; neither do they deal with any of the difficulties encountered when this and some other moral rules come into conflict.

I willingly acknowledge that the biblical writers lay down certain basic rules, especially those enshrined in the Ten Commandments. But do these by themselves provide specific direction in many contemporary situations? They remain as applicable and relevant as they ever have, but they need to be fleshed out by more specific moral values. There may be times at the very beginning and very end of human life, when it is far from clear how the moral rule against the taking of human life can best be applied. It is then that the moral principles of justice, love, and the dignity of each individual human being may be of considerable assistance in determining what is the most ethical course of action to take in these circumstances.

Once we have some idea of biblical directions, they have to be applied, and it is at this point that we need Christ to guide us. Jesus was the perfect synthesis of justice and forgiveness, responsibility and understanding, commitment and love. We are to seek to be as Christ to others, as we work hard at applying the biblical directions to the specifics of the modern world.

Some people may regard this as a 'woolly' position, in which far too much decision-making is left to the judgement of the individual. And yet this is what one finds in the New Testament. The attitudes of Jesus towards such 'hard-and-fast' issues as the observance of the Sabbath day, divorce and adultery, reveal an intriguing mixture of unequivocal principles. The basis of Jesus' dealings with people was concern for human and individual well-being when surrounded by the unyielding legalism of others, accompanied by standards far in excess of those expected by even the religious leaders of his day. The totally revolutionary attitudes of Jesus cannot be neatly encased within a few absolute regulations, such as 'observing the Sabbath day to keep it holy', even though he had no intention of overturning such a regulation. His concern was with the impact of a particular principle on people, so that it would benefit people (as it was intended to do) rather than become a meaningless burden for them. Take for instance the following illustration.

> *Toni always does her best to keep Sundays different from all other days. She has a high view of Sundays, goes to church, refrains from working in the university library, and enjoys the time it gives her to spend with friends, read, and generally relax. But she's not legalistic about it. If she has to buy a few items in a shop, she will; if her car needs petrol, she will fill it up. And occasionally she will go to a Sunday afternoon concert. From time to time, she will help a friend's parents who own a corner shop, by serving in the shop for two to three hours on Sunday evenings. This isn't her ideal way of spending Sunday evenings, and she would prefer not to work, but she knows that her help is greatly appreciated. Unfortunately, Jeni – another friend – is very critical of Toni for some of her 'liberal' ways. Jeni thinks Toni is letting down the cause of Christ by failing to keep Sunday as special and holy as it should be kept.*

Toni and Jeni have similar goals and values as far as Sunday is concerned, but their approaches differ. Whereas Toni is looking at the meaning of Sunday and is attempting to work out how best she can put this into practice in her surroundings, Jeni's actions are more specifically determined by regulations. Toni is also aiming to act in ways that will help others, even when this breaks across the special nature of Sunday. My own preference is for Toni's approach, although I have considerable respect for Jeni's feelings and for her commitment to the principles she thinks she should abide by. Nevertheless, her legalistic approach has limitations.

We have to ask how the approaches we use affect people. While the Bible provides very important guidelines, it does not provide black-and-white answers on many of the specific issues we meet today. Neither should we expect it to do so. It did not provide our forebears with answers to some of their questions: should a woman in labour be given an anaesthetic? should babies be vaccinated? In the same way, we shall not find in its pages a statement as to whether IVF should be used to provide an infertile couple with a child, or at what point an individual with a very severely damaged brain may be allowed to die.

To expect specific answers from the Bible to such questions is to misunderstand the purpose of the Bible. It is also to ask the wrong sort of questions. What the Bible provides is a true understanding of the human condition in relation to God's purposes for individuals and the community. This provides an accurate insight into the value bestowed by God upon human existence, the dignity of individual human beings, and the ways in which we should treat each other. These values constitute the bedrock upon which a Christian ethical system has to be based. It is to these and related values that I shall return repeatedly throughout these pages.

Biblical perspectives on human life

Human life is invariably seen by the biblical writers as constituting a *unity*. For them, a human being cannot be isolated into a series of independent units. While there are references to body, soul and spirit, or to body and soul, or to flesh and spirit, these are not isolated segments of the human individual. They are integral components of what it means to be human.

Neither can any human being be viewed in isolation from God, since one of our supreme characteristics is a potential for responding to the overtures of God. We are beings who achieve significance and freedom within the designs of God. However, we are not just individuals standing before God; we are people *living in community*. It is in community that we are to live out our God-relatedness and put into practice our response to God. In the same way as we need God, we need each other, whether this be in families, social groups, churches, cultures, or whole societies. We are both biological and spiritual beings.

When we turn to the Old Testament we find that its emphasis is consistently on the whole life of a human being, never on the body as the material element and a soul as the spiritual element. Additionally, we find that individuals' relationships are indispensable – to others in the human community, and also to God. The capacity for forming personal relationships is present in all human beings, and it is a capacity that needs to be developed if human life in all its fullness is to be experienced.

In the New Testament the concept of the human person is more difficult to unravel because of its dependence upon certain Greek modes of thought. The emphasis, however, is on the quality of the life of a person in relation to God and to other human beings (see Chapter 5). This is well illustrated by reference to three New Testament words.

The first of these, _bios_, is used principally to denote bare subsistence, survival, and the means of keeping alive (Mk. 12:44; Lk. 15:12–30; 1 Tim. 2:2), although on some occasions it is equated with the lusts of the flesh (1 Pet. 4:2) or with the pride of life (1 Jn. 2:16). This aspect of human life has something in common with biological life and with the basic necessities and drives of life. The second word, _psuche_, appears to have three major connotations. The first describes a human being's vital functioning, that is, life as opposed to death. Jesus urged his followers not to be unduly anxious about their _psuche_-life (Mt. 6:25). In its second sense _psuche_ describes aspects of a person's inner life such as the mind, will and emotions. Jesus told his followers to love God with all their _psuche_ – heart, strength and mind (Lk. 10:27; Mk. 12:30; Mt. 22:37). Third, _psuche_ is also human life transcending present reality: 'whoever would save his psuche will lose it, and whoever loses his psuche for my sake and the gospel's will save it' (Mk. 8:35–6; Mt. 10:39; 16:25–6; Lk. 9:24–5). This is life transcending time and mortality through faith in God's grace and power. The third word, _zoe_, is life in full abundance, the life that only Christ can give (Jn. 10:10). This is life with an eternal quality, and it is inseparable from faith in Jesus Christ.

These various facets of human life are not three distinct kinds of life, but are three dimensions of the quality of one human life. They underline the intrinsic value of human life, regardless of its condition, simply because it is from God. All human life has worth, no matter how privileged or demeaned by society's standards. Nevertheless, these words point to differing levels of the realization of the potential of human life, depending upon its stage of biological development, the richness or paucity of the relationships established with other human beings, and the closeness or otherwise of a living relationship with God. All human life is not the same, although it always has worth derived from the value bestowed upon it by God. This will not solve all problems in the ethical realm, but it provides an important base from which to work.

Theological themes and human value

Created in God's image

One biblical theme is crucial: human beings are made in the image and likeness of God. This was expressed vividly by John Calvin when he wrote that 'God looks upon himself . . . and beholds himself in men [people] as in a mirror.' This suggests that as God looks on people, he recognizes that they are icons (images) of himself. In people God finds his own perfections and characteristics mirrored back to himself. Consequently, when we see another human being we see another creature who delights God by mirroring him. We also mirror each other.

People are like God, in that we relate to the world, to other people, and to God. We make choices and act upon them; we have values and value systems; we are aware of ourselves and of others; we are held responsible for our actions. We are aware of God and are capable of responding freely to his call. Therefore, it is clear that all of us have some of the relational features of a personal God.

This principle is foundational to an understanding of people, and as we delve deeper, we find within it a number of more specific *themes*. The first of these is that, like God, we are capable of *understanding*: the more we understand, the more like God we become. This is a pivotal mark of human existence, and all of us have something of this capacity, either actual or potential, or in the form of the memories others have of us.

The second theme is that of *control*. God has placed humans in control of themselves and their world, and this in turn is control of God's world. From this stems yet another theme, *responsibility for other people*, for human welfare in general, and for all facets of the environment. Responsibility is essential if the control bestowed upon us is to be harnessed for good ends. Such responsibility, far from depicting humans as rebellious creatures, emanates from our creation in the likeness of God; it is built into what 'being human' is all about. In other words, to 'be human' is to act responsibly: it is to take decisions, to forge new paths, to be creative, and to seek new solutions to old problems.

A final theme is one of *our dependence upon each other within the human community*. Whenever confronted by other human beings we are in the presence of images of God, who make claims on us. We are dependent upon them, and they upon us, because of our likeness to each other, and our mutual likeness to God. It is this interdependence that should constitute the basis of our response to other humans, rather than any 'rights' they (or we) may possess. In other words, justice, equity and fair dealing stem from our joint mirroring of God; we are to value others because of what both they and we are in the sight of God, and because we depend upon each other within the human community.

Christ's redemption

Our creation in God's image is an important place to begin, but it is only a beginning. It assumes even greater significance when seen against the background of the Son of God assuming human identity, and becoming human like us. The man, Jesus, revealed the image of God in human form. In Jesus we see God incarnate, God in truly human form – real God and real man.

In becoming a human being, God brought about the redemption of lost humanity, but that was not all. This very act also *bestowed unequalled value upon the human race*. In identifying himself with the human race, Jesus, the God-man, acknowledged the value of all human beings. In other words, God's concern for humankind was so great that Jesus Christ, his Son, became a vulnerable human and then gave his life on behalf of human beings. Although this remarkable self-giving is generally stressed from the viewpoint of salvation, it also has profound implications for the ways we view each other – we are all of immense value from God's perspective, a value that should be reflected in our ethical systems.

Both the creation and redemption of humankind demonstrate that *human life is precious to God*. We are accountable to God for our own lives and, where we are responsible for other human lives, we are accountable to God for those lives. Consequently, once people are undervalued, we fail to take seriously the work of God, negating the incarnation and Christ's commitment to humanity in becoming one with God's creation. We adopt values diametrically opposed to those of Christ for whom human life was worthy of his own life.

Dignity of people

From this it follows that everyone has *an intrinsic dignity*, resting not on what they can accomplish in material, social or spiritual terms, but on the basis of God's love. Consequently, human dignity is based primarily on what individuals are in the sight of God and never on what they can or cannot do for society, for humankind, or even for God. Those who are of no functional value to society still retain a dignity, since they remain important in the sight and purposes of God. It is in this light that we who come into contact with them are to deal with them.

From here it is but a short step to the notion of *servanthood*, by which we give ourselves for others, serving them in a self-sacrificial way, and putting their interests before our own. Such a lifestyle finds its warrant in the worth of others, and in the claims others make upon us because they are so like us and because they are of such value in the sight of God. These 'others' are not simply our friends and those who will repay us fully for our concern, but include our enemies – those who have little interest in our welfare, and perhaps would even do us harm if given the chance.

If individuals have a dignity bestowed upon them by God, they are never to be valued simply because of their value to another individual, an organization, or society. To treat people in this way is to treat them as nothing more than means to an end, and therefore as the property of another. Attitudes of this kind deny to individuals a worth and dignity of their own.

Human beings are one with us in the human endeavour, they are like us, and we all have significance in God's sight. In this sense human dignity is indiscriminate, pointing towards a flowering of human abilities that should be encouraged and developed wherever and whenever possible, since it reflects what God wants for people.

Namelessness

The flip side of human dignity is what I shall call human namelessness. As I contemplate bestowing dignity upon human beings, what impresses me is that a central element in practice is the recognition that people have names. They are individuals to whom we can relate in ways that are meaningful for both them and us. By contrast, lack of dignity is evident when people are treated as though they have no names; they are anonymous; they have become nameless.

We all know what happens when there are vast tragedies and thousands are killed or slaughtered. There is no way even those close to the scene can respond to situations like this in other than an impersonal fashion. The deaths become little more than statistics; the people are nameless. Some of course will mourn the loss of real people, but the human sense of mourning is quickly overtaken by the brutal statistical nature of the event. These people, whoever they may have been, are not seen as those who had individual relationships to God;

they lose their worth and dignity as the sheer magnitude of the occasion overtakes everything else.

People become nameless when no one cares about them. They may have potential worth, and yet are treated as cogs in a wheel. This transformation into namelessness occurs, as I have just indicated, in tragedies of huge magnitude, and yet is also found in families, societies, hospitals, and work situations.

Namelessness is also a frequent accompaniment of illness. As dignity is lost through illness, especially when the illness is debilitating and catastrophic, enormous effort is required to maintain a feel for the individual as a person. Unfortunately, this condition can be precipitated by impersonal health-care systems, as a result of which the situation becomes even worse. How can someone 'be someone' when they appear to have lost their status within society? Relationships break down for the nameless ones, since relationships with a nameless individual cease to be meaningful. In other words, the nameless are also 'relationless', and this is the antithesis of any Christian understanding of the human condition.

The challenge for Christians is to recognize this condition, and the ease with which it can occur within impersonal institutions that so readily depersonalize people by the ways in which performance, redundancy or illness are tackled. None of this is inevitable, and our task is to advocate systems that insist on giving people names, and that recognize and empathize with people in their suffering, struggles and hurts.

Relevance of human suffering

When considering human suffering, we generally limit our thinking to the suffering of human beings. Obvious as this sounds, and eminently sensible as it may appear, it has immense limitations. A Christian perspective broadens the whole approach by arguing that God's suffering and human suffering are inextricably linked. The suffering of a human being has direct implications for God, since it is one of God's images that is being hurt. In a sense, therefore, God is himself violated when a human being is destroyed or injured. And so, when one person injures another God himself is wounded.

It is against the background of this close linkage between human and divine suffering, that we can conclude that illness and injustice bring sorrow to God. If this is so, the relief of illness and the pursuit of justice are important means of helping relieve not only human suffering, but also, in some way, God's suffering. This is why the suffering of others should be of immense concern to us. All attempts at relieving suffering are responses to the vulnerability of God's love for people, who are his images. Not surprisingly, they are to be given high priority by the followers of Christ.

The repercussions are immense. Everyone is to be viewed within the context of a suffering world, from the immediacy of the human suffering which implicates all of us, to the suffering of the creator and redeemer who loved humans so much that he became one with us and died for us. That act demonstrates that God is not immune to the plight of humanity, and this in turn shows how much we ourselves should value humanity.

Misuse of human responsibility

Although human beings are capable of understanding, control and enormous responsibility, we are prone to debasing our understanding, to exercising control selfishly, and to acting irresponsibly. The ease with which we misuse our many abilities lies at the heart of our problems, giving rise as it does to strife, enmity, selfish excesses, inequality and injustice.

It is this misuse of responsibility that leads to the existence of conflicting moral claims, since there are some situations in which we cannot act in ways that are wholly good and totally free from guilt. We need to beware, therefore, of establishing idealistic standards, and judging everyone by those standards. Much as we may desire such standards, and the absolute goodness they depict, the reality is that neither others nor we ourselves live by absolute standards. We fail, and frequently we fall short. As a result, we often need to work with a hierarchy of moral claims, according to which we evaluate lesser evils and greater goods. To acknowledge this is not to denigrate human value or attempts at upholding human dignity; neither is it a means of introducing situationalism and relativism into ethical discussion. It is simply an acknowledgement of the world in which we find ourselves – a broken world, where the images of God are in rebellion against God's authority.

Humility

As we realize the need for *humility*, we realize the immensity of our dependence upon God. We recognize that we are not our own, but belong to God to be used according to his purposes. Allen Verhey (*On Moral Medicine*) has argued that humility in this sense is not fatalism, since it reckons with the brokenness of our world and accepts that there are events beyond our comprehension. There are no easy answers, but in the midst of all we fail to understand, we have to live with the brokenness and tragedy of our world in hope and faith and love. Alongside this distinctively Christian vision, is another: *heroism*. For Verhey, this enables us to risk new beginnings, and to share the sadness of our world and our lives for God's cause and someone's good.

What we are doing here is walking a very fine line. We are learning to accept the brokenness and tragedy of the world – our world, our lives, our families, our hopes and our dreams. The world lets us down, and the temptation is to cry out against God and all that can make sense of the catastrophes. The way of humility and heroism is to acknowledge the brokenness and tragedy, to stare at it, and through it see the suffering of God, suffering that touches us and that can bring us healing. What we see is the *relevance* of God for those enmeshed in hurt and deprivation, and our place in relating this relevance to those in desperate need. We come to see that God sometimes interrupts lives and hopes, but that even these interruptions have to be faced up to in the spirit of Christ. We come to see God's presence in places we would never have chosen, and in circumstances that repel us. But, even here, God can be known, sometimes much better than in palatable and happy circumstances.

Who is my neighbour?

Are we inconsistent in the value we place on human lives? We may accept that some lives actually *are* worth more than others. For instance, a healthy thirty-year-old is worth more than a seventy-year-old with advanced Alzheimer's disease; or a healthy three-year-old in the United Kingdom is worth more than a severely malnourished three-year-old in the Sudan. Alternatively, we may not accept this: all human lives *have* the same value, but we fail to live up to this standard in practice. We should care as much for the seventy-year-old with Alzheimer's as for the healthy thirty-year-old, and this implies we should direct as many resources to the one as the other. And we should care as much for a starving child in a region with endemic poverty and starvation as for a healthy child in an affluent suburb in our own country. In practice the latter rarely occurs, and there are pressures against the equal distribution of resources in the former.

What do we do about the chronically ill, the retarded, the demented, the unemployed, those with social problems, the outcasts of society? What value is to be ascribed to all these? As far as they are one with us in the human endeavour, they are to be valued as others value us and as we value others. There is to be no discrimination. Does this lack of discrimination continue to apply when there are not sufficient resources to go around, when hard moral choices have to be made between one group and another, or even one individual and another? Can we continue to *act* on the presumption that all are always to be valued at precisely the same level?

As far as I am concerned, no group is to be stigmatized as valueless, or even as of only limited value. Every group is of value, and is therefore to be assisted in whatever way we would assist a privileged member of society. Every effort is to be made to put this anti-discriminatory ethic into practice, and to render it public policy. Nevertheless, a point may come where invidious choices have to be made, and where all courses of action will involve loss and suffering. Perhaps we have then to seek the lesser of the two evils. But if we do this, human dignity will be sacrificed whichever course is followed. At this point of unavoidable tension, we may well find that, in practice, the value being ascribed to some human beings is being downgraded. Perhaps there actually *are* limits to the protection we can give to the value of some human beings in situations of unavoidable conflict. However, any course of action that downgrades human value is never the course of choice – it reflects the plight of humans in a suffering world.

All human beings should be valued, but can *all human beings be of equal value to me*, in the sense that I am in a position to serve and help them? I am to feel at one with all humanity, but I cannot rescue all humanity however much I may wish to do so. I am never to close my eyes to those in need – after all, whenever I see need about which I could do something to help, my responsibility is to assist such people. We are also to remember that all human life is interrelated, so that we cannot completely ignore *any* human beings. However, we cannot be responsible for *all* human beings. There *is* a differential, and there *are* limits.

In attempting to unravel these issues, we have obligations to take seriously the dignity of all human beings; all human beings are to be valued *if at all possible*. That is the furthest we can go. We have enormous responsibility to help a person if nothing obstructs us from doing so. If we are in a position to help we must do so – we are duty bound. For example, an elderly couple living next door, will on occasion need practical help and perhaps emotional support, and we should help them accordingly. People with whom we have direct contact are our *near* neighbour(s); this may include our family, friends, church, neighbourhood, work situation, and (within limits) our community. Our near neighbours are the people to whom we have considerable responsibility.

At the other end of the spectrum is a person far from us, in a situation over which we have no control. Here our responsibility may be negligible. Consider an elderly couple living in a nursing home in another country. We know they exist only because we are aware that elderly people do live in nursing homes in other countries. These are people with whom we have no direct contact at all, those in other countries, in other communities. We know about these through the media but our knowledge of them is limited to them as a group and not as individuals. These are our *far* neighbour(s) and our responsibility to them is very limited indeed.

In the middle of the spectrum there is the responsibility we have towards those we know but with whom we have no direct contact; our control of their well-being has been mark-edly reduced. We can think of elderly parents living in another city; we are unable to help them on a daily basis and we should not be expected to do so (although we may be able to provide considerable indirect support). People whom we know and care for, but who are geographically removed from us are our *personal* neighbour(s). We do have a responsibility to them, even though it may be largely exercised at a distance.

This is a parochial view and yet a practical one. We do not ignore our *far* and *personal* neighbours although our respon-sibility is inevitably a limited one; our focus is on our *near* neighbours. Clearly, there is a tension here, but it should be a productive tension. It is a way out of the paralysis of feeling 'I am responsible for everyone', but knowing that in practice this is impossible. Our responsibility first and foremost is for our *near* neighbours, those whom we can truly help. If we fail here, we fail totally as human beings. If we succeed here, we enlarge the scope of our neighbourliness.

Interpreting the theological themes

These themes open up new dimensions for an understanding of our relationship to our fellow humans, and underscore the high priority to be placed on efforts to improve the welfare of those around us. We are to see others as those who are imaged after God, as those to whom we are to commit our-selves as fellow images of God, and as those who are one with us in the suffering of a world at enmity within itself and also with God's designs. We are to see people as individuals who merit our concern because they merit God's concern. The next step is to draw out from these themes more specific conclusions regarding human value.

The first of these is that human life is on loan from God; it is a gift from God. Our own lives, as well as the lives of oth-ers, should never be viewed as having only biological value. Life belongs to God, even more than it belongs to us. And so whenever we consider the value of a human life we have to bear in mind its relation to God. In assessing how to deal with difficult ethical questions in the realm of bioethics, we need to recognize that human life is life-derived-from-God, not life-in-isolation-of-God.

A second conclusion is that, as we emphasize the wholeness of human beings, their biological-spiritual unity has to be treated with seriousness. Individuality is lost when there is no scope for growth and fulfilment as a being in one's own right. It is less than Christian to live as though all that matters is the existence of human life regardless of its quality. Such an attitude leads to mediocrity in our own lives and to a gross neglect of the welfare and aspirations of others. The mere existence of human life in its barest essentials is hardly sufficient. This applies through all stages of human existence from the earliest beginnings of human life in the uterus to the end of human existence in extreme old age. A corollary of this is that, although human value may be severely jeopardized in extreme situations (as in very severe brain damage), there is generally never any time when human life has no value at all.

A third element is that the quality of an individual's life is important. It is unfortunate that the term 'quality of life' has, in the eyes of some, become confined to the biological or medical quality of life. This is sad, since it reduces human existence to physical dimensions alone; this is a complete antithesis of the biblical picture of human life. When life is defined in the various ways suggested previously by the words *bios, psuche* and *zoe*, the quality of human life in this broad sense is an essential attribute of a Christian perspective. The goal for the lives of individual human beings is an adequate physical existence, and a satisfactory day-to-day experience of family and social obligations, work, recreation, moral responsibility, and a whole range of challenges and expectations. It also incorporates spiritual experience, the service of God and one's fellow human beings, and interaction with other humans in love, forgiveness and hope.

A fourth observation is that the undervaluing of human life takes many forms. It stems from the widespread destruction of foetal life for superficial reasons. But it may also be the result of the irresponsible creation of new life, from pregnant women smoking or drinking alcohol, from unjust social or commercial practices, from an inequitable distribution of resources within our society or between societies, and from gross inequality of opportunities within a society.

Tragically, human life is easily wasted, and all instances are an implicit denial that human life is precious to God. Wastage of human life is everywhere, as millions of people are killed in wars, automobile accidents, earthquakes and famines, by other people in homicides or by themselves in suicides, and by smoking cigarettes and drinking alcohol. Malnutrition has killed countless human beings, as have epidemics of infectious diseases, while the loss of prenatal human life through spontaneous and induced abortion outstrips all other forms of human wastage put together. The widespread loss of human life in these ways leads to a debasement of human existence, which is seen as being readily expended and of little value. This, in turn, engenders a callousness towards human life. So much of this wastage is preventable, but we have learnt to live with it and accept it as a normal part of human life. Automobile fatalities are accepted with little questioning of their futility, but they as much as any of the other forms of pointless human wastage question the value placed upon human life by God.

In the fifth place, choices sometimes have to be made between one human life and another, or one group of humans has to be favoured above another group. Any such choices are invidious, and social and economic systems should not precipitate these dilemmas with their overtones of injustice, exploitation and despair. But in a sinful world, there is no escape from ethical ambiguity, moral imperfection and errors of judgement.

With these themes in mind, we are in a position to see what direction we can obtain from the Bible.

Four

The Bible and Human Value

The Bible and human life

It would be foolish to set out on this chapter with the expectation that biblical writers will provide us with a definitive viewpoint on human value. We will not encounter any such thing. Indeed, the issues may be far more murky than we would have wished for. For instance, what about those numerous statements in the Old Testament dealing with God's people killing their enemies, sometimes in what to us are abhorrent ways? How can these be squared with a high view of human life, let alone with bestowing absolute value on human beings? It may even be argued that the Bible projects a low view of human life, and all the emphases we hear about the sanctity of human life are based on a selected reading of the biblical record.

But there are also apparent problems in the New Testament. Consider Matthew 2:16.

> When Herod realized that he had been outwitted by the Magi, he was furious, and he gave orders to kill all the boys in Bethlehem and its vicinity who were two years old and under, in accordance with the time he had learned from the Magi.

Herod, of course, was not one of the Lord's people, but what we have here is the death of innocent infants resulting directly from the birth of Jesus. One may argue that this was the act of a desperate power broker, with no interest in human value or human dignity. While this would be true, it still represents an uncomfortable anomaly, intimately associated as it was with the coming into the world of the Saviour. These infants were as innocent as any others; they were just in the wrong place at the wrong time, and they were slaughtered. There was no way in which they could benefit from the message that Jesus was bringing. Perhaps they should have been accorded absolute value, but the sinfulness of the world saw to it that they were denied this. The question we have to answer is whether there was any way in which they could have been saved, living as they did when Jesus was born in a country where the ruler thought the birth of Jesus threatened his own survival.

The early church period raises similar dilemmas. Peter's miraculous escape from prison (Acts 12:6–19) led directly to the deaths of the guards who were accused by Herod Agrippa I of allowing them to escape. Their innocence did not protect them from an untimely death, giving the impression that Peter's freedom and consequent ability to direct the extension of the church were more important than their continued existence. In turn, Herod lost his life for blasphemy (Acts 12:21–3). In neither of these instances do we get the impression that physical life per se is an ultimate state of being. Neither does this come through from the first in this series of episodes, which started with Herod's persecution of the church and the death of James (Acts 12:1–3). None of the deaths here can be justified, but by the same token, it is not the deaths that shine through as being of supreme significance.

Alongside these episodes can be placed Jesus' apparent lack of concern about slavery, the early church's apparent acceptance of slavery as an institution even though Paul was concerned with slave–master relationships, and the lack of political action on the part of Jesus and the early church against political oppression. If these are examples of a denial of human value, what do they tell us about the early church's emphasis upon valuing human beings? It is true that Jesus, in particular, had radical views on the role of women within society and the church, and that his every action asserted human dignity and integrity, but this was at the individual level rather than at the level of social structures. These examples are not characterized by the loss of human life, even though some loss would probably have occurred. Nevertheless, the systems that, apparently, escaped specific condemnation would have been exploitative, in that the dignity and worth of some would have been seriously downgraded. While there is no hint that Jesus or Paul approved of this downgrading (in fact, the opposite is the case), neither do they emphasize human dignity to the exclusion of other priorities.

Moving to the Old Testament, we are confronted by a myriad of culturally difficult issues. In Exodus 32, following the giving of the Ten Commandments and various other laws, the description of the tabernacle and a range of offerings, the people of Israel committed idolatry by worshipping the golden calf. In the light of this, Moses pleaded with God, he destroyed the calf, and then determined who was on God's side (Ex.32:25–9). As part of this process, he gave the Levites a word from the Lord: 'Each man strap a sword to his side. Go back and forth through the camp from one end to the other, each killing his brother and friend and neighbour.' This was done, and three thousand people were killed. Moses' own interpretation of this slaughter was that the Levites had 'been set apart to the Lord today, for you were against your own sons and brothers, and he has blessed you this day.'

In this instance, the people who were slain had been guilty of idolatry; sufficient reason for them to be killed in Old Testament times. People were also put to death for adultery, for other social misdemeanours and of course for murder. The precise theological significance of these actions is not of concern in the present context. What does emerge is that some values were of greater importance than human existence. In this sense, therefore, it is difficult to assert on biblical grounds that 'human life is of absolute value'.

Look at Psalm 139. After the sublime heights of this psalm when David extols the wonder of how he has been kept safe through a host of circumstances, including during his foetal existence, he concludes by asking God to slay the wicked and by expressing his hatred for such people (Ps. 139:19–24). The contrast within this psalm is almost too great for us today, who know little of this hatred. Its essence is hatred of iniquity and of those who oppose God, a hatred that is demonstrated by physical means. The spiritual and physical are more closely intertwined than we understand. We are confronted here by a view of human value that places far less stress on mere existence than we tend to place on it today. We would, therefore, be foolhardy to press the biblical record too far in the direction of an absolute value of human life.

But the supreme constraint is that provided by Jesus himself. He did not consider his earthly life as the pinnacle of existence. For him humility, servanthood and obedience were more important. He humbled himself and became obedient to death; he died on a cross (Phil. 2:8). This was something he accepted for himself; it was not foisted on him. Nevertheless, it again emphasizes that human life has relative, rather than absolute, value.

One gets the impression from the biblical record that human value can be measured in a variety of ways. It is not only measured by life, as opposed to death, since it is not simply viewed in physical terms. The meaning of human existence is a God-centred meaning, in which faithfulness to God is of as much significance as the continuation of a human life. The challenge for us is to interpret this in bioethical terms at the turn of the millennium. On the one hand, no human being can conclude that some people should be put to death because of unfaithfulness or idolatry – that is God's prerogative alone. On the other hand, do we keep alive all human beings, no matter what the circumstances, on the grounds that they are of absolute value? Neither position is tenable.

The Bible and prenatal value

Since the biblical writers do not concern themselves directly with life before birth, how can the Bible be of assistance when seeking direction for dilemmas rooted in processes taking place in the months before birth? Surprisingly, however, Christians of many persuasions appear to be more definite about where they stand on matters at the beginning of human existence than at almost any other stage. In other words, despite what I have just stated, they claim to obtain clear guidance about the significance of fertilization. The reason for this is that the Bible is far from silent on references to human life before birth, even if its framework is a markedly different one from that of scientists.

As we come to the biblical evidence, we need to remember that the distinction between embryos (first eight weeks of gestation) and foetuses (remainder of gestation until birth) was unknown to the biblical writers. Perhaps this demonstrates the irrelevance of such a distinction. Nevertheless, today we use these terms for biological reasons. Therefore, I shall use the terms 'embryos' and 'foetuses', as well as the rather unwieldy 'prenatal life', although on most occasions any distinction between embryos and foetuses will not be relevant in biblical terms.

In many discussions regarding biblical thinking on foetal life, considerable emphasis is placed on a few biblical passages.

> Your hands shaped me and made me. Will you now turn and destroy me? Remember that you moulded me like clay. Will you now turn me to dust again? Did you not pour me out like milk and curdle me like cheese, clothe me with skin and flesh and knit me together with bones and sinews? You gave me life and showed me kindness, and in your providence watched over my spirit.
> Job 10:8–12

> For you created my inmost being; you knit me together in my mother's womb. I praise you because I am fearfully and wonderfully made; your works are wonderful, I know that full well. My frame was not hidden from you when I was made in the secret place. When I was woven together in the depths of the earth, your eyes saw my unformed body. All the days ordained for me were written in your book before one of them came to be.
> Psalm 139:13–16

> Before I was born the Lord called me; from my birth he has made mention of my name.
> Isaiah 49:1

Before I formed you in the womb I knew [chose] you, before you
were born I set you apart; I appointed you as a prophet to the
nations.
Jeremiah 1:5

When Elizabeth heard Mary's greeting, the baby leaped in her
womb, and Elizabeth was filled with the Holy Spirit. In a loud
voice she exclaimed 'Blessed are you among women, and blessed
is the child you will bear! But why am I so favoured that the
mother of my Lord should come to me? As soon as the sound of
your greeting reached my ears, the baby in my womb leaped for
joy.
Luke 1:41–4

The significance of prenatal life

What can we glean from these passages? Although considerable care is required to ensure that too much is not demanded
of them, and that they are not torn from their context, we will
not go too far wrong with a series of general statements.

The first of these is that the biblical writers include prenatal
life within the human community. They recognize that the
beginnings of adult human life are to be found in the unborn,
and that there is continuity between life before and life after
birth. Consequently, there is a continuity, spanning birth,
within the life of individuals. One instance of this may be surprising. In the Old Testament, when Esau and Jacob were
twins in their mother's womb, they struggled with one
another, and this was interpreted as prefiguring their struggles
in later life (Gen. 25:23). In another situation Samson's
mother was told to abstain from alcoholic drinks during her
pregnancy (Judg. 13:7). Sensible as this advice may appear to
us today, the reasoning then was quite different. The relevance
in Samson's case stemmed from what he was destined to be as
an adult; he was to be a Nazirite and Nazirites were forbidden
to drink wine. What is significant is that there is a perceived
linkage between foetus and adult; what happens to the foetus
has major repercussions for its life as an adult.

A second point is that the knowledge and care of God extend back to the foetus. This is most clearly brought out as God's servants, such as David and Jeremiah, look back at his concern for them throughout their own foetal lives. They were aware that the person they now are, and the foetus they were before birth are one and the same individuals (Ps. 22:9, 10; 139:13; Jer. 1:5). These statements had a spiritual thrust – the God whom they experienced as being faithful in the present had also been faithful throughout the whole of their earthly histories. He had been with them from the time they first came into existence. For David there was also a link between his present sinful nature, and what he interpreted as his sinful nature before birth: 'Surely I have been a sinner from birth, sinful from the time my mother conceived me' (Ps. 51:5). David was so impressed with his sinfulness that he could see no way in which this had not been present from his very earliest beginnings long before he was actually born.

And yet this theological confession only partly expressed the concerns and purposes of God, who had been with David and Jeremiah from eternity. God 'saw' David long before he was formed in the womb (Ps. 139:15, 16); God 'chose' Jeremiah and consecrated him as a prophet long before Jeremiah's body took on the form of a human being (Jer. 1:5). In similar vein, Paul argues that the followers of Christ were chosen by God, not at the beginning of their earthly existence, but before the creation of the world (Eph. 1:4; 2 Tim. 1:9). Clearly, then, our prenatal existence is not seen by these writers simply as a matter of embryos and foetuses (even if they had been able to use these terms). It is God's work, expressing his purposes, and directed towards his glory. The physical part reflects only one part of God's plan for his people; there is far more, and it is this 'far more' that is neglected when we concentrate our vision solely on the physical side of development. An understanding of the beginnings of individual existence takes us into theological realms as much as (perhaps more than) into scientific and biological ones.

A third characteristic of the biblical record is that the beginning of an individual's existence (we might use the term 'fertilization') is recognized as a gift of God (Gen. 4:1; 16:2;

29:31,32; 30:22, 23; Ruth 4:13). It is viewed as an act of creation in which both humans and God have their essential roles to play. It is not purely a human act, from which God can be totally excluded; neither is it purely a spiritual transaction devoid of human participation. It is the gift of new life to the one who has come into existence, a gift that springs from human decision-making and actions, whether responsible or irresponsible. In the Old Testament, God is frequently seen as opening or closing the wombs of individuals, not as illustrations of biological bravado, but within a context of faith. What is relevant here is not obstetrics, but God's purposes, his gift of new human life, and the rewards of faith. Great care has to be taken to ensure that we do not downgrade these principles, making them little more than directions for dealing with infertility. That would be to confuse theology with biology, and once that happens very important guidelines for our thinking about God and his purposes are lost.

What we have learned so far is that God protects his people before birth as they develop in their mothers' wombs, and then after birth. The context for this is that of a living relationship between God and his people. What this means is that those biblical passages touching on foetal life are confessions about God and his purposes, and are not designed to impart information about the precise status of foetal life. To expect the latter is to impose upon the Bible a particular scientific world-view, foreign to any of the writers or their cultures. But even when this is acknowledged, these passages still provide pointers of relevance to us. In particular, their context is always that of living people looking back on the way in which God had looked after them since their earliest beginnings, and about God's purposes for them from eternity. God's purposes are always central; any biology we may glean from these passages is incidental, since their aim is not to provide biological data or even ethical directives. We always have to seek their theological purpose, since this is their primary intention.

Where does this leave us in our thinking about God's dealings with embryos and foetuses in general? Can we move from expressions of praise by God's people regarding God's faithfulness to them before birth, to a detailed understanding of how God views all embryos and foetuses? If we do this, what we are doing is moving from the specific to the general, from the community of God's people to the world at large. Once we use passages such as the ones I have quoted, and especially Psalm 139, to demonstrate that every single embryo ever conceived is a human person of precisely the same value and status as adult humans, we have generalized from the personal history of God's servants, and the unique events surrounding the incarnation of the Son of God. Is a generalization like this valid?

This is where different perspectives emerge, even among Christians. I would prefer to refrain from generalizing like this, and adopt a more tentative conclusion, namely, that God is concerned about embryos and foetuses, as he is concerned about human life after birth. What this leads to is a serious commitment to the welfare of embryos and foetuses. Uninteresting as this may sound, it ensures that we never treat human life before birth frivolously and that we never underestimate the dignity and worth of those who will be like us in the future even though now, in their unlikeness, they are in need of our nurture, care and protection.

One of the striking features of the biblical writings is that they leave a great deal unsaid that would have been of interest to us today. Passages such as the ones I have touched on provide few clues about the significance of determining precisely when human life begins, since the biblical writers did not think in these terms, and they do not address the question of whether a very early embryo is a person with the rights of a person. The writers did not think like this, and were not interested in questions such as these. They are our problems, and it is our responsibility to decide what response is appropriate for those seeking to be faithful to God. Just as we have no idea what it means to claim that an embryo has consciousness, we have no idea what it means to ascribe spiritual dimensions to an embryo's existence.

Silences and the benefit of doubt

On a number of occasions I have referred to silences in the Bible: the lack of specific references to topics and issues that interest us today. The biblical writers are silent on these matters. How do we cope with these silences, since they are a hindrance to us in our endeavours to construct an adequate biblical basis for our thinking? The difficulty we have to face is that these silences would not bother us if we were not committed to taking the Bible seriously. It is only because we long to be faithful to the biblical revelation that we feel compelled to fill in the gaps, a compulsion that applies regardless of any specific positions we adopt on the precise status of embryos or foetuses.

And this is where the problem comes to the surface. No matter where we stand on any particular issue, the temptation is to interpret these silences on the basis of viewpoints we already hold on other grounds. These other viewpoints may be conservative, moderate or liberal. Unfortunately, our own viewpoints can be made to fill a biblical silence and if we are not very careful, passed off as a biblical viewpoint. We are all capable of doing this with the best of intentions. Is there, then, any way of avoiding this pitfall? As far as I can see, it is imperative that all of us acknowledge biblical silences, and leave them as areas where the biblical writers make no precise contribution to the topic in question.

But does this satisfy us as Christians? If we acknowledge that there are topics to which the biblical writers make little contribution we will have to adopt one of two approaches. In the first of these, we will have to go as far as we can using our own understanding and judgement. When this is the case, there will be a diversity of perspectives among Christians, and all of us will have to work hard at seeking the best direction we can from general biblical guidelines and even from constructive secular approaches. Many will regard this as a dangerous approach, and will turn away from it. I understand their apprehension. There is an alternative approach, and this is one of silence. If these are biblical silences, there can also be Christian silences. We acknowledge we don't know, and we say and write nothing.

I view both approaches as being acceptable for Christians, as long as we openly acknowledge the approach we are adopting. My own approach is the former of the two. As a scientist I consider it imperative to suggest ways forward at very specific levels, but there will be considerable interpretation in some of the positions I adopt. I do not claim infallibility theologically, scientifically or ethically. The most that can be asked of Christians is that they strive to apply biblical guidelines and theological perspectives as faithfully and consistently as they are able.

Biblical silences serve as a warning against undue dogmatism and triumphalist interpretation on issues of little concern or relevance to the biblical writers. Humility of interpretation and speculation is the only way forward for Christians.

Another relevant consideration in this context is what is sometimes referred to as a 'benefit of doubt' interpretation. According to this, whenever there is any doubt about the ethical position to be adopted, the traditional moral position should be given the benefit of the doubt. In practice, this leads to protection for embryos, children and disabled individuals. Not surprisingly, this approach has great attraction for many Christians, and it is an attraction with which all Christians should have sympathy. Unfortunately, while its commendable aim is that of protection for the weak and defenceless, it is too general an approach to be of assistance when confronted by very hard dilemmas. These have to be worked through as systematically as possible, since choices sometimes have to be made between two weak individuals, both of whom the benefit-of-doubt approach wishes to assist.

There is also another consideration, and this is that the benefit-of-doubt approach is a conservative approach rather than a Christian one. This does not invalidate it, but it reminds us that it is not biblical *per se*. Consequently, there should be no hint that it is superior to approaches that ignore this consideration. It is a helpful approach, rather than an exclusive one.

Are the foetus and adult morally equivalent?

Consider Exodus 21:22–5, since this is freely used to teach the parity of the mother and foetus, and yet it has lent itself to a variety of opposing interpretations by biblical scholars. A pregnant woman becomes involved in a fight between two men; she is hit and the result is a miscarriage. The critical issue concerns the nature of the penalties to be exacted by the husband for injury to the woman and death of the foetus. According to one group of scholars a distinction is made between the death of the foetus and the death of the woman on the ground that foetal life is not equivalent to adult human life. If a foetus died a fine was exacted, the level of the fine being determined by the husband and judges. On the other hand, if the woman was injured or died, the law of punishment in kind (*lex talionis*) was applied. According to Exodus 21:12, anyone killing a baby, child or adult was considered a murderer, for whom the death penalty was exacted.

An alternative interpretation is that, where injury or death occurs, *lex talionis* applies to both the foetus and mother. Hence, in the case of Exodus 21:22, there was to be a demand for damages for causing the woman to go into premature labour. The following verses exacted further compensation if either mother or foetus suffered physically. Consequently, mother and foetus are considered of equal value.

Whatever interpretation is the more appropriate (and this depends a great deal on the translation consulted and on the biblical scholar followed), I regard this as a slender basis on which to build a whole theology of the foetus. The biblical writer was dealing with the regulations within a covenant community, and his primary concern at this juncture was with the nature of the punishment to be inflicted for injury following accidents or fighting. He was not dealing with the status of the foetus as such, nor with its importance relative to that of an adult human life. This passage deals with unintentional abortion brought about by personal conflict.

There are even greater difficulties in applying this passage to the status of the embryo and early foetus. The miscarriage at the heart of Exodus 21:22–5 must have been of a relatively well-developed foetus, perhaps six months or older. Had the miscarriage been of an embryo of just a few days' or a few weeks' gestation, the woman would probably not have been aware of her pregnancy, let alone of a miscarriage. To extrapolate from the miscarriage of an older foetus to the status of an embryo a few days old involves a major leap, which has to be justified on the grounds of legitimate biblical interpretation. I do not consider that such justification exists.

A second argument is that Jesus' incarnation bestows upon all human embryos an inviolable status from the beginning of their physical existence. As we have seen previously, the incarnation stresses that foetal life is integral to the lives of human beings. Our lives as individuals commenced at fertilization, just as the life of Jesus as a human being commenced at fertilization. Nevertheless, there is a major jump from here to the position that the incarnation demonstrates the ethical and spiritual significance of a few days of embryonic life in the absence of any ongoing human life as an individual. To argue like this in no way underestimates the significance of Jesus' commencing his life as an embryo. However, the attempt to derive from this statement specific biological principles about fertilization or genetic uniqueness, is an interpretation that owes far more to perceived needs within contemporary society than to biblical interpretive principles.

An additional problem is that the fertilization of Jesus was quite different from that of all other human beings: it did not involve the fertilization of an ovum by a sperm. Why, then, should Jesus' fertilization as a biological phenomenon be used as the basis of a theological statement about the status of all normally conceived foetuses? The one does not lead to the other, no matter how important each may be in its own right. A biological difference of this dimension cannot be ignored when biological issues are at stake.

A third issue concerns the use of biblical data to justify the significance of the foetal existence of Jesus. The account in question is that in which John the Baptist as a six-month-old foetus in his mother's womb 'leaped for joy' (Lk. 1:41–4). One interpretation of this is that it was a special movement inspired by the Holy Spirit, and that the six-month-old foetus was Spirit-endowed. Another interpretation is that the foetus's joy was prompted by the two-week-old embryo of Jesus, although the interpretation could equally well have been that the foetus responded to the coming of Mary.

This passage undoubtedly indicates that God was at work in John the Baptist's life, even prior to his birth. However, yet another major leap is involved in moving from this passage, with its description of a unique event, to the viewpoint that all foetuses ever conceived have precisely the same status as humans after birth. That could well be true, but even if it is, it does not come out of this passage. If there is a direct application of this passage relevant to us today, it probably teaches that all foetuses are filled with the Holy Spirit. Not only is an interpretation along these lines unwarranted, it also detracts from the spiritual significance of the account, that the six-month-old foetus of John the Baptist was endowed with the Holy Spirit. Such an interpretation is also of no relevance to contemporary biological debate.

A fourth point emerges from Luke's account, where the word *brephos* used to describe the unborn John the Baptist is also used to describe the newborn Jesus and the infants brought to Jesus for blessing (Lk. 1:41; 2:12, 16; 18:15). This is said to favour the humanity of the foetus, and especially the beginning of personal identity at fertilization. Interesting as this conclusion is, it does not necessarily follow from use of this particular word, which refers to a single instance of older foetal life and on other occasions to infants and children. It may emphasize the spiritual and moral significance of older foetuses, but by itself should not be used as the basis of a vast generalization about the inviolability of all foetal life. Those who advocate the latter are arguing far more from silence than from this one word.

Another issue is raised when it is noted that Levi was in the loins of his ancestor, Abraham his great grandfather (Heb. 7:9, 10). These verses appear to recognize an individual human being before fertilization, since the genes that will eventually form Levi are still in Abraham's testes. Does this mean that Levi was recognized as a unique individual before he was a fertilized ovum? John Medina (*The Outer Limits of Life*), in making this point, goes further and claims that Abraham's sperm cells could only have contained bits and pieces of genetic information, that generations later would become Levi. From this he concludes, 'This Scripture, examined rigorously, appears to say that God recognizes future genetic information as distinct, protectable humanity before formation of eggs and sperm.'

Tongue in cheek, he contends that if we use this passage in the same literal way as some other passages are used, we will end up having to save the product of every ejaculation on the planet, since God appears to recognize individuals as distinct beings before they are germ line cells. Perhaps, he argues, as I have been arguing, that biblical passages were never meant to be used to interpret the beginnings of human life.

The prenatal existence of Jesus

The incarnation of Jesus brings us face to face with prenatal existence, since Jesus himself commenced his human existence as an embryo. Like all other human beings, Jesus developed gradually and for nine months was a foetus. For example, the angel of the Lord told Joseph not to be afraid to take Mary as his wife, 'because what is conceived in her is from the Holy Spirit' (Mt. 1:20). Jesus, like us, experienced the whole of foetal existence, in that his incarnation encompassed prenatal as well as postnatal life. This, in turn, introduces us not to some theoretical piece of data, but to a very human set of possibilities.

The pre-birth narratives, such as Luke 1:26–45 and Matthew 1:20–3, introduce two women – expectant mothers – acting as we might expect such women to act, but also knowing that they were experiencing quite extraordinary pregnancies. As we read these accounts, it is easy to forget how uncertain these events were for both Elizabeth and Mary. Of these uncertainties, one was the possibility that something could have gone wrong during development of the foetuses. There is no reason why this could not have happened to the foetus that would develop into John and also to the foetus that would develop into Jesus.

We have so wrapped the baby Jesus in swaddling clothes, that we fail to see the risk God was taking in allowing Jesus to become fully human. This was no fail-safe pregnancy and birth; this was real drama with the possibility of failure. After all, consider the actions of Herod after his birth. Herod did his best to kill the infant Jesus, and the little family had to flee for their lives in order to escape. Even then, the consequences for other baby boys and other families were tragic; so many were killed. Jesus was not immune from danger as an infant, and there is no reason for thinking he was immune from danger before birth. If we fail to see this, we overlook what God had to overcome in order to bring about the salvation of human-kind. Of course, God would protect Jesus as he developed and grew, and yet this was against a background of much that could have gone astray. Some assume that God will use instant remedies to fulfil His purposes, particularly in difficult situa-tions. Yet we see that in Jesus' life this was not the case. Jesus' life was not a smooth and straight road to travel – the pathway of faith never is.

The meeting between Mary and Elizabeth illustrates that both pregnancies were very fragile and very dangerous processes. In becoming a human being, God undertook an exceedingly dangerous journey, and he did this for humankind. God works through all the things that can go wrong in human life, the major point to emerge being that he establishes cer-tainty in the midst of uncertainty. God worked through the very real dangers inherent in life before birth in order to appear as that baby in the manger. The world of the womb was just as dangerous for Jesus as for anyone else, and yet God allowed him to develop through these immense dangers so that he could experience every aspect of what it means to be human.

The importance of context

We have to be exceptionally careful that we do not manipulate Scripture to provide us with ideas we already hold. I have great sympathy with those who want everyone to treat foetuses as inviolable. This is a commendable moral position, one that fits comfortably with Christian aspirations, with a bias in favour of embryos and foetuses whenever possible. I have no doubt whatsoever that the biblical revelation bestows enormous value upon prenatal as well as postnatal human life. However, the revelation has to be seen as a whole, and we are in great danger when we emphasize the inviolability of prenatal human life but are silent on the inviolability of postnatal human life.

We also have to interpret Scripture in context. Consider Psalm 139, and verses 13–18. We take this passage out of context when we apply it to the status of foetuses, since it is dealing with the psalmist's response to being attacked by godless foes, a response that is fourfold. These particular verses constitute one of the four responses, in which the psalmist looks back at his own journey as a human being, and at the way in which God had been with him up to the present time.

What we have here is the psalmist, as one of God's servants, praising God for the way God had cared for him throughout his own prenatal existence. This exposes an element of the psalmist's thinking that is often foreign to us: he was poignantly aware that God had created him. God had brought him into being, or in picturesque language, God had put him together in his mother's womb. God was looking on, and indeed God was involved in forming what he now is, physically and psychologically. God was there, and because he was there and because he was an active participant in all that went on, he has an intimate knowledge of this human being who is now his servant and who is in trouble. And so, as the psalmist looks back at his own life, from long before he had any personal recollection of it, he sees God at work; he sees God protecting him and caring for him. And the only conclusion he can arrive at is that if God cared for him then, he must still care for him now. The psalmist recognizes continuity from the foetus he was before birth to the adult life he experiences now, but he also recognizes another form of continuity and this is the one he is emphasizing, namely, the continuity in God's care and provision for him.

What is more God 'saw' the psalmist before he was born; in some way he knew him then. But he also knows, in some mysterious way, the days that lie ahead for the psalmist. God who has cared for us in the past goes on caring for us into the future. Just as we can now affirm that he cared for us before we were even aware of our surroundings, let alone of God, he will go on

caring for us well beyond any future we can ever imagine. As
we look back, and as we look forward, we are aware that God
is with us, always going before us. This is a much deeper affir-
mation of the constancy and care of God, no matter what may
befall us in human terms. These verses affirm that God is *my*
creator, as well as *the* creator.

These emphases, which come through these verses with
such startling clarity and power, tell us nothing directly about
how to deal with embryos in the laboratory, or to utilize
foetuses that have been aborted (either spontaneously or
induced). On the other hand, they tell us a great deal about
how God's people are to face tribulation and the attacks of
those who would destroy them; they are enormously useful in
helping us appreciate God's concern for his faithful followers.
As such we are given pointers about how we are to treat others, especially those who are also God's faithful followers.
The psalm is silent beyond this, since the psalmist was far
more concerned with God's glory than with his ethical obligations towards those who care little for God's name (verses
19–22).

Celebrating life before birth

The status we ascribe to foetal life reflects a mixture of theological, ethical and biological presuppositions. The duty of
Christians is to be as loyal as possible to the diverse range
of principles and teaching found in the Bible, alongside which
they are to hold consistent ethical principles and reliable
biological interpretations. It is this diversity that presents
problems. Many Christians feel there is a hierarchy, with the
biblical principles placed at the top. This is fine, as long as
the biblical principles are not detached from the science and
the ethics. All three are required if we are to gain a coherent
perspective of our world, and of human beings within the
world.

Problems arise when biblical principles alone are given cre-
dence for arriving at Christian ethical solutions. The silences, as
I have indicated, have to be left as silences, or filled in as

constructive a fashion as possible. Over against this approach is one where Christians rely solely on secular ethical principles, and leave no room for biblical insights. I am equally unhappy with this approach, since it leads to a denial of any Christian input, or at best to the insertion of isolated Christian precepts. Biblical, scientific and ethical principles, held in tension, are all essential, no matter how demanding the tension at some points. With these thoughts in mind, let us unpack various ingredients of what I view as a viable Christian perspective.

This starts from the fundamental assertion that foetuses are human beings; they are genetically part of the species *Homo sapiens*. Foetuses are one of us: they are the earliest versions of ourselves. We would be foolish to deny the continuity between ourselves as embryos, ourselves as foetuses, ourselves as children, and ourselves as adults. As we look back at our own histories as human beings, we have to learn to recognize the significance of our lives as embryos, foetuses and neonates, even before we had any memories of being 'us'. We existed for a time on the knife-edge of existence dependent on our mothers, and known to God far more than to any humans. The ambivalence of these early stages is unnerving, and yet we would not be what we are now without these tentative stages in human existence. Then we were only barely 'known' as members of the human community.

Our humanity now, with all we confess and acknowledge and celebrate, owes a great deal to our dim humanity then. And so, it is appropriate that we celebrate the prenatal stage of human existence, ascribing value to it. As we do this, we are stating that foetuses have a value in and of themselves, just as we have a value in and of ourselves. They achieve significance because they are one with us within the circle of humanity. Foetuses throughout development are important, and it is fitting that we who are able to ascribe significance and dignity to others should ascribe significance and dignity to foetuses. An unborn human has the potential to become a fully developed, mature human being, and therefore we ought to treat all foetuses with seriousness and concern. A new human life has commenced, and under all normal circumstances that life is to be nurtured and protected.

Closely associated with this resolve is an awareness that our responsibility as human beings is to protect other humans, especially the weak and disadvantaged. This protection should extend to the foetus, which straddles the borderline between life and death, sufficiently immature not to warrant protection and barely mature enough to be treated as a human being. This is what one would expect of this knife-edge period of our existence. To deny protection to these early stages, but strive for it later on, is to deny the significance of the biological continuum, let alone the continuum of God's care, that extends from the foetus to old age.

This is the general principle, and it is a principle with immense repercussions. As we focus our attention and start asking specific questions, we have to acknowledge that we are moving into territory where there are no precise biblical directives. This is where the interpretation and extrapolation of the principles become critical, and where we have to rely on general ethical and theological principles, and where we have to seek the guidance of the Holy Spirit for our thinking and actions.

Are there any differences between what we were as foetuses and what we are as adult humans? Obviously there are: foetuses manifest few of the characteristics of human persons; their intellectual and rational abilities are limited or non-existent. They may be one of us, but they have yet to manifest the characteristics we expect of personhood and of beings made in the image and likeness of God. Nevertheless, the embryo and early foetus are human beings, with the full potential of growing into adult human persons. But this does not resolve the issue of whether we as adults are morally obligated to protect them under every conceivable circumstance. Where does this leave us?

Our responsibility for embryos and foetuses should lead under all normal circumstances to their protection. It is our duty to protect them from wanton and needless destruction. The recognition of foetuses as 'the last of the unemancipated', and as some of the weakest and most defenceless members of the human community, leads inevitably to horror at the widescale slaughter of foetuses in which many societies indulge.

Neither should we go to the opposite extreme and conclude that foetal life is of greater value than postnatal human life. Human life in general does not receive absolute protection. It is not only foetuses that are weak and defenceless: so are children brought up in impersonal institutions, beaten at home, malnourished, enticed into smoking cigarettes or drinking alcohol by sophisticated advertising, or born with appalling physical deformities. Any ethical system needs to pay serious attention to all endangered human life, and not just that of foetuses. Since the foetus is part of a human continuum extending from well before birth and ending many years after birth, it should never be made the sole object of ethical attention. In a fallen world there are often conflicting demands and interests, all of which need to be taken into account. All human life is precious, and as far as possible, our actions should bear testimony to the dignity and value of all individuals – foetal as well as adult, adult as well as foetal. Conflict will, however, sometimes arise between the good of the embryo or foetus and the good of the mother and family, and perhaps even the good of society. Our ethical principles have to address such conflict.

Embryos and foetuses are never simply means to an end, whether this end be that of the pursuit of scientific and medical information, or the perceived welfare of another human being. The perspective I have developed leads to respect for an embryo for what it is now and prospectively. The early embryo is not nothing, even if it is not a mature human person. To isolate an embryo or foetus from its future dimension, and to treat it as though it was an end in itself as an embryo or foetus, is to fragment the history of an individual human being. An embryo or foetus is something, even if not yet somebody, although this something is mainly due to its potential in the future to be somebody.

We should be honest and admit that there is ambivalence, both ethically and scientifically, about the embryo and early foetus. We do not have a biblical warrant for undue dogmatism in this area; neither do we have sufficient scientific information to make categorical assertions. Faced with the mystery of our own beginnings, we begin to realize something of the mystery of human existence itself.

The way in which we treat human beings is critical, and as long as this is emphasized, all humans, prenatal and postnatal, healthy and unhealthy, young and old, mentally retarded and demented, are to be provided with considerable protection. This is one expression of the biblical principle that we are to live for others and are to give ourselves for others. The great conundrum is the extent to which this incorporates embryonic and foetal life.

Five

Personhood and the Image of God

Clearing the ground

Throughout this book it is impossible to avoid reference to 'persons' and 'personhood'. This upsets some Christians who see the use of these terms and the ideas that go with them, as driving a wedge between what it means to be a human being and what it means to be a person. Once this is done, their fear is that some human beings will be treated as non-persons, and that the equality that should exist between all humans will be lost. In other words, the use of a concept like personhood may lead to the single population of human beings being divided into two subpopulations – persons and non-persons, those who are truly human and those who have failed to make it. Let me illustrate by reference to embryos.

All human embryos are human beings, in that they belong to the species *Homo sapiens*; they are undoubtedly human material, they are formed of human tissue, and if allowed to develop will one day become like the rest of us. Christians also contend that human embryos in some senses image God, and so any procedure that results in embryos and postnatal humans being classed differently may undermine embryos as images of God. On this basis, many would argue that human embryos should be looked at and valued in exactly the same way as those of us who are reading these words. Since no one has the right to kill us, no one has the right to kill human embryos. We are of absolute value, and so are they.

What is significant about these statements is that not one of them has made any reference to whether or not embryos are persons, and some think there is no need to do so. For them, the notion of personhood is anathema because it is seen as threatening basic Christian values. After all, once embryos are deemed to be anything other than human beings like us (perhaps non-persons or potential persons), the prospect opens up that they will be valued less than we are valued.

The concern is that, just as embryos may be devalued, a range of other vulnerable groups, such as imperilled infants, retarded children and adults, seriously brain-damaged individuals, those in a persistent vegetative state, and those with severe dementia, may also be devalued. In all these groups there are some who are so unlike us that questions are raised about the continued value of their existence. The best way to protect these at-risk groups, so the argument goes, is to regard them as human beings on exactly the same level as all other humans: they have to be treated precisely as the rest of us are treated. No distinction will ever be made between the value of a brilliant thirty-year-old and the value of a severely mentally retarded thirty-year-old, and therefore the resources to be directed towards each of these individuals will be identical. The other side of the argument is that, if the notion of personhood is used it becomes possible to bestow greater value on the brilliant individual than on the mentally retarded one, so that the former will be given more health-care resources than the latter. It may even be suggested that it would be better for the mentally retarded individual if he or she did not go on living. This may or may not be the case, but the question raised by many Christians is that even the merest such possibility is unthinkable since both are images of God. It becomes intolerable even to contemplate a distinction between these or any other human beings, regardless of their stage of development, quality of physical or mental life, or their wantedness by others in the human community.

This is the sort of testimony brought to bear against using a notion like personhood, and on the surface it is a most attractive approach within a Christian perspective. But is this attraction illusory? While I would prefer not to talk about persons and personhood, I have come to the conclusion that I have no option but to do so.

Thinking about dead bodies

As an anatomist I am used to dealing with dead human bodies, since my university department always has bodies for teaching and research purposes. The bodies are generally kept for a few years, and before they are eventually cremated they will have been extensively dissected. I am also used to going into our museum where there are parts of bodies in pots, as well as slices through bodies that have been preserved and treated so that they are virtually indestructible. Then there are the human brains that are used in our neuroanatomy classes.

These are real people; they are someone's grandmother, aunt, father or husband. There are people in the community for whom these were once their loved ones; they remember them and may still be grieving their death. And yet here we are cutting them up, and we can do this because the people themselves bequeathed their bodies to the department so that they could be studied in these various ways. There are many issues that have to be considered before we can act in these ways, the most important of which are ethical issues.

But are these bodies people? Are they persons? Are Dick and Felicity still there, or are they the remains of Dick and Felicity? Are we dissecting people or bodies? Those of us involved in this area have no doubt that we treat these bodies with immense respect, since they are all that we now have to remind us of the people who once spoke, laughed, ate and joked as we do today. These memories are especially pertinent for those who once knew them and loved them, but even for those of us who never knew them they are reminders that we ourselves will one day be cadavers (dead human bodies). One day we will no longer be able to strive for those things that mean a great deal to us, even though our bodies may continue for a time.

Dead bodies force us to recognize that there are circumstances where we are forced to distinguish between a human being and the person who once made that human being something of immense worth and significance. Generally we do not separate the two, since we recognize a person by their body, appearance, voice, and actions. But there are exceptions, of which death is one, and if this is an exception there may be others. Exceptions do not question the assertion that human beings are in the image of God, but what they do tell us is that we often have to make judgements about how people are to be treated. The simple fact that they are God's image does not settle ethical questions. Consider the following:

Stephanie has extremely severe brain damage after a motor car accident. She is in a persistent vegetative state, and will never again be able to communicate in any way with anyone. Before the accident that led to this condition, she was a writer and effective speaker; she looked after her two children, and she regularly led Bible studies. Her family now have no idea whether she can respond in even the simplest way to them. Never again will she write or speak a word, never again will she see her children, and never again will she have a thought about the Bible. But her body is alive.

Dougald has also been injured in a car accident, and has brain damage. The after-effects are severe, and he has difficulty in reading and writing. Indeed he has had to be taught to read and write, and he is making very slow progress. Never again will he stand in front of a class of students or carry out an experiment in his laboratory. But he is able to get around, and he shows immense determination to make as much as he can of his severely limited abilities. He is coming to accept that he will never again be the person he was before the accident, but he is making for himself a new life and he is grateful to be alive.

Is there any difference between Stephanie and Dougald? Both have been badly damaged by their respective accidents. Neither will again be able to do what they did before, and yet one has no awareness of being alive whereas the other does. Can they both be described as persons? There is no doubt that Dougald is a person; even if his accident had changed his personality, he would be a person. But what about Stephanie? She presents us with a problem. Is her condition closer to that of the dead bodies in an anatomy department, or to that of Dougald? What do her relatives think, and what would they think if she remained in this condition for five, ten or 20 years?

We may not wish to be confronted with the issue of personhood, but when faced by situations such as these, it seems very difficult to avoid. It is hard to imagine how people like Stephanie and Dougald can be regarded in exactly the same light. If they are, we will find it extraordinarily difficult to make decisions about appropriate health care for each. It is imperative then to look further into this matter.

What is a person?

Robert Wennberg (*Life in the Balance*) identifies personhood with the ability to engage in acts of intellect, emotion and will at an appropriate level. For him, persons are individuals with a developed capacity for rational, moral and spiritual agency, that is, they can think, reflect, make plans, fall in love, worship, make decisions and have regrets. Writing from a Christian perspective, he distinguishes between the terms 'person' and 'human', because while God is a person he is not a human being. On the other hand, a dead corpse is still a human corpse even though it is no longer a person, since its capacity for rational activity has been irrevocably terminated. For him, a foetus is human but is not a person, since it has not yet developed the functional ability to engage in personal acts. He also argues that personal life does not begin to emerge until some time after birth, when the socialization process begins. Both foetuses and newborn infants possess biological human life, but neither possesses personal human life. This statement by itself does not tell us whether or not foetuses have a right to life; that has to be determined on other grounds.

Theologically, Wennberg virtually equates the terms 'human person' and 'image of God', although the latter is a more encompassing term since it includes the notion that we are finite replicas of God, having a special value and also special responsibility before God. It points to persons as those capable of responding to God, worshipping him, and being transformed into his moral likeness. Hence, he views the image of God as something individuals become as they gradually acquire the ability to engage in personal acts; it is not something that is instantaneously present before birth when they lack intellectual and moral capabilities. Not only this, infants and foetuses cannot respond to God or worship him, and therefore cannot image him.

From this it follows that one's status as a special object of God's love and grace is tied to one's nature as a person who can respond to God, enter into a personal relationship with him, and be morally and spiritually accountable to him. Human beings are special because they possess the possibility of reflecting the moral character of God himself.

Wennberg's qualitative stance is a fairly extreme one within the Christian community, since he is prepared to spell out in precise detail the relationship between being a person and the possession of specific abilities. However, even if foetuses and some other groups of humans are not persons, they do not become valueless. The decision as to what should or should not be done to them has to be made using a range of well-grounded ethical criteria.

A modified version of this position distinguishes between when human beings attain personhood and when they should be treated as if they had attained personhood, the consequence of this being that society has to decide when to confer personhood on developing human beings. This position lends itself to a gradualist position, according to which if, in the normal course of development, beings will become those who image God, then by virtue of this potential they already deserve some of the reverence due those who image God.

Alternative stances

The first alternative is the most conventional of the three. Teresa Iglesias (*Embryos and Ethics*) argues that to be a human being is to be a person, so that this identity holds even at the very earliest stages in human existence. In the case of human embryos, personal abilities, including self-awareness, choice and creativity, are all potentially present from the earliest stages of development; they are not added to any particular stage of development. All the capacities we now have as personal human beings developed from what we were at the beginning of our existence, since an inherent capacity for those abilities must always have been present in the human organism from its beginning. Any actual capacity we currently possess (such as self-consciousness and self-determination) must have existed prior to its manifestation. This argument from potential leads to the view that the kind of life an embryo has is personal life, simply because of its capacity for personal life (unlike a dog's potential).

In this manner Iglesias aims to bypass any problems inherent in development. No matter where an entity may be along a developmental continuum, it is still a complete entity. Hence an early embryo, a late foetus, an infant, and an adult are single entities, not because they all possess the same abilities, but because they possess the capacity to develop from one stage to the next. But does this approach assist in distinguishing one phase from another, especially when there is conflict? Interesting as it may be to hold them up as identical, this is deceptive. It is also pertinent to ask why we should view this approach as inherently Christian. It is a conservative approach, and this may appeal to many Christians, but it has little by way of the theological to offer.

A more nuanced approach is that of Oliver O'Donovan (*Begotten or Made?*), who starts from a similar position, but views the early developmental stages from the viewpoint of human appearance and identity. He firmly rejects the sort of qualitative analysis espoused by Wennberg. In his view, a person is not a genetic or biological category, and human personality cannot be understood from an experimental scientific perspective. There is, therefore, no point in looking for scientific measures of personhood, all of which are irrelevant and probably misleading.

Instead, in order to gain an understanding of what the term 'person' means, one has to look to identity that which makes us beings with histories and names. According to O'Donovan, we discover the significance of people by interacting with them in love, and by committing ourselves to them and their welfare. In this way we come to appreciate that particular human beings are irreplaceable. Although we are only able to discover these things in just a few human beings, we subsequently have to generalize from these few to all others. This generalization, he argues, is essential if we are to commit ourselves in personal relationship to children in the womb or to the severely handicapped.

O'Donovan is prepared to use the term 'person', although his use of it is based squarely on relationships. As long as relationships are positive and supportive, I have a great deal of sympathy for his position, since relationships are fundamental to what we are as beings in the image of God (see Chapter 3). The problem comes when relationships are isolated from other aspects of what it means to image God. When relationships go wrong, when foetuses are not dealt with in love, we have to have other means of deciding how persons are to be treated. Useful as this approach is, it does not seek to come to terms with detailed decision-making; no matter how great our commitment to individuals, that commitment will not answer specific ethical questions. Commitment to persons is a helpful pointer, but conflict between respective treatments for different persons requires resolution at a more precise level.

Another interesting Christian contribution is provided by Gilbert Meilaender (*Bioethics*), who starts from the standard position that we are persons throughout our history. Those humans who lack certain cognitive capacities are regarded as simply the weakest and most needy members of our community. We care for them and we care about them as we seek to discover in their faces the hidden spirit, the face of Christ, and the call to community.

On this basis, he contends that while we should not allow people to die, useless treatments can be refused. The distinction he draws is 'Will the treatments benefit the life this patient has?' as opposed to 'Is this patient's life a beneficial one, a life worth living?' He concedes that some treatments may be excessively burdensome, so that withdrawal of this burden amounts to refusal of treatment, but not rejection of life. This distinction is a crucial one for him, illustrated with regard to the persistent vegetative state, where the withdrawal of feeding is, in his view, aimed at taking life. The same seems to apply to the severely retarded, and the permanently unconscious. This position stands or falls on definitions of useless and excessively burdensome treatment, and hence on the distinction between taking life and choosing life. The withdrawal of feeding in the persistent vegetative state is a case in point, since it is not self-evident that this is taking life (the person may be dead, even if the body is still alive).

Is this approach successful in bypassing use of the term 'person'? In order not to distinguish between human beings and persons, a distinction has to be made between different forms of treatment. This is ambiguous at best, and in my view raises as many problems as does the notion of personhood. Not only this, it fails to provide a means of resolving conflict situations where two individuals or groups of equal value come up against each other.

The image of God

We have already seen how some writers practically equate the image of God with personhood, and this is not surprising since both centre on the attributes of human beings (actual or potential). A few of the features of being imaged after God's likeness were outlined in Chapter 3.

The phrase 'image of God' occurs principally in the early chapters of Genesis (1:26, 27; 9:6), as well as in a small number of New Testament passages (1 Cor. 11:7; 2 Cor. 4:4; Col. 1:15). There is also reference to people being in the likeness of God (Jas. 3:9). Other New Testament passages refer to the transformation of Christians into the image of Christ (Rom. 8:29; 2 Cor. 3:18; Col. 3:10).

The image of God has been interpreted in a variety of ways historically: to refer to the spirituality, rationality and morality of human beings; to their dominion over creation; to their capacity to enter into relationship with God; and to physical attributes such as their physical bodies and upright posture. It is these capacities taken together that bestow upon humans their uniqueness.

No matter which aspect we consider, we are confronted by developed attributes, whether these be the human ability to make choices, make moral judgements, or reflect on their situation. The same applies to human relationships with others, with creation and with God. What, then, is their relevance for ethical concerns? The presence or otherwise of these capacities during development (and following catastrophic injury) presents exactly the same issues as does personhood during development. Emphasis will be placed on either the sufficiency of potential or the necessity of the actual. It is not surprising that the relationship between talk about personhood and about the image of God is a very close one.

One possibility is to stress the importance of acting in a neighbourly fashion towards all human beings, including those unable to demonstrate the capacities associated with images of God. In acting thus, we act as true images of God, and we also treat these others as images of God. This is akin to O'Donovan's emphasis on human appearance, and it constitutes an important element within a Christian approach. However, it leaves untouched detailed ethical decision-making.

Personhood at the edges of human life

It should have become clear that we have a choice to make whenever confronted by human beings such as embryos, foetuses, handicapped infants, or those with very severe brain damage. When unable to respond or express preferences because of their early stage of development or the extent of their damaged brains, we shall stress either that which is currently present in these individuals, or their potential for reaching a level of responsiveness characteristic of normal human existence. This applies whether we talk about personhood or the image of God.

In my estimation there is no escape from this dilemma once we are in a position of having to make precise ethical decisions. If we have the luxury of confining our attention to a general level, vague general assertions may well suffice.

Indeed, Christian directives may prove very instructive. But as soon as precise guidelines become inevitable, these general directives and assertions have to be fleshed out as we struggle with weighing up one set of values against another. And it is here that references to persons and personhood may come into play.

Some Christians will attempt to avoid such references, and I have no problem with that as long as they also provide sufficiently detailed guidance to be of assistance to those having to make extremely demanding decisions. My own conclusion is that there are occasions when this is not possible, and when reference to persons and personhood, and also to potential persons or the potential for personhood, is helpful. These occasions will generally be at the extremes of human life, when the level of intellectual, moral and spiritual abilities displayed by an individual is minimal or even non-existent, and when taking account of the lack of these abilities will assist decision-makers. In such situations we are operating on the brink of moral and spiritual ambiguity, and person-based guidelines may assist when Christian emphases based on neighbourliness, humility, servanthood, integration and community have set the scene, but seem unable to take us any further.

Six

From Non-Existence to Existence

Conceiving children

An imaginary family: part I

In 1980 John and Jean had two children. Up until the mid-1980s John and Jean were not convinced their family should be extended beyond two children. Most of their friends and contemporaries had just two children, and they had already passed the stage of even questioning that decision. But John and Jean did decide to have a third child. Then, a few years later they had a fourth child.

Today, John and Jean have four children – three teenagers, and one a little younger. The first two children, James and Susan, were always contemplated. What though about numbers three and four, Clive and Sandra? They exist today because John and Jean changed their minds about having them.

Clive and Sandra are unique individuals, both biologically and in God's sight. Very easily, though, they may not have existed – not because of any obvious rebellion or sinfulness on the part of John and Jean, but because of a sincerely held viewpoint. Clive and Sandra almost failed to make it. If they had not, they would never have risen beyond the realm of hypothetical beings, with no more substance to their existence than occasional wistful longings on the part of either John or Jean.

Clive and Sandra bring us face to face with a mystery: philosophical, theological and biological; the 'control' of fertilization. Fertilization is frequently depicted as the absolute dividing line between the absence of an individual and the appearance of a new individual. Consequently, many Christians place a great deal of moral weight on this process. The emphasis is almost always on the moral significance of interrupting the development of an embryo or foetus after the occurrence of fertilization. If this is done, there will be no individual in the future, whether this is due to induced abortion, spontaneous abortion, or some accident during prenatal life. However, exactly the same result is obtained by a decision on the part of the would-be parents against conceiving any future individuals.

Let us imagine some alternative scenarios for our imaginary family, keeping in mind that James and Susan do exist.

An imaginary family: part II
'Clive' and 'Sandra' were conceived, existed for a matter of three or four days as embryos, but then failed to implant in the wall of the uterus. Indeed, Jean may never have been aware that they even existed for that short period of time, and would have been disappointed had she known.

An imaginary family: part III
We can suppose that John and Jean did not want any more children, and so Jean was using an intrauterine contraceptive device. By this means, any embryos that might have been produced would have been prevented from implanting.

An imaginary family: part IV
We are informed that John and Jean employed an oral contraceptive, thereby preventing fertilization from occurring. Although John and Jean were quite capable of producing embryos, and of giving rise to a 'Clive' and a 'Sandra', they decided against this.

An imaginary family: part V
John and Jean are using the rhythm method, a 'natural' form of contraception, and thereby once again avoiding fertilization. A 'Clive' and a 'Sandra' would not have been given

existence, although in this instance no artificial methods of contraception would have been resorted to. (Precisely the same result would have been obtained by ceasing to have intercourse, or by either partner being sterilized.)

These scenarios all have the same end result, and yet there are many differences – in motives, in the use or otherwise of contraceptives, in the adoption of natural or artificial forms of contraception, and in the occurrence or non-occurrence of fertilization. Beings whom we now call Clive and Sandra would have been prevented from coming into existence, and would never have become one with us in experiencing what 'being human' means. Can we conclude from these scenarios that John and Jean would have been morally culpable in those instances in which they decided against conceiving (regardless of the manner in which they accomplished this)? My answer is 'no', unless we have moral obligations to non-existent beings.

Non-existence

Given we do not have moral obligations to non-existent beings, what are our *theological* obligations to non-existent beings? Does God expect married couples to 'bring forth' children, and if so, is there any limit to the number of children? Is it more spiritual to conceive ten children rather than four, or four rather than two, or two rather than one, or one rather than none? Unless one believes that the *primary* purpose of marriage is the production of children, it is difficult to understand how Christian couples can have theological obligations to non-existent children. If it is argued that one does have such obligations, it follows that contraception (whether *natural or artificial*) is contrary to the purposes of God, with natural forms of contraception being just as objectionable as artificial ones.

The number of children conceived is not a simple matter of morality or theology. It is the result of a complex interplay of biology, culture, economics, and peer group pressure. Christians should approach fertilization in a spirit of awe and reverent wonder, since it is the supreme creative act with which we can be associated. We are doubly responsible: first, for bringing into existence new lives, and second, for guiding and directing those children throughout their growing stages until they can assume responsibility themselves for responding to God. This form of creation is something we do in conjunction with God; we are creating beings who are the icons (or images) of God, in precisely the same way as we ourselves are.

Clive and Sandra, therefore, are 'gifts of God'. They are God-like beings, regardless of the manner of their fertilization. They would also have been gifts of God if they had been conceived outside marriage, by donor insemination (DI), by IVF or by gamete intrafallopian transfer (GIFT), or if genetic manipulation had been involved. Whatever we may think of the morality of any or all these procedures, the resulting children are to be treated as we should treat any image of God.

However, if Clive and Sandra had not been given human expression, would John and Jean have been guilty of rejecting a gift of God (since they would have overridden their biological ability of conceiving)? Most married couples are guilty of that, since at some point and in some way, they have not had as many children as they were capable of having. In fact, so are single women and single men. If we approach their ability to procreate only in biological terms, we shall end up with a moral perspective far removed from any Christian one. The reason we do not move in this direction is that we view childbearing not simply in biological terms, but within the much broader context of marriage and, therefore, of moral and social obligations.

The 'gift of God' concept is to be viewed within a framework provided by moral principles (is it within the context of marriage?), human decision (is it responsible in our circumstances?), and physiological capabilities (are we capable of having a child?). Together, these three components comprise God's gift of a child. To emphasize one at the expense of the others is to have a misconstrued view of what God's gift amounts to. In other words, to emphasize the ability of a married couple to conceive at the expense of making responsible decisions, is to demean God's gift, just as it is to have a child outside the marriage (commitment) relationship. The decision to have no children *at all* within a marriage, in spite of an ability to have them, also has to be looked at very closely, for it too may demean God's gift.

If, then, human decision-making is of crucial importance in conceiving, it has to be accepted that the bringing into existence of children like Clive and Sandra is a legitimate function of human beings. We are co-creators with God in the creation of human life (as well as of other life), and there is no escape from the consequences of such decisions.

We have to come to terms with the idea that our own non-existence is a non-question. I can only say that God had purposes for me, and that is why I was conceived, and why two humans 'decided' to have me. I am here as one of God's people (someone who has been created individually by God), with all the possibilities of enjoying God and of extending his kingdom on earth. One can only conclude that God does not have purposes nor a specific intention for the unconceived, that is, the non-existent. Therefore, his intention is not thwarted by the use of contraceptives or simply by a human decision to refrain from having a child.

Fertilization

What about all those embryos that were conceived, but existed for a few days or for a week or two, before being unintentionally discarded? They never had the opportunity of reflecting as I have done. They could never have written a psalm, sung a song, or loved another person; and they were never even recognized as images of God. They were almost as non-existent as if they had never been conceived. Did God have a specific intention for such as these, and was this thwarted by the spontaneous abortion?

Some argue that God's general intention becomes specific at fertilization, since the prospect of a specific embryo developing into a person is much higher than either a specific sperm or a specific ovum will have of developing into a person. This is true, and yet there is only a 50 per cent chance that a specific embryo will develop into a fully developed person. Not only this, but for the first four days or so of development there is no hint of the cells that will give rise to the foetus and future individual. Between 4 and 14 days, it becomes increasingly possible to recognize a small number of cells that are destined to grow into the future individual, although most cells over this period will form the placenta and associated support tissues for the foetus. At the same time, the mother does not perceive this growing embryo as an individual. It is not unreasonable to argue, therefore, that the embryo up to approximately 12 to 14 days of gestation is only part of God's general intention as opposed to his specific intention. Therefore, I suggest that there is very limited theological distinction between those 'beings' which were never fertilized and those which experienced no more than a 'millisecond' of existence. My deep sense of humans as images of God, prevents me from doing otherwise. In what sense are embryos lost early in development any more a Clive and a Sandra, than a sperm and an ovum that could have united to become a Clive and a Sandra, but that did not? Either way, Clive and Sandra did not eventuate; they did not even develop far enough for their mother to experience their presence. They were never one of us; they never became (or even nearly became) one of John and Jean's family. Their lives as human beings had hardly started. There is a difference between the two groups, but it is dangerous to make the differences much larger than they actually are.

Looking backwards and forwards

Another aspect to consider when discussing God's purposes for individuals, is to distinguish between *retrospective* and *prospective* arguments. We can be categorical in saying that God has purposes for both Clive and Sandra. As we look back at their lives we can say that God has been with them from the time of their fertilization, and that he even had purposes for them prior to that (just as he was with Jeremiah and David; see Chapters 3 and 4). This is the *retrospective* certainty that applies to all God's people. However, we cannot say anything about God's purposes for an ovum that *failed* to

be fertilized by a particular sperm. Neither can we say anything about his purposes for an embryo aborted early on in its
existence. We may regret that such an embryo failed to
develop further (and the loss may be grieved), but to argue
prospectively that God had purposes for that embryo, and
that these purposes have now been thwarted, is to assert
something for which we have no warrant. This takes us into
the realm of biblical silence.

The theological rationale we use to back up our ethical
perspective on any issue needs to be well worked out. For
example, we cannot claim that God had further purposes for a
pastor who dies at the height of his ministry, when he
appeared to be in his prime. Humanly speaking, we may
deeply grieve his death and the loss of a ministry that – to us –
had a great deal more to give. But we cannot claim that God's
purposes have been thwarted.

Then there is the distinction between the replaceable and
the irreplaceable. Clive and Sandra are irreplaceable individuals. They have been with us and we have known them; we have
felt and seen them growing and developing, and coming to
occupy a place in the human community (within the family,
neighbourhood, church and school). Their interrelationships
with us affect us and we are changed by them. This is true to a
lesser extent when children die at a very young age; it is also
true to a limited degree of late spontaneous abortions, and
sometimes it may even be true of early abortions. It is not true
in anything like the same way of very early natural abortions
(within the first two to three weeks of gestation), and it is not
true at all of any occurrence prior to fertilization.

In other words, the younger a foetus or embryo is when it
dies, the more it is capable of being replaced by a different individual. This may mean that, in practical terms, many people
regard the young foetus or embryo as having fewer of the
definitive features of an individual than do older foetuses and
children. In these terms, the borderline between replaceability
and irreplaceability is not at fertilization. It is later; how much
later probably depends on numerous factors. I would suggest,
however, that these owe more to biological than to theological
considerations.

What this means is that the value we place on people, including prenatal humans, depends on the extent of the contact we are able to have with them. We cannot value humans who do not exist, and may never exist. We may value the possibility of their existence, but that carries different responsibilities from those we have towards humans who actually exist. What about humans who exist for very brief periods, a few days or so, when the termination of their existence has nothing to do with human actions? How much can we value them? My conclusion is that our valuation of them depends more upon the possibilities they hold out for future human life than upon any inherent value they have as immature embryos. This valuation parallels what I have suggested may be the lack of God's specific intention for them. However, as development proceeds, and as we become more and more aware of the prenatal as people like us, our valuation of them increases. We value them as we are able to relate to them as members of the human community, and as those who are one with us. We recognize, too, their God-likeness, and from this stems our responsibility towards them as neighbours and friends.

Preventing fertilization

Turn now to the methods used by those not wanting a child. Do the different methods used have significance from a Christian standpoint, especially as far as any embryos are concerned? Consider the following.

Imaginary couples I
Imagine four couples: Evans, Thomas, Phillips and Lewis. Not one of them wishes to conceive. Couple Evans decides not to have intercourse, thereby preventing a possible future child from coming into existence. Couple Thomas has intercourse; an oral contraceptive is being used, fertilization does not occur, and no child results. Couple Phillips has intercourse. Since the wife is using an intrauterine contraceptive device, fertilization does occur, but the embryo is prevented from implanting; no child results. Couple Lewis

*has intercourse. No contraceptive is being employed since
they think they are infertile and have no reason to expect to
conceive. However, on this occasion fertilization occurs. A
child is not wanted on account of the wife's serious and
chronic ill health, and so a first trimester abortion is carried
out; no child results.*

These four couples pose immense challenges to our ethical
decision-making, and demonstrate clearly the stress placed on
fertilization. The intention of all four couples is the same, since
not one of them wishes to conceive and bring a new human
being into existence. The result in all four cases is the same,
and yet in two of them fertilization occurs. This immediately
poses a challenge. Is there any moral difference between the
actions of these couples?

An intuitive response is that there appears to be a difference
between the actions of couple Evans and couple Thomas on
the one hand, and couple Phillips and couple Lewis on the
other, since in these latter cases, an embryo or foetus has been
prevented from developing further or has actually
been destroyed. Are either of these actions tenable for Christians? For many people, the actions of couple Phillips and
couple Lewis may sometimes be acceptable, although the
actions of these couples are more problematic than those of
couple Evans and couple Thomas. In turn, the actions of couple Lewis pose greater problems for many than do those of
couple Phillips. If, however, fertilization is used as an absolute
landmark, the actions of couple Phillips and couple Lewis will
be regarded as unethical.

Should Christians regard fertilization in these terms? The
biblical principles that emerged in Chapters 3 and 4 are not
very specific, and they have a family context. And it is precisely this context that is so important for these illustrations,
each of which revolves around a couple demonstrating their
love for each other but not wishing to conceive at this time.
This may be supremely ethical and deeply spiritual. In the
case of couple Lewis, the love of the two for each other leads
them to want to protect the life of the wife. Her life is seen as
being of greater value than the possible life-to-be of the

foetus. Their desire to maintain intact a loving and committed relationship is a profound act of human commitment,
even though its accomplishment involves sacrificing the
future life of a foetus.

The value system I am developing points to the actions of
couple Phillips being more acceptable than those of couple
Lewis, since the embryo of couple Phillips is far less mature
than is the foetus of couple Lewis. In addition, the embryo of
couple Phillips has not implanted. Alongside this, it can be
argued that the actions of couples Phillips and Lewis should
never be courses of choice.

Achieving fertilization

A second illustration refers to couples McDonald, McGregor,
McIntosh, McMillan and McLeod. In this case the couples
wish to conceive.

Imaginary couples II
*Whenever the husband and wife of couple McDonald want
to conceive they know they will be successful within two to
three months. Couple McGregor is also fertile but there are
certain sexual problems requiring counselling. With help,
they overcome these problems and are able to conceive. With
couple McIntosh the male partner has an infertility problem.
However, the use of artificial insemination by the husband
(AIH) helps to circumvent this problem, and fertilization
occurs. In the case of couple McMillan there is an infertility
problem on the female side. This is solved by microsurgery
on her uterine tubes, and fertilization subsequently occurs. A
similar problem exists with couple McLeod; surgery is
unsuccessful in this instance, but fertilization is brought
about using IVF.*

In each of these cases the couple wishes to have a child derived
from their own genetic material. The husband and wife do not
want to introduce a third party into their marriage relationship. Each of the couples is successful, although different

avenues are used. Each of them, ideally, wants a child in the simplest, easiest and most natural fashion – just like couple McDonald – and yet they are unable to do so. The question is, have couples McGregor, McIntosh, McMillan and McLeod acted less ethically than couple McDonald? Is there any distinction between the actions of couples McGregor and McIntosh, both of whom have received therapy and yet only couple McIntosh has had artificial assistance in the reproductive process itself? Is there any distinction between couples McMillan and McLeod, both of whom have the same problem (blockage in the female partner's uterine tubes) and resort to the same initial treatment (microsurgery to repair the blocked tubes); and yet couple McLeod had to go further and employed IVF? I touched on these procedures in Chapter 2, when considering the legitimacy of controlling fertilization using technological means.

Yet again, there is ethical uncertainty. The goal of all five couples is the same – the production of a child from their own bodies, a child who is the outcome of their marital love. In none of these instances has there been any abrogation of the marriage bond or any desire to do so. In each case the desire has been to raise a family of their own, to care for and to bring up any resulting children within the confines of the love and warmth of a couple committed to each other and also to others for whom they have responsibility. Any differences between these couples stem from the extent of their fertility, and the intrusion of therapy into the reproductive process. In terms of the information I have just presented there appear to be no ethical differences between the actions of any of these couples. However, if natural fertilization is regarded as definitive, even AIH becomes unethical, and IVF will definitely be viewed as such.

In these illustrations technology intervenes far more than with the first set, and in some cases there is also separation of the sexual act and fertilization. Are these procedures going beyond the bounds of Christian actions? All the couples desire a child, and they would all like to accomplish this in the simplest way possible. The choice for some of them is no child, or a child brought into being using artificial means.

While artificial means can be pursued for unworthy motives, or in a grossly excessive manner, neither is inevitable and neither applies in these illustrations. It is difficult to accept, therefore, that there is no place for any of these procedures in the lives of Christians.

What is emerging is that considerable emphasis on fertilization does not eliminate conflict and uncertainty. What has happened is that the nature of the uncertainties has changed, and this itself may have a variety of repercussions.

Fertilization and doomed embryos

Let us now move on to look at three other married couples all of whom want a child. We shall follow them through different situations, keeping an eye all the time on the embryos involved in these events.

Imaginary embryos I
Couple Stewart has conceived without any technological assistance. However, let us assume we know a great deal about what has gone on in this particular case, with one embryo being lost after a week or so. The woman knew nothing about it, and had no idea that she had been momentarily pregnant. After a couple of months, a second embryo is fertilized, everything proceeds well, and a baby is born.

Is couple Stewart morally culpable in any way at all? Most would say 'no'. The fact that human embryonic life has been lost is due to the normal process of fertilization, and of the massive number of chromosomal and genetic abnormalities implicit in so much early embryonic development. Loss of this nature is an unavoidable facet of development. This is the way things are; embryos such as these are doomed. I shall argue that we are not justified in giving these embryos a high rating on any scale of human value: they are doomed embryos. Perhaps we should regard them as doomed human material, rather than human beings with potential or even potential human beings.

If we accept this assessment, we are accepting that doomed embryos are a subset of human embryos that cannot be set alongside other human beings, and that cannot be valued as we value other human beings. An alternative is to reject this assessment, since the fact that many embryos are biologically doomed is irrelevant to their moral value. They are as valuable as all other human beings.

I do not think there is one clear answer from a Christian angle. No matter what our view of the status of human embryos (see Chapter 7), doomed embryos have no prospect of becoming people like you and me. And there is nothing we can do to alter this. Even if we think they should be given the value we give to children and adults (they are inviolable), we are unable to do that in this instance. We are unable to change the facts. Doomed embryos will never be able to demonstrate even the remotest glimmerings of ordinary human life.

How do we respond to this possibility? My response is that the biblical principles encountered in Chapter 4 cannot be applied in any direct manner. Embryos that never make it beyond a few days or so are not Davids or Jeremiahs in the making. They are not even Clives or Sandras, or you or me in the making. They are, simply, embryos that never made it.

Doomed embryos are of concern to us because they are human material. By the same token, we are not to bestow upon them value they do not possess. A doomed embryo with its unique genetic make-up is still nothing more than human material, especially when, as with couple Stewart, it failed to develop for reasons beyond the scope of human control. The prospects for such embryos could change at some time in the future, but there is no escape from this conclusion or from this categorization at present.

Imaginary embryos II
Couple Taylor has experienced severe fertility problems, and has resorted to IVF. Four embryos have been fertilized in the laboratory, and all four have been transferred to the wife's uterus. Of these, two have survived and continue to develop; two have been lost. The result is the birth of twins.

Some of the same considerations apply to couple Taylor as to couple Stewart. We do not know the reasons why the embryos were lost, although it is quite likely that some were lost because of chromosomal and genetic abnormalities. Others, however, may have been lost because of deficiencies in the IVF procedure, in that some damage may have been done to the embryos at some stage in the process, or the timing of the transfer to the woman may have been slightly wrong. The precise reasons are not known in the present state of knowledge. If it proves possible to improve the efficiency of the procedures, it may theoretically be possible to minimize the loss of embryonic life. Nevertheless, as with couple Stewart, there will still be loss. In view of this, I do not believe there are any significant ethical differences between this situation and that of couple Stewart, as long as the procedures are carried out with the greatest degree of scientific and clinical expertise available, with embryonic loss being kept to a minimum. The involvement of technology has no ethical implications for the value we ascribe to embryos. After all, there is human involvement in natural fertilization, which leads to an inevitable loss of embryos. In our present state of knowledge, there is no escape from this doomed embryo syndrome, whether the fertilization is natural or artificial. It is true that the loss of embryos in IVF-related procedures is up to four times greater than with natural procreation. However, this figure may be deceptive, since one is dealing here with a subpopulation having infertility problems, where the loss of embryos may be occurring at a higher rate than in those with normal fertility.

Couple Taylor's situation has introduced an awareness that embryos are doomed not only because of chromosomal and genetic abnormalities of unknown origin, but also because of environmental factors. These include not only deficiencies in IVF procedures, but also a vast array of problems during natural fertilization – hormonal imbalance in the mother, and extrinsic factors such as high levels of radiation, the mother smoking during pregnancy, damage caused by a large range of recreational and pharmaceutical drugs, and other aspects of the mother's lifestyle. Some of these are controllable, others may not be. Any serious ethical perspective having the good of the embryo and foetus at its core, will seek to diminish these factors as much as possible, because together they lead to an unnecessary wastage of embryonic life.

Imaginary embryos III
Couple Walker has also experienced fertility problems, but in this instance treatment produces eight embryos. Of these, three have been placed in the woman's uterus, and one survives. The other five embryos are frozen and two years later, another three are used; on this occasion, one again survives, and a second baby is born. The remaining two frozen embryos are not required by this couple, and are disposed of. In all, therefore, six of the original embryos have been lost, four within the woman's uterus, while two have been allowed to perish.

Couple Walker takes us further, since five of the embryos have been frozen, and the two embryos surplus to requirements have been deliberately discarded. Four embryos have been lost in exactly the same way as with couple Taylor, and the same considerations apply. However, two may have been at greater risk of dying due to having been frozen. That is a technological matter, and good ethical practice will ensure that the loss is not excessive. The ethical status of these embryos is not placed in jeopardy by this procedure.

The surplus embryos are the unintended end result of a life-affirming process, in much the same way as the lost embryos are. As we have already seen, some embryos are inevitably doomed whenever attempts are made to procreate human life. To expect otherwise is to fly in the face of biological reality. The issue facing us is whether this particular method (employing hyperstimulation of the woman's ovaries, and the production of a large number of eggs and subsequently embryos) is acceptable ethically and spiritually.

Once again we should not be surprised if simple answers elude us. This is because whatever answer we give will have to take account of the well-being of the woman herself, and also of the ethical demands placed upon her and her partner in making decisions about the fate of surplus embryos. Of course, it is possible to ignore these considerations, and concentrate solely upon the embryos. Tempting as that approach may be, it ignores the desires of a couple for children of their own, and is in danger of placing more value upon embryos than occurs in natural fertilization. If couples Taylor and Walker go ahead as in the scene I have depicted, we are again faced with the doomed embryo syndrome. Is this extending the syndrome needlessly? We may not have major ethical qualms about producing 6 embryos for each living child, but what about producing 50 for every living child? Does the number of doomed embryos have ethical significance? There is no assured answer to this question, although our moral intuition often hints that numbers are significant. In view of this, the number of doomed embryos should be kept as low as possible.

Does the discarding of human embryos take us into an 'embryo destruction syndrome' as with couple Walker? Or is this transgressing some imperceptible boundary that opens the gate to the wholesale destruction of human embryonic life, and perhaps even human life in general? This is a very serious question for Christians, and I have enormous respect for those who answer in the affirmative. If in doubt, please answer 'yes'. For myself, I am not so certain.

In all probability, many of these embryos could never have developed into human beings: they too are doomed. Since so little is known about them at present, it is not possible to determine which are healthy and which are not – beyond some very rudimentary and inadequate indicators. This still leaves some embryos that could have developed further, and that had the potential to become fully developed human beings. These are being deliberately destroyed. What can we say about these? In view of their potential, they should never be discarded without very careful thought indeed. But is destroying them equivalent to murder? If we think it is, we will have to accept that natural fertilization frequently involves the murder (or at the very least, manslaughter) of some embryos. We are also making very early embryos morally equivalent to adult human beings. As far as I am concerned, this is not the case in our present state of knowledge, and Christians have no grounds for arguing that it is. We have no idea whether it will ever be the case.

I am not convinced there is any biblical mandate for according exactly the same value to discarded embryos as we do to later foetuses, children and adults. My argument has been that there is no significant ethical difference between the processes that resulted in the loss of embryos in any of the three imaginary situations. While there are nuances, of which we should be aware, and while the procedures involving technological intervention are capable of being used to exploit embryos (and incidentally the couples themselves), they do not automatically debase the value we place on embryos. We are moving in a grey area, characterized more by ignorance than by definite knowledge. Wisdom tells us to acknowledge what we do not know, and to decide where the boundaries of moral behaviour should be drawn.

The Bible has nothing specific to say about human embryos, for the simple reason that this was not a concept known to the biblical writers. As we saw in Chapter 4, we find references to human life before birth, and these provide helpful, if general, clues about the value of early forms of human existence. But when it comes to weighing up the value of a couple wanting a child and the value of the embryos brought into existence by this desire and whose future existence is placed in jeopardy by it, we would be foolhardy to expect explicit biblical direction. We cannot extrapolate ethical guidelines from biblical silence to solve dilemmas at the frontiers of contemporary scientific debate. Silence is silence, and nothing more. Biblical evidence should neither be pushed too far nor wrenched too vigorously out of the culture of the time in which it was written.

Seven

Coming to Terms with Human Embryos

Thinking about embryos

As we have just seen, many embryos are lost as part of the process of fertilization, a loss that may be greater when artificial forms of fertilization are employed. Embryos may be discarded if no longer wanted, they may be transferred to a couple who had no part in producing them, or they may be used for research purposes. Regardless of what actually happens to embryos, we cannot avoid asking a fundamental question: What value should be placed on human embryos? Consider a young, pregnant woman, Jocelyn.

Jocelyn has just become aware that she is pregnant, since she has missed two periods and has had the pregnancy confirmed. An embryo has been in existence for about six weeks. There is no doubt there is new biological life within Jocelyn; this will either keep on developing or something will go wrong and she will miscarry. Either way, she will be aware of it. Jocelyn has three options.

Option one
Jocelyn is delighted at being pregnant, and she refers to this embryo as her child. But what does she mean by this term? She knows what children are like, of course; her sister has a three-year-old. But is her six-week-old embryo a child in the same way as the three-year-old is a child? It will probably become a child, but is it one now?

Option two
Jocelyn never intended to become pregnant, and now wants to have an abortion. For her, the embryo is nothing like a child; it is a nuisance since she has other plans for the next two years and these do not include having a child. An abortion presents her with no moral difficulties, since for her a six-week-old embryo is nothing special in human terms.

Option three
Jocelyn wants her pregnancy to continue. However, she has no desire to refer to the embryo within her as a child. She hopes everything will continue satisfactorily, but she is unable at this early stage to feel she is carrying a complete new human being. If anything goes wrong, she will probably be upset, but she will not actually consider she has lost a child.

These three options correspond to the three major viewpoints on the moral status of prenatal human life: that embryos and foetuses are persons, non-persons, or potential persons (see Chapter 5). Which one satisfies your viewpoint?

Embryos and foetuses are like us

According to this viewpoint, the embryo is to be regarded (and therefore treated) as a human person from the time of fertilization. Some argue that, since it is impossible to prove that personhood begins later than fertilization, we should err on the conservative side and conclude that personhood begins at fertilization. In other words, from fertilization onwards the embryo is to be treated in the same way we would treat a mature human being.

It is considered that the process of embryonic development is nothing less than the development of a person. There is no stage in human existence when we are not persons. Consequently, embryos and foetuses are to be treated as if they are persons and are to be regarded as having absolute value. As some would put it, they are inviolable. Underlying these conclusions is one idea, potentiality: whatever we now are, was present in potential form in the embryos from which we developed. Since we now have self-consciousness, the potential for self-consciousness must be present in all embryos. On this argument, all embryos possess personal life; all embryos are nothing less than actual persons (see Chapter 5).

This is fine as far as it goes, but arguing like this has its problems since we do not think like this in any other area of life. What this is saying is that if a has the capacity to develop into A, a is exactly the same as A. When you think about it, this is a bit odd. After all, we never get confused between acorns and oak trees; we acknowledge that the one develops into the other, but we do not actually think they are the same. Similarly, a caterpillar develops into a butterfly, but one would not dream of considering them interchangeable. Even though they are the ends of a continuum, they are very different from one another. Likewise, a three-day-old human embryo is not the same as a thirty-year-old human adult, even though the one develops into the other. An embryo has the potential to become an adult, but this does not happen instantaneously; in fact it is a long way from realization in a three-day-old embryo.

As an analogy think of a student commencing a course of study. At this early stage the student has the potential to pass the final examinations, a potential that may be realized when those examinations are ultimately passed. But this will not come about without a great deal of study, learning and hard work, and it is these alone that convert the potential for success into actual success. Along the way, the student is changed by the learning, with the result that the student who passes the examination is *different* from the student who turned up at the first class full of potential. However, we do not regard the student as a 'failed' student prior to passing the examinations and in the same way we should not view the embryo as a 'nothing'.

The intentions of those who hold the 'foetus is a person' position are exemplary, with their desire to enhance the value and moral standing of embryonic and foetal life. Nevertheless, it is far more arbitrary than some would have us believe. I have great sympathy with the intentions of this position, but I am not convinced it can be sustained in practice (I consider it is inconsistent). From a Christian perspective, it is a very important position since it is frequently seen as the one most in accordance with biblical teaching. In Chapters 3 and 4, I attempted to show that the issue is not this simple, and that biblical principles cannot be neatly encapsulated in positions such as this one. Nevertheless, its absolute facade has enormous attractions for many Christians. However, in the final analysis, I fail to see how I, or anyone else, can in practice provide the degree of protection for early embryos demanded by this position, and if I cannot reasonably assure them of an appropriate level of protection, the position itself becomes untenable.

Others will disagree with me, and will hold that an inconsistent position that aims to protect all embryos is preferable to a consistent position that does not aim to give the same level of protection. These two stances reflect different ethical approaches, but neither is implicitly Christian. These different approaches have nothing whatsoever to do with differences in fundamental attitudes towards biblical teaching; both, I believe, are possible approaches for Christians.

Another important argument that some Christians employ is what we might describe as 'the benefit of the doubt' approach (see Chapter 4). According to this, if there is any question about the value to be ascribed to an embryo or foetus, give it the benefit of the doubt by ascribing greater rather than lesser value. In other words, always take the side of the embryo or foetus (or any weak or disadvantaged individual). If there is uncertainty about when 'human life begins' err on the side of conception rather than some time later in gestation. Once again, I sympathize with this conservative response, since its aim is protection of the weak and disadvantaged. But I also have my doubts, since this response can be used to bring an end to serious thought. By all means let individuals use it when its aim is to uphold human value in notoriously uncertain circumstances, but as a general principle it has serious limitations.

Embryos and foetuses are very unlike us

In this case there is no way in which embryos and foetuses can be regarded as even remotely resembling persons. They are non-persons, a position that stems from the generally held viewpoint that we do not consider it wrong to destroy either the ovum or sperm before they have united. On this basis, some conclude that we are not morally obliged to preserve the life of the embryo or foetus. Either can be regarded as a thing, and not a person, until that point in development when brain function can be detected (this is a debatable point, and also one open to highly variable interpretations).

According to this viewpoint, the first few weeks of gestation have no moral significance. The complete lack of any personhood (either actual or potential) or sentience means that the embryo has no moral rights. The acquisition of sentience is the ability to feel pleasure or pain. Once this has been acquired, an embryo or foetus has sufficient moral status to make it wrong to inflict unnecessary pain upon it. There is much confusion when it comes to timing, and stages from six weeks of gestation all the way through to 28 weeks of gestation have been quoted as the beginning of what I will call a pain-detecting brain.

Considerable emphasis is placed by some writers on the acquisition by the embryo or foetus of consciousness, which, in turn, depends on some minimum degree of nervous system development. The problem is that consciousness in any meaningful sense will not become evident until well after birth. Hence, the task of determining at what neurobiological stage an embryo can be regarded as possessing consciousness is a difficult, if not impossible, one; and yet, it is a crucial one if the embryo or foetus from this point onwards is to be the bearer of moral rights.

Both these views indicate that for a number of weeks (or even months), the human embryo or foetus is a nothing. In practice it probably has less rights than a rat or mouse embryo, since these are protected to some extent by regulations governing experimentation on animals. The point at which this situation changes is open to debate. These widely divergent appraisals cast doubt on the advisability of using either of these possibilities as the definitive beginning point of meaning or significance.

And so we are back at the distinction between an embryo on the one hand, and sperm or ova on the other. Are they more or less the same? While it may be tempting to minimize the differences, on the ground that the moral distinction between a newly fertilized embryo and almost-to-be-fertilized ova and sperm is not that great, it is even less satisfactory to argue that there is no moral difference at all. The chances of isolated ova or sperm becoming human beings are much less than the chances of an embryo doing so: their potential is of a quite different order. To argue, as some do, that if it is not wrong to refrain from producing additional persons (that is, contraception is acceptable), the killing of a foetus (a potential person) is no worse than using contraceptives, is taking the argument to a logical but unhelpful conclusion. The potential of these different categories varies enormously, so much so that ova and sperm are better described as possible persons rather than potential persons. These early differences in embryonic development cannot be ignored, because if they are we are left floundering in a moral sea.

Another problem with this approach is that it ignores our moral obligation as people to nurture the very young within our midst. It fails to take account of the commitments we have to the welfare and survival of infants and also, to varying extents, of foetuses. The human family has obligations to the prenatal and neonatal, and in more general terms to those unable to look after themselves, since all these are totally dependent on the actions of responsible moral agents committed to their care (a position running alongside the biblical directive to care for the weak and defenceless). Apart from such actions, neither foetuses nor the newborn would survive. The importance of relationships within the human community, including relationships with those who, using neurological and behavioural criteria, are barely members of that community, must be emphasized. In other words, neurological and behavioural criteria alone are not sufficient to tell us how we should act towards foetuses and infants, since they fail to take account of the commitments so crucial to our life together within the human community (another biblical directive). Even when the neurological and behavioural features of the foetus or newborn are inadequate on a biological scale of values, our commitment to love and care for one of our own kind is basic to what we are as humans living in community.

This provides an important perspective, although it does not tell us whether our commitment to love and care for embryos, foetuses and neonates is indiscriminate, or whether it depends to any extent on their stage of development. Are people in general as committed to nurturing a three-week-old embryo, as they are a six-month-old foetus, or nine-week-old infant? Undoubtedly some are, but probably most are not. There is an open-endedness here that we shall have to explore further, since it fails to provide any precise practical guidelines to the value we place on developing embryos and foetuses. For assistance with this important task, we have to move to the third position.

Embryos and foetuses are growing like us

This third perspective occupies a place between the other two. It is based on the idea that the embryo or foetus is an entity with the potential to develop into a being with full personhood. What this says is that in the normal course of its development, this embryo or foetus (as a potential person) will acquire a person's claim to life, although even very early on in its development it already has some claim to life. In terms of this principle, a human embryo or foetus is a potential person.

In using this expression a contrast is being made with actual persons (normal adult human beings), beings with a capacity for personhood (temporarily unconscious persons), possible persons (human ova and sperm), and future persons (persons in a future generation). In practical terms, potential persons, such as embryos or foetuses, have some claim to life, whereas possible persons have no such claim (the difference between existence and non-existence – see Chapter 6).

Emphasis on this sort of potential takes seriously the continuum of biological development, and refuses to draw an arbitrary line to denote the acquisition of personhood. At all stages of development the foetus is on its way to full personhood, and, if everything proceeds normally, it will one day attain full personhood in its own right.

According to this viewpoint, there is no point in development, no matter how early on, when the embryo or foetus does not display some elements of personhood – no matter how rudimentary. The potential is there, and because of this both the embryo and foetus have a claim to life and respect. This claim, however, becomes stronger as foetal development proceeds, so that by some time later on in development (probably during the third trimester for practical purposes), the claim is so strong that the consequences of killing a foetus are the same as those of killing an actual person – whether child or adult. Consequently, the foetus in the last trimester will, when necessary, be treated as a 'patient'. This mirrors most people's responses in ordinary life, where we recognize a difference between the accidental loss of an embryo or early foetus and the birth of a stillborn child. Both entail the death of a human being, and yet under most circumstances the loss of a life which almost made it is felt much more acutely than that of a life which had hardly begun to develop.

As with all intermediate positions, the potential-person position satisfies neither extreme. It is seen as being too liberal by those advocating a 'foetus is a person' viewpoint, and too conservative by the 'foetus is not a person' school. Not only this, but the 'potential person' stance is itself open to varying interpretations. Nevertheless, its gradualist emphasis strikes a chord with many, on biological, philosophical, intuitive and pragmatic grounds. It helps many through the maze of problems in the difficult prenatal and neonatal areas, and constitutes a helpful ethical basis for tackling specific ethical issues here. I find myself at ease within the broad limits of this position.

But is this a Christian position? Have I forgotten all about the biblical principles I touched on in Chapters 3 and 4? Have I become humanistic in my desire to work out a specific position?

In my assessment of the biblical accounts touching on prenatal human life I concluded that they did not take us nearly as far as some Christians would like. Embryos and foetuses are extremely important, they fit within the human community, and are to be treated with a great deal of seriousness. Nevertheless, we cannot emerge with watertight rules regarding their precise value under difficult, competing situations.

I do not believe one can put forward any specific position as definitively being *the* Christian position. In this sense, I do not consider there is one Christian position. However, there are limits to a Christian perspective, and I consider 'the foetus is not a person' position falls outside these limits. Similarly, a very liberal interpretation of the 'foetus is a potential person' position will probably also pose difficulties for Christians. This leaves the 'foetus is a person' and more conservative renderings of the 'foetus is a potential person' positions as being suitable for Christian interpretations. My own preference is for the latter, since I believe it is a more helpful position in practice, but I have no desire to downgrade the Christian merits of the former. We should now ask whether the approach I have adopted is as helpful as I am making it out to be.

Embryos and foetuses deserve protection

The use of the concept of personhood has come in for a great deal of criticism, since it is viewed as introducing a distinction between two groups of people – those who display personhood and therefore are to be valued, and those who lack personhood and so need not be valued. In other words, it appears to suggest that some people need not be valued as much as others. While there is an element of truth in this criticism, it also needs to be stated that such a distinction is only bowing to reality, namely, that in practice we do not appear to value all human beings indiscriminately. It is useful, therefore, to look at human embryos and foetuses in terms of the degree of *protection* we wish to afford them.

In Chapter 6 I referred to the impossibility of protecting most miscarried embryos. I suggested that we should not wish to protect very badly damaged embryos; however, even if we wished to do so, we would usually be unsuccessful. There is, therefore, a class of embryos that cannot be protected as members of the human community: our protection of humans cannot be absolute. Even if we banned all induced abortions and all research on human embryos, there would still be human embryos lying outside our ability to protect them. They lie outside the sphere of human protection. Consequently, whatever absolute value we wish to place on early embryos is of little more than theoretical interest, since it fails to protect them in practice.

Given this is the case, how do we determine which members of the prenatal human community should be protected? Consider the principle of *commitment*. As human beings we commit ourselves to other humans, and others respond to us in a similar fashion. Generally, therefore, commitment is two-way. There are exceptions, as with later foetuses, neonates, or adults who are unconscious or have suffered severe brain damage; in these instances, the symmetrical relationship is incomplete. Nevertheless, even here there are elements of a two-way interaction. However, with very early embryos, the situation changes. Some embryos, which I shall call *Gs*, will never be in a position to commit themselves to us in any way at all. They are biologically incapable of developing any further, and so any commitment to them on our part is entirely asymmetrical. There can be no hint of a two-way commitment. Other early embryos, let us refer to them as *Hs*, are capable of developing further, and so as time passes these will gradually enter into a two-way commitment relationship. This will only be fully realized three or four years after birth, but it will begin to make itself felt during gestation.

Our commitment to the *G* early embryos is the sort of commitment we show towards many groups of animals, cultural artifacts, or the environment. We are to protect them in a general way, since they constitute important facets of what 'being human' means. Nevertheless, this cannot be the special commitment of one human to another. The *H* early embryos, however, are different. They present us with the challenge of recognizing and responding to other humans, that one day will be in a position to commit themselves fully to us. We do not know which early embryos are *Gs* or *Hs*, until six or more weeks into development in normal (not technological) pregnancies. As we become more and more certain that we are dealing with an *H* embryo, we become increasingly obligated to protect and nurture that embryo, and later that early foetus, as one of us.

Prenatal human life is to be protected. As embryos and foetuses develop, the hope is that they will one day be able to contribute to the human community, and every effort is to be made to ensure as far as possible that this will eventuate. To demean such members of our community is to diminish what we are as members of that same community. Relationships between prenatal and postnatal humans mirror relationships integral to the human community itself. They reflect what we *are* as human beings.

Deepening and growing commitment to protect embryonic and foetal lives, and to work for the welfare of those lives, may not appear as convincing as one committed to their protection from day one of gestation. In practice, however, it may amount to a commitment that is as close to an absolute one as it is possible to attain. Nevertheless, it takes seriously the limitations within which we all have to function, and which circumscribe the developmental potential of numerous embryos, and this too is an important commitment to human well-being.

The possibilities of research

We now move into even more difficult territory: embryo research. Should research be conducted on human embryos, or is this taking society into a barbaric wilderness? Does research on the smallest examples of human life constitute the most heinous of all crimes against God's world and the work of his hands? If that is the case, this is somewhere we dare not go.

For many Christians embryo research marks a point of no return. To carry out research on such defenceless beings is the worst possible way of treating humans as a means to an end, and this is morally indefensible. To choose between embryos, destroying some but preserving others, is seen as an abhorrent form of exploitation. In these terms, it appears as if a strong case can be made against any form of research on human embryos, and yet a moment's reflection shows that these sentiments only hold water if embryos are treated as having the same value as adult humans. They can be defended if embryos are equivalent to us, but the argument loses some of its weight if this is not the case. We are inevitably back at the status we ascribe to embryos, a debate that is far from cut and dried. Consider the following:

Laboratory one
Research is being carried out on human embryos and foetuses (up to 12 weeks' gestation) that have been spontaneously aborted. They are difficult to find, but the research workers have managed to obtain a supply. They consider this as ethical research since the embryos and foetuses are dead, consent has been given by the mother, and the cause of death is accidental.

Laboratory two
The embryos are surplus to the requirements of couples in an IVF program. They have been produced in order to give rise to new human life, but these particular ones are not needed for that purpose. The couples have donated them to a research program. The research hopes to provide information on the causes of infertility.

Laboratory three
Here the embryos have been produced quite specifically for research purposes. They have been fertilized from the sperm and eggs of men and women in an infertility program, but the only reason for doing this is to provide embryos for the needs of a research team, which is looking for new ways of treating male infertility.

In all these laboratories, the research is aimed at providing basic information on the way in which the human embryo develops, at providing a better understanding of infertility and of treating it through IVF, at preventing genetic disease, and at improving contraception.

Laboratory four
Research is aimed at providing therapy for the embryos. All these embryos are from couples involved in an IVF program, and the hope is that the treated embryos will be returned to the woman for further development. The therapy is gene therapy, and the aim is to replace a defective gene with a normally functioning one.

These are hypothetical scenes since some of them are scientifically impossible at the moment, and some are contrary to most currently accepted guidelines on embryo research. They illustrate the spectrum of possibilities in embryo research. Laboratory one involves research on dead embryos; laboratory two, research on spare or surplus embryos; laboratory three, research on embryos produced specifically for this purpose; and laboratory four, research aimed at improving the health of the embryos on which the research is being conducted.

For most people, the laboratory one example does not raise ethical problems since induced abortion is not involved and embryos are not being destroyed as part of the research. Laboratories two and three are examples of non-therapeutic research, that is, research that will not benefit the embryos in question. This is of major concern to many people. Laboratory four illustrates therapeutic research, and so does not raise the same set of problems as the previous two. But gene therapy itself may be of concern (see Chapter 8).

Research: the need to know

Before delving into details, consider this. Research on human embryos has been essential in providing any knowledge at all about early human development. Without such research over the past one hundred years, little would be known about any of the stages in the developing human being. However, there is no way of obtaining embryonic material other than by abortion, either spontaneous or induced. Further, this material has been used without the consent of either the mother or, of course, the embryos or foetuses themselves. If this is regarded as unethical, there is no ethical way of obtaining any definitive knowledge of human prenatal development. As one surveys the literature of the past, there is generally no way of knowing how some of the material was obtained, and even if one did know and decided that some had been obtained unethically (from induced abortions), there is no way of isolating unethically derived data from ethically derived data. The two sorts of data, assuming there are two sorts, have become completely integrated into one within the literature. Hence, to attempt to pay attention to some embryological studies and ignore others on ethical grounds, when all are intermingled, is absurd.

Imagine a situation whereby no research had ever been conducted on human embryos and foetuses. There would be no knowledge about early human development, and there would be no control over early development. There would be little obstetric knowledge. The science of human embryology would hardly exist and one imagines there would be very high rates of foetal and infant mortality. For me, science in these areas is to be welcomed, since it reflects responsible human control and it brings with it the prospect of decreasing illness and disease. This has immense repercussions for good for both foetuses and children. Therefore, if we look back to the first laboratory scene I do not find any ethical problems here. I also approve of research conducted on induced abortions, provided the stringent conditions necessary (including complete separation of the clinical and research procedures) are rigorously adhered to (see Chapter 11).

I admit that in making these statements, I am speaking as a scientist (see Chapter 1). However, many scientific advances have ushered in vast benefits for humankind, and are to be regarded as part of God's providential dealings with the human race. This is one area where we need to look closely at applauding scientific endeavours, and encouraging those that increase knowledge and understanding. As long as clear ethical guidelines and Christian essentials inform our science, the latter is to be welcomed rather than opposed.

Therapeutic research

Laboratory four introduces therapeutic research, with its objective of treating individual embryos. For now, let us assume there are no scientific or ethical problems with gene therapy (see Chapter 8). This is *therapeutic research* in its simplest form, and has much in common with far more traditional clinical research on adults. The embryo is being treated as an end in itself, with the prospect of benefiting from the research procedures. Treatment like this is an illustration of extremely sophisticated medical technology, and as such poses no especial ethical problems.

What about research aimed at benefiting *embryos in general*, as in research aimed at decreasing the incidence of, or treating, infertility? This is where the second and third laboratories come in. Is this therapeutic or non-therapeutic research? At first glance, it is non-therapeutic research, since its aim is not to benefit the individual on which the research is being conducted. We have to ask whether it is warranted to move from a principle worked out for adult patients to one involving four-, eight- or 16-cell embryos. This is important when it is considered that only 1 to 5 per cent of IVF embryos will give rise to living human beings, and of the naturally fertilized embryos implanted within a woman's uterus, 30 to 40 per cent will survive and develop into adults.

Against this background, I think it is reasonable to suggest that this can be equated with therapeutic research, because in my view we are not able to equate each individual embryo with an individual foetus, child or adult. There is no way at present that more than about 40 per cent of these embryos can develop further. This situation may never change, but if it does, it will only come about through research on embryos and subsequent advances in our understanding of the causes of the numerous genetic and chromosomal abnormalities that give rise to spontaneous abortions. Here is the dilemma.

Which course of action will best reflect a high view of human embryos as beings created in the image of God? Should it be a refusal to carry out any research aimed at understanding, and perhaps eventually treating, spontaneous abortions? This is the view of many Christians. On the other hand, there may be a place for research using *certain* human embryos in an attempt to minimize the astronomically high wastage of embryos caused by chromosomal abnormalities. This possibility is far less readily accepted by Christians. However, is it obvious which of these two courses of action is more conducive to an emphasis on the dignity and value of human life?

Both courses of action are fraught with danger, since both are a bewildering mixture of good and evil. Either way, we shall be choosing what we consider to be the lesser of two evils. If human embryos are considered to have the same value as later foetuses and adults, each embryo on which research is carried out will be seen as the needless and tragic destruction of human life. Such research will, therefore, be repudiated and opposed, but by the same token it will offer no prospect for enhanced understanding of spontaneous abortion and the inevitable destruction of vast numbers of embryos in future. On the other hand, if embryos are not viewed as being equivalent to adults, some research may be feasible, with the possibility of decreasing the destruction of embryos in the future. Take your pick: each way has its problems, and the problems on both sides should be acknowledged.

But what about unfettered research on countless millions of human embryos? However noble its goal, this may have detrimental effects on society's attitudes towards human life in general and it would be unwise to move in this direction. The wastage of embryonic human life through spontaneous abortion is of catastrophic proportions, and this questions the dignity of the early stages of human existence. Nevertheless, moderation is essential, since research using human embryos is replete with moral and spiritual dilemmas.

In laboratory two, *spare or surplus embryos* were used in research. These are incapable of further development as long as they remain in the laboratory. These embryos were brought into existence for the express purpose of providing a couple with a child, and therefore were destined to become fully developed human beings. If not required by the couple concerned, they will die unless donated to another couple. Can they, as doomed embryos, be used for research purposes? If they are, their potential for further development is obviously cut off. But they will die anyway. If we accept that they can be discarded, and if we view them as being like dead bodies, research on them may be ethically acceptable. This is not an easy conclusion to reach, and perhaps we should never reach it. But I believe it should be debated – even by Christians.

The question of the *deliberate production of embryos* for use in research programs, as in the third laboratory, has no parallel in any other medical research. It sets out to produce embryos with the potential for developing into full human individuals, but which will never be more than objects to serve the purposes of others. I reject the deliberate production of embryos in this way. If human embryos are produced simply to provide scientific information, that information has already taken precedence over the significance of human existence. And that is not a prospect either Christians or societies in general should relish.

Embryos and the human community

The biblical principles regarding foetal life dealt with in Chapter 4 (and to a lesser extent Chapter 3) have informed the whole of the discussion up to this point. Against this background, it seems to me that embryos and foetuses are victims of a world in conflict: they are destroyed and disfigured by disease, greed, envy, accidents, the unjust actions of individuals or societies, and selfishness. Embryos and foetuses mirror what we *are* far more accurately than we often like to admit. They are one with us in the human endeavour; they benefit by our creativity and scientific expertise, and are put at risk by our technological misadventures and short-sighted self-centredness. As embryos and foetuses live with us, they experience the results both of our faithfulness to God and of our rebellion against him.

Embryos and foetuses are weak and in need of protection. They are due the profoundest of respect because they are human just as we are. In their weakness and defencelessness, we are called to place a wall of compassion and protection around them and also around pregnant women, just as we are around the handicapped and mentally retarded, the aging and the senile. However, as I have already argued, this cannot provide either embryos or foetuses with absolute protection. That is an impossibility. Nevertheless, it is incumbent upon us to be biased in favour of their protection whenever feasible. The problems are especially acute in the case of very early embryos, and we have to be realistic enough to accept this. But is realism falling short of absolute biblical standards (the 'what ought to be' approach)? It may sound pious to insist on complete protection of early embryos, when we are generally unable to protect them. Realism (the 'what is' approach) is called for, since there are limits to the protection we can afford prenatal human life (see Chapter 3).

Embryos and foetuses are to be valued as highly as possible, remembering that they are somewhat removed from our experience of what constitutes humanness – they are removed in appearance, in relationships, and in time. The result is that we cannot come to terms with them in the same way, or to the same extent, as we come to terms with someone far more like us. This does not convert embryos into nothing; neither does it render them valueless. That would go against the biblical guidelines I have alluded to. Nevertheless, is it feasible to value them exactly as we value those like ourselves?

Consequently, when conflict arises between the interests of embryos and of those of people like us, I have argued that we are to place greater value on people like us than on embryos. The way in which we do this and the ethical guidelines we erect will be crucial, since embryos are to be protected and their interests are to be forwarded as actively as possible. This position does not demean embryos, since it has another consequence: they are to be protected against the irresponsible actions of people like us. The considerable value I am ascribing to embryos, linked with our responsibility to protect them as weak and defenceless members of the human community, take priority over the irresponsible actions of adults. This ensures a considerable level of defence in practice, and stringent protection against the irresponsible forays of the human community.

My hope is that in the future a time will come when each embryo brought into existence, whether naturally or artificially, will have an opportunity to develop into an adult human. Such a hope is profoundly Christian, with its basis in the resurrection and hence the renewal of creation and its liberation from the anguish and turmoil of the fall. While there is no theological reason to believe that this hope will be fulfilled in the world we know now, it forms part of the Christian perspective for assessing the perplexities of early embryonic development. As such, it provides us with an auspicious context for the specific debate on what we do now to embryos and foetuses.

Eight

Genetic Dilemmas

Genetics, medicine and genetic manipulation

Genetics is frequently considered in isolation, as though it constitutes a stand-alone domain, far removed from all other parts of clinical medicine. However, this is grossly misleading since genetics is part of the modern medical endeavour, and it cannot be pushed to one side without also pushing to one side many of the other branches of conventional medicine and medical biology. Genetics, like the rest of medicine, brings under our control biological systems, which is not of necessity a bad thing.

Nevertheless, the potentially negative side of genetics is the one frequently highlighted, and so it is hardly surprising that genetics is often equated with genetic engineering. The emphasis here tends to be on the 'engineering', the manipulation of humans, and for many years this has been the stuff of exciting science fiction. Vague as the term 'genetic manipulation' is, it frequently refers to two areas of genetic control, namely, cloning and eugenics (negative and positive).

Cloning which is so frequently equated with genetic technology has recently hit the limelight again. Therefore, the next chapter will be devoted solely to a discussion of this contentious topic.

Negative eugenics involves the elimination of defective genes, and hence of the prospective possessors of those genes, from the population. While negative eugenics does not actually change individuals, its potential for changing the genetic make-up of a community is considerable. Although its aim is not to improve future generations, it is a means of selecting healthy as opposed to unhealthy individuals, by preventing the existence of foetuses (and, therefore, future children and adults) who are seriously malformed in one way or another. It achieves this using abortion, a crude tool at the best of times. This may be for the supposed good of the foetuses and future individuals themselves, of the family of these future individuals, or even of society. While many Christians may have little sympathy with negative eugenics because of the involvement of abortion, there is no escape from the serious nature of some of the decisions that have to be made.

Positive eugenics has invited a great deal of idealistic support, with visions of improving attributes such as intelligence and personality. This emphasis on improving human design stands in stark contrast to conventional medical approaches with their emphasis on rectifying abnormalities and combating disease. This form of eugenics has a long history, extending from 1883, when it was based on the notion of encouraging reproduction of the select. Although current emphases are on genetic approaches, the concept has changed little. The difficulty has always been to identify the select, and then to promote only those genes considered to be desirable. It is not surprising that eugenic approaches have proved disappointing, since traits, such as intelligence, are controlled by ten to one hundred genes, as well as by environmental factors. Apart from deciding which traits to promulgate, control of this order lies outside the realm of feasible science, and may always do so. Consequently, positive eugenics is far weaker scientifically than once imagined, while its ethical base leaves a great deal to be desired. Any attempts to impose it on society (no matter how crude) would be at the expense of individual freedom of choice.

Because of this potential to manipulate human nature, genetics encapsulates people's fears regarding future abuses of science. It is seen by some, including some Christians, as nothing less than 'playing God' in the most objectionable of ways. For Christians as much as for anyone else, it often represents all that threatens human welfare; it may even be regarded as the antithesis of what Christianity stands for. It is going where humans have never been before, and in the eyes of some it is going where humans should not go. It is moving into forbidden territory, territory open to God but not to created beings. Christians are encouraged by some to rise up and denounce the whole of the genetic enterprise, but this demonstrates a serious misunderstanding of the science of genetics, as well as a simplistic approach to a Christian view of genetic advance.

The problem here stems, in part, from the perception that present-day human genetics is monolithic. In fact, genetic technology ranges from genetic screening and the use of DNA probes on the one hand, to pre-emptive intervention and selective abortion on the other. It also ranges from genetic counselling to somatic-cell gene therapy and possibly in the future to germ-line gene therapy; it also encompasses the Human Genome Project (HGP, with its efforts to produce the complete nucleotide sequence of the human genome).

These possibilities have been made likely because contemporary molecular genetics allows for the manipulation of the genetic content of human cells. As a result, it holds out prospects both for dramatically extending the range of current medical therapies, and for bringing about radical changes to the way in which medicine itself is practised. Hitherto intractable genetic diseases, such as cystic fibrosis, muscular dystrophy, Huntington's disease and amyotrophic lateral sclerosis, are being unravelled and the genes involved have been defined. Not only this but many forms of cancer lend themselves to genetic treatment.

From embryos to genes

With these thoughts in mind, think about a couple, Shane and Sarah, who we will follow for a few years.

Illustration: part I
In their first pregnancy some years ago there were reasons to be concerned that the foetus may have cystic fibrosis. At 16 weeks an amniocentesis was carried out, and a small amount of amniotic fluid was removed so that some foetal cells could be tested using a recombinant DNA-based gene probe for cystic fibrosis. They knew beforehand that if this

turned out to be positive they had a choice to make – either continue with the pregnancy knowing that the child would be afflicted with this debilitating and distressing condition, or have an abortion. If their pregnancy had occurred more recently, this testing could have been carried out at eight weeks, with a chorionic villus biopsy. The choice, however, would have been exactly the same. As it turned out, the test for cystic fibrosis was positive, but Shane and Sarah decided not to abort. As a result, Catherine was born.

The possibility of aborting in this situation immediately raises a query. Is a foetus with the gene that will result in having cystic fibrosis to be valued less highly than a foetus without this gene? Those who abort appear to be stating that the one foetus is of less value than the other. However, the issue does not end here, since an affected foetus will become an affected child, and this affected child will, in the present state of medical therapy, have a limited life expectancy. Hence, in considering the possibility of abortion, should we think only of the foetus, or should we also take into consideration implications of the disease for the future child (and even adult)? We will also have to ask whether non-existence is preferable to knowingly bringing an affected child into existence. These issues are well-known ones, revolving around the abortion of foetuses with congenital abnormalities. While these abnormalities are genetic in origin, the ethical debate is dominated by considerations of abortion and not of genetics.

If we now move a little into the future, we encounter Shane and Sarah hoping to have another child.

Illustration: part II
Understandably, they are worried about the prospects of another child with cystic fibrosis. On this occasion they are informed that the embryo itself can be genetically tested before it has a chance to implant in the uterus. This is the technique of embryo biopsy. They are told that fertilization will have to take place by IVF, and that one cell will be removed from an early embryo, and will then be tested with the same genetic kit used previously. If this shows that the embryo does not have any indication of cystic fibrosis it will

*be transferred to Sarah's uterus in the normal way. On the
other hand, if it tests positive for cystic fibrosis, it will be
discarded and the same procedure will be carried out on a
second embryo. This will be repeated until a negative result is
obtained.*

Shane and Sarah are now confronted by a different set of
dilemmas. They have to ask themselves what value they attach
to the embryo if they agree to discard affected embryos (also
referred to as *in vitro* abortion). They realize that the choice
has changed; they are no longer comparing the respective values of a foetus and child, but of a four- or eight-cell embryo
and a child. If they agree to discard a human embryo, is this
equivalent to destroying a human life? Is it in some way like
sacrificing a human life? According to another viewpoint, it
may be far less significant than this and may have far more in
common with contraception. Either way, the dilemma has
shifted. It is not yet in the genetic realm, but it is not that far
away. It has little to do with conventional abortion, since foetuses are not being destroyed, although it does focus attention
on early embryos (see Chapter 7).

Illustration: part III
*Shane and Sarah have made their choices. They have two
children – Catherine who has cystic fibrosis, and Rebecca
who hasn't. Rebecca was the result of implanting a healthy
embryo following gene testing. Two embryos were
discarded prior to this. Should Shane and Sarah have any
ethical qualms? They could have avoided the birth of
Catherine, who is now thirteen, is far from well and has a
poor life expectancy. That would have meant a late abortion. Two non-existent beings could have existed, but did
not. If they had existed they would have had cystic fibrosis.
Rebecca is a delight. Both children are deeply loved and
cared for. In a different age, and with different medical
technology, the situation would have been very different.*

Our couple decided against a conventional abortion (when
Catherine was born), but agreed to the discarding of two

embryos which, had they been implanted, would have resulted in the birth of two further children with cystic fibrosis. They are aware they have allowed their embryos to be manipulated, and are aware they have gone down a tenuous technological path. Their Christian friends are divided in their responses to what Shane and Sarah have done, although most accept they have acted with integrity and honesty, and that they place great store on the welfare of their family.

Illustration: part IV

In a futuristic scenario, Shane and Sarah plan to have another baby. Again they are advised to use IVF, but the emphasis on this occasion will be on testing the embryos with the intention of correcting any genetic defect that may be found. There will be no question of an in vitro abortion; instead, if the first embryo tested is positive for the cystic fibrosis gene, that gene will be replaced or will be overridden in some way by inserting some other gene. This is the realm of germ-line gene therapy.

We are now well and truly into the area of gene manipulation. What should have emerged, though, is that the transition from conventional approaches to genetic ones has been a gradual one. Should germ-line gene therapy become a practical reality it would be far more difficult and far more costly than refraining from implanting defective embryos. What we need to enquire about are the ethical objections to this form of gene therapy if it becomes feasible. At one level, it appears to be an extremely sophisticated means of overcoming a deficiency, but would it have any detrimental effect upon our valuation of human beings? It may actually enhance it, by eliminating a disease trait from the population.

Assessing the perplexities

In part I of the illustration, we are dealing with a being of whom the mother, Sarah, is very much aware, especially when amniocentesis is used. Shane and Sarah have a serious ethical decision to make. This is inescapable, especially in view of its magnitude. After all, it involves the *destruction* of a human life. Is this word 'destruction' an appropriate one? After all, the foetus is aware of nothing at a conscious level (due to the relative immaturity of the cerebral cortex even up to 20 weeks gestation), and if an abortion is carried out, that existence will hardly have started. Is there, then, any ethical difference between the non-existence resulting from contraception (see Chapter 6), and non-existence resulting from the destruction of an 8–9 week or even a 16–19 week foetus? I have no doubt there is a major difference.

But acknowledging this difference may not bring the discussion to a close, since the good of the foetus and future child is a consideration. The medical condition may be so severe that some will conclude that non-existence is actually in the best interests of the future child. In some very extreme cases this is a serious, albeit highly debatable, argument, especially for Christians.

The second decision facing Shane and Sarah brings them face to face with knowingly going ahead with a pregnancy, using an embryo with a known defect that will result in a child suffering from a serious medical condition. Alternatively, they may decide that *that* embryo should not be allowed to develop any further, and so they proceed with an embryo that, as far as this particular disease is concerned, is healthy. What is the nature of this choice? Is it choosing between two human beings, as one would choose between two children, or is it choosing between two kinds of potential?

This question may strike us as highly theoretical and of little interest. But that would be misleading. We have to press ahead and ask an even more difficult question: is there any reason why a defective embryo (with a debilitating condition) should be implanted in a woman's uterus for further development? Or to phrase this question slightly differently: is there any reason why anyone would decide at an early embryonic stage to bring into the world a child with a serious ailment, when an alternative is available? To decide in favour of an embryo with a serious medical condition amounts to a form of genetic predestination, since it is known that *this* embryo will give rise to a child with a lethal ailment. In an instance like this, the ethical focus has been narrowed down to a specific individual, with a specific future. How do we respond? What Christian guidelines do we possess? I claim no definitive, let alone, Christian answer. I can only put forward possibilities. My inclination is to suggest that, ignoring what we definitely know about an embryo's *future* is to ignore an important aspect of that individual's well-being. This can only be justified if the value of a particular embryo is regarded as being higher than that of the resulting child, and if the quality of the resulting child's health is ignored.

But is this a Christian conclusion? Are Christians tied in to genetic predestination, having to accept whatever turns up in the genetic 'lottery'. Most Christians utilize medical treatment to alleviate or cure illnesses (even when these have a genetic basis), suggesting that they do not accept the inevitability of genetic predisposition. We do not believe in genetic predestination, and therefore should not accept that embryos with destructive genetic predispositions are to be preserved at all costs. We are to value the human-in-the-making, the human who will be, the family of that individual, and the relationships of all involved.

But we are not finished. How important is health versus debility? Are we far too concerned with the quality of human beings, and with the integrity of their bodies? The choice of a healthy embryo rather than an unhealthy embryo may reflect a bias against the disabled, and from a Christian angle may contort all our values about the intrinsic worth of human beings in the sight of God. We should be concerned at these trends, although the queries focus on the sort of people with whom we have dealings. When confronted by a person with a disability, that person is to be treated as someone imaged in God's likeness, since the essential characteristics of God are present even when the disability or damage is considerable. However, when discussing a three-cell embryo, we are not discussing such a person. Not only this, but we have to decide whether we will bring a damaged person into existence. What mandate do we have as God's stewards to do that? This is not a matter of *coping* with a disability, but of *creating* a person with a disability, with which he or she will have to cope in the future. This is a new realm, demanding new approaches.

Of course, there are numerous conflicting arguments about whether a couple, such as Shane and Sarah, should opt for IVF under these circumstances, the dangers of quality control in this type of procedure, and the drive towards perfection with the repercussions this could have for society's treatment of the unhealthy. While these are serious issues for ethical debate, they cannot shelter us from having to determine whether there is a moral distinction between the fate of a three-cell embryo carrying the gene for cystic fibrosis, and of a child suffering from cystic fibrosis. I am inclined to think that such a distinction does exist.

Somatic-cell gene therapy

The correction of gene defects in a patient's own body cells (that is, somatic cells) is known as *somatic-cell gene therapy* and was first approved in humans in 1989 and first used in 1990. The strategy involves gene replacement or gene correction with the genes being introduced via vectors. These may be viruses which have had the gene of interest included in their genetic material and will transfer the gene of interest by their usual infective mechanism. Injection of packaged genes directly into human cells may also be a possibility. The aim of this form of gene therapy is to modify a particular cell population and so rectify a particular disease in a particular patient. As such, it is similar to procedures like organ transplantation, but is far more powerful than any indirect genetic therapies. However, there are technical difficulties associated with the expression and appropriate regulation of new genes in somatic cells. Enormous care has been taken, both procedurally and ethically, in undertaking studies on human patients, and very specific guidelines have been elaborated.

In other words, somatic-cell gene therapy amounts to little more than putting genes directly into patients. This is illustrated by the first human trial involving a four-year-old girl with severe combined immune deficiency (SCID) disease.

People with SCID lack the gene which enables cells to make a protein called adenosine deaminase (ADA). The lack of ADA damages the immune system, making it almost completely useless and therefore exposing patients to repeated infections. In this study copies of the ADA gene were infused intravenously at various intervals into the girl's white blood cells. A marked improvement in her condition was still evident a number of years after the treatment.

Far more significant is *cancer gene therapy*, the goal of which is to enhance the patient's anti-tumour response. Since 1989 a number of patients suffering from advanced melanoma (life expectancy of less than 90 days) have received gene-modified cells. In some of these patients the cancer regressed, and this appears to be a safe and practical method for introducing foreign genes into humans. It may well be that within a few years gene therapy will be accepted as an effective treatment along with surgery, radiotherapy and chemotherapy.

Other conditions that may be alleviated by this approach are some forms of heart disease, cystic fibrosis, and Duchenne muscular dystrophy.

This form of gene therapy is a very sophisticated way of alleviating disease. At face value, therefore, it fits admirably within Christian goals for health care, since it is an extension of many currently accepted practices. As it is used to treat those with serious genetic conditions, it has as its goal the enhancement of the welfare of individuals: curing where possible and always caring. We should applaud this use of gene therapy, because there is no virtue in being complacent when conditions can be altered for the better.

When confronted by gene therapy something very important has altered, and this is the boundary between the alterable and the unalterable. This shift is a significant one, since much that was until recently in the unalterable category has now entered the alterable category, or at least will enter that category within the next few years. It is extremely important for Christians to understand this transformation, since we make a mockery of our faith by objecting to good developments for bad reasons. Upholding the *status quo* in a rapidly moving scientific area is not a mark of faithfulness; it is a mark of temerity. There is no biblical reason for arguing that the unalterable must always remain unalterable. If that were the case, we would still be objecting to anaesthetics and I can see no reason why that would be inherently biblical. The unalterable regularly becomes alterable, and our response should be one of rejoicing unless there are well-delineated moral and spiritual reasons for thinking otherwise. There are no such reasons in somatic-cell gene therapy, from which I conclude that our Christian responsibility is to encourage the developments in this area, seeing them as a mark of Christian stewardship.

This is one side of the coin; what of the other? Although there is no virtue in living with deformity or debility that can be rectified, we must not fall into the trap of thinking that a deformity or debility makes an individual's life meaningless. While much of the research in somatic-cell gene therapy is of benefit and should be encouraged, we must not forget that there is a great deal we cannot do and will not be able to do in the foreseeable future (and perhaps ever) in the genetic realm. It is at this point that we are to learn to live with the unalterable, realizing that God's grace is shown in numerous ways that are in no way dependent upon medical advance.

Care is required at this point, since our genetic make-up is something we inherit. Our inheritance may be a fortune; it may be a disaster. Either way, we are not responsible for our own genetic blueprint. We take what we are given; we learn to live with the genetic raw material we brought into the world. Similarly, we have to accept the genetic advantages and disadvantages of others, as we take seriously God's indiscriminate love for all no matter what their genetic deficiencies.

In other words, it is imperative that the pursuit of physical perfection is not placed above the enhancement of specifically human characteristics. Biology can appear very cruel, and there are gigantic biological inequalities from which we can never escape and with which we have to learn to cope. This is as true of genetics as anywhere else. As humans we have to learn to live with, and share, the total genetic burden of humankind. In Christian terms, this implies we are to become one with the afflicted, suffering with them and giving of ourselves in love and practical concern. Somatic-cell gene therapy constitutes one important element of this concern, but it is only one element. Equally important are social systems that protect and support the genetically disadvantaged, and community efforts that imbue the genetically disadvantaged with meaning as human beings of worth and dignity.

Somatic-cell gene therapy, therefore, has a crucial role to play in coping with many forms of genetic disease. Its potential usefulness within medicine is considerable. Having stated this, however, it would be misleading to suggest there are no problems. It is imperative that potential benefits and harms are balanced, while there is an ongoing need to assess the safety and effectiveness of new techniques. There must be unequivocal evidence from animal studies that inserted genes will function adequately and will have no deleterious effects. New genes have to be able to be placed accurately into the target cells and remain there long enough to be effective. New genes also have to be expressed in cells at the appropriate level and only in the correct tissues, and neither the genes nor the retroviruses must harm the patient. The benefits of gene therapy have to be compared with current alternative therapies (such as bone marrow transplantation), and to ensure that the interests of patients are always paramount. For the foreseeable future, this form of gene therapy should be viewed as a treatment of last resort. To date, protocols in major medical centres have used exemplary ethical criteria and these are acceptable within an overall Christian perspective of somatic-cell gene therapy.

Germ-line gene therapy

I shall deal in far less depth with germ-line gene therapy, not because it will not emerge as of major importance in the future (I believe it will), and not because there are not serious arguments in support of it (there are), but because at the present time it is not permitted by existing guidelines.

Germ-line gene therapy involves inserting the gene into the germ line (sperms, eggs and embryos), so that when the modified individual reproduces all offspring will have the inserted gene instead of the original defective one. The original defective gene is either removed or its expression is masked. This form of gene therapy attempts to manipulate an early embryo so that the individual it will become is not affected with a fatal disease. From animal experiments there is evidence that this form of gene therapy is risky, because gene expression may occur in the wrong tissues. In addition, since the foreign gene is inserted randomly into the host DNA, various stages of normal embryological development may be disrupted with serious adverse consequences. Yet again, any damage to the DNA caused by this procedure will stay in the germ line and be passed on to subsequent generations, unlike the situation with somatic-cell gene therapy where only the single individual treated is affected.

So, at present there are scientific problems in using germ-line gene therapy, problems that sound forbidding. Yet, with further experimentation and research these problems may well be overcome; if this proves to be the case, enormous possibilities will ensue. In the event of this happening, what objections would there be to embracing this technology and providing individuals and their offspring with an almost 'disease-free' life? The response of Christians to such technological advances should not automatically be a negative one.

There are various arguments in favour of germ-line gene therapy, were it to become scientifically feasible. Some genetic disorders, such as those affecting the brain would only be open to treatment in this way. This is because brain cells in hereditary central nervous system disorders cannot be repaired after birth; as a result, genetic repair would have to take place a long time before birth, by targeting the germ cells. A second reason in favour of germ-line gene therapy is that it would dispense with the need to repeat somatic-cell gene therapy in different generations of a family with a genetic disorder. By eliminating the defective gene from the population, the treatment would be a 'one-off' and so would vastly improve the efficiency of gene therapy.

Arguments like this are scientific and clinical ones. However, before rushing too enthusiastically in the direction of this form of gene therapy, even in the future, there is another issue to be raised. This is that germ-line therapy involves obtaining embryos via IVF, determining which ones require treatment, and then carrying out the therapy. However, the far simpler procedure of refraining from implanting defective embryos achieves some of the same therapeutic aims without running the risks of inserting a new gene into a defective embryo. However, this would not satisfy those wishing to eliminate a defective gene from the population.

What are we to make of this? We appear to have an intriguing ethical conundrum, from which there may be no escape one day. The simpler course of action, utilizing IVF, requires the disposal of defective embryos, a procedure we have met earlier. Some may reject this approach on the ground that it is unethical to select healthy embryos and reject defective ones. Those who respond in this way are then left with the option of germ-line gene therapy, which traditionally has posed far greater problems for those with reservations about manipulating human embryos.

True, both possibilities can be bypassed by refusing to have anything to do with any procedure that tackles health problems at the embryonic stage. This may be an appealing approach to some, but in Christian terms one is left with a nagging doubt. Why place the embryo off-limits when the procedures are aimed at improving human welfare? Indeed, their aim is to increase our valuation of human beings, not to jeopardize it. The choice confronting us is a stark one – to draw an absolute distinction between human embryos and all other humans, or to accept that a fuzzy distinction is more appropriate, with the rider that human embryos cannot be totally protected from the concerns, interests and ill health of older members of the human community.

Enhancement genetic engineering

A different application of somatic-cell or germ-line therapy, known as enhancement genetic engineering, involves the insertion of a gene into an individual in an attempt to improve on a particular trait in an individual. The aim in this case is modification (improvement) of a *healthy* individual in a permanent manner. This is similar to providing growth hormone to normal individuals in order to improve their sporting prowess. What is happening here is that the genetic engineering would be employed, not in the treatment of a disease, but in an attempt to improve a perfectly healthy individual. This gets us into real genetic engineering, and into the heart of the usual concerns so many people have about genetics in general. This is a totally different area from everything considered up to this point. Christian concerns will legitimately come to the surface here, since this takes us very close to abrogating our role as stewards of God's creation. It may not inevitably do this, but it takes us very close. There are also potentially grave scientific and clinical consequences, for example, the extra gene (whether normal or modified) may have adverse consequences resulting from protein imbalance (concerns currently expressed for germ-line gene therapy).

But is this the end of the debate? Let us imagine we can improve an individual in the sense that they will not suffer from heart disease in 50 years time. When the genetic enhancement is carried out, the individual is healthy, and in the absence of the enhancement would continue to be healthy for many years. Is the avoidance of heart disease at the age of fifty years, an improvement? The answer has to be 'yes', since disease is being replaced by health. Should such enhancement be condemned? I doubt it. What, then, if one could improve an individual's athletic performance by gene replacement? This is improvement in the sense that good exercise and coaching constitute enhancement. Ill health does not come in to this, but by the same token is there anything wrong with exercise and coaching? Not in principle, although there may be when the exercise and coaching become excessive.

What emerges is that even genetic enhancement is not such a clear-cut issue as sometimes envisaged. Although there are substantial reasons to object to it, care is required. What are the reasons for attempting it? Do the anticipated changes amount to improvement in any meaningful sense, or are they ephemeral? Are they directed at benefiting the individual or at serving someone else's interests? These questions emerge directly from the biblical principles outlined in Chapter 3, and they bring us back to a Christian framework. Genetic enhancement by itself may not be at fault; what does require assessment are our own motives and goals.

Insurance, genetic screening and patents

The possibility of providing genetic information to insurance companies has proved a highly contentious area. The majority of insurance companies are profit-making corporations, their aim being to insure the healthy at cheaper rates than the ill, or those likely to become ill. For this reason, insurance companies discriminate according to age, gender, occupation, blood pressure and many other health-related factors. In current discussions concerning the possibility that genetic data will become available to insurance companies, issues of equality and fairness immediately come to the fore, with critics arguing that this will lead to discrimination. However, it is difficult to see any difference between this and their traditional discriminatory practices. In other words, would the use of genetic information by these companies signify a radical departure from their current practices? If it is ethical for companies to weigh insurance premiums against those who smoke cigarettes or who have a known history of heart disease, is it any less ethical to do the same to those with known genetic disease?

These brief considerations bring us up against the fundamental issues in underwriting. Should information be used in setting insurance rates? Is genetic information any different from any other medical information? A central issue is the degree to which genetic differences among individuals count as morally relevant reasons for treating people differently with respect to insurance. Even if it is accepted that most of the common disabling diseases have a complex variety of causes, including genetic ones, can it still be argued that a genetic test differs in some profound way from, let us say, a cholesterol test?

People cannot be said to be responsible for their genes, but the genetic component in cholesterol level is probably substantial. This leaves us with an even more fundamental question, and this is whether the central notion of health insurance is morally sound, since much of it is not dealing with voluntarily assumed risks. Ultimately, the debate revolves around the moral acceptability or otherwise of insurance cover itself, particularly when applied to health insurance. The focus of the debate has shifted from genetics *per se* to health insurance, in that it is forcing us to challenge the fundamental premises behind insurance underwriting in the health domain. This surprising conclusion is also a disturbing one, for Christians as much as anyone else.

Genetic screening comes in various forms. There is presymptomatic testing, in which individuals are tested before any symptoms have appeared, in an attempt to determine whether they are carriers of a particular genetic condition. They are not themselves ill and may know nothing about their susceptibility to a genetic disease without specific testing in this way. Whether or not they will eventually become ill will depend on their genetic constitution. Then there is prenatal screening, in which an individual's genetic predisposition for a particular disease, such as Huntington's disease is detected well before birth. This may result in the affected foetus being aborted (or eventually treated or even cured).

Both forms of testing represent a type of medical and even social foreknowledge, since one is looking ahead to what may happen to an individual's health at some time in the future. This knowledge may be highly desirable, since it may help individuals avoid disaster and suffering, and it may also make available preventive health services. But it also forces those afflicted with genetic diseases to face up to their predicament and make choices they would not otherwise have to make, and may prefer not to have to make. This is not an easy predicament for Christians.

Genetic screening should contribute to improving the health of those with genetic disorders. It should allow carriers of an abnormal gene to make informed choices about repro-duction and it should help alleviate the anxieties of those faced with serious genetic disease. There are, however, many potential problems, including ensuring adequate prior consent, adequate confidentiality, and that there is no stigmatization of the genetically disadvantaged. Not only this, unsolicited and sensitive information about an individual should not be forced onto that individual, since a person has the right to refuse testing and so prevent knowledge about himself or herself from being generated.

What about information in the workplace? Employers may use genetic screening as a basis for discrimination against employees with health problems. This would simply be a more sophisticated means of discriminating against people than is currently available. Employers may wish to use genetic screening to detect whether workers are genetically susceptible to unavoidable hazards in particular occupations. A programme of voluntary testing of this nature to inform workers of risks is ethically defensible. On the other hand compulsory genetic testing could be used in socially undesirable ways.

Genetic screening for susceptibility to common diseases such as many cancers, cardiovascular disease and diabetes is emerging, and could lead to health benefits if those at high risk modify their lifestyles. Alternatively, it may lead to stigmatization of those susceptible to these diseases. It may also lead to fatalism, and to the exacerbation of risk factors. It also has to be admitted that the close relationship between susceptibility tests and commercial interests may lead to the testing being driven by market forces.

There is also another, even more subtle force, and this is that undue emphasis on individuals with genetic diseases may result in a lack of social action. Were this to occur, the brunt of the problems created by genetic diseases would be borne by individuals rather than by society. For instance, in a workplace characterized by toxic chemicals in the environment, emphasis on individuals may lead to their relinquishing their jobs, allowing the organization to ignore its own responsibility for removing the health hazards themselves.

The final issue I shall look at here is that of patenting human genes, since patents may be issued on individual genes as well as on micro-organisms into which human genes have been inserted. They may also be issued for the discovery of a human gene or gene fragment, and for the products (proteins) and mutations of these genes.

Consider the patenting of the genes BRCA1 and BRCA2, linked with inherited breast cancer. Considerable scientific and financial resources have been spent by biotechnology companies in the search for a diagnostic test for breast cancer, suggesting that it is not unreasonable for them to recoup this money. However, other research groups have also devoted time and effort to the search for these genes. If the competition were to be threatened by patenting, the whole nature of the scientific endeavour could be altered in molecular genetics research.

Vigilance is essential. Commercial interests could win out and restrict freedom of investigation. They could also price genetic therapeutic products out of the reach of ordinary people and even out of the reach of whole societies. On the other hand, if these investigations do not take place, the potentially beneficial products will not be available to anyone.

This area is characterized by frequent disagreement between industrialists and environmentalists. Large pharmaceutical companies, in particular, contend they must be free to patent genes and human cells where these have been isolated and characterized outside the human body. They argue that they need to be able to profit from the resulting new diagnostic techniques or therapeutic treatments to cover the very high development costs. Allied with this pragmatic approach is the argument that neither isolated genes nor large quantities of purified proteins occur naturally, and should as a result be patentable. The contrary position is summed up by arguments opposing ownership of human life and commercialization of the human body, leading to the position that parts of the human body, including genes, cannot be patented when they remain in the human body.

At a more global level, there is concern that patents on living organisms remove distinctions between living and non-living matter and so undermine the unique status traditionally accorded to life – including human life. In more specific scientific terms, the case is frequently put that genetics research should be a co-operative search for new knowledge, rather than a self-interested search for profits. Once patenting comes to the fore, researchers may become increasingly reluctant to share information, thereby diminishing the transfer of information between laboratories. It is also feared that patenting will slow the development of gene therapy by forcing royalty agreements from researchers developing screening kits.

Considerations such as these leave us with perplexing and unclear predicaments, since we are walking a scientific, ethical and commercial tightrope. Issues from which there is no escape include the dignity of human beings, fairness in dealing with individuals, whole groups of people and companies, the integrity of nature, and the freedom to remain oneself alongside the freedom of scientists to experiment. It would be foolhardy of me to suggest there are straightforward solutions, whether from a Christian or any other perspective. What is required is a balancing of arguments, and a continual awareness that we are not to live for our own ends at the expense of the interests of others.

Playing God

The notion of playing God raises its ugly head in most scientific domains, the intended message being that this is forbidden territory. However, from a Christian standpoint we are made in God's image, and so are to function like God. No matter how much our God-likeness has been shattered by sin and rebellion against God, we are still images of our maker, albeit tarnished images. As such we demonstrate a great deal of his creativity and his inquisitiveness (see Chapter 3). We are to exercise control over the created order, and this is to be done in a responsible fashion. Humans as scientists are humans as God's images, probing and thrusting into the creation, attempting to understand it and make it accountable to God's stewards. Within the medical sphere, the desire is to exercise at least limited control over evil in the form of disease, disease that would ravish and destroy all that is beautiful and worthy in God's world.

This, of course, is just one side of the picture. The other side is that scientists may be arrogant and unworthy, with motives of self-aggrandizement and personal glory. They may show little regard for the welfare of individual humans, even when the realm within which they are working is that of medicine. Nevertheless, these negative images fail to negate the overall thrust of much of scientific advance, genetic advance in this instance. Genetic advance in and of itself is not synonymous with pride and arrogance. It is not an aping of God's power, since gene therapy owes its rationale to this power. As long as the aim of gene therapy is the alleviation of human illness, it has the potential to elevate God's images. This is where therapeutic interventions fit in. By contrast, the attempt to create some new creature with superlative powers would be to play God in the wrong way, since it would stem from human conceit regarding the unlimited nature of human resources, including the ability to create and control in far-reaching ways. A more balanced view is that playing God should remind us that we tamper with fundamental biological processes with caution and great humility; there is much we do not know, and there is much over which we have only limited control. We are to play God, but we are to do it with intelligence and compassion.

This also reminds us that we are not to use massive scientific powers for superficial and frivolous ends. There are always dangers, and to risk these for minor gains is dangerous and irresponsible. So much of the criticism of genetics revolves around its possible insubstantial uses, such as gene manipulation for eye colour or facial features or whatever. Such criticism is justified, but this is criticism of the misuse of genetics rather than of genetic advance itself. Similar criticism can be made of the misuse of many other technological developments, and even of human abilities themselves. Humans playing God only becomes dangerous when they fail to utilize their God-like capabilities in appropriate ways.

Tinkering with nature

Perhaps genetic technology is more than this, since it goes further and tinkers with nature and what is even worse, with people. This is true, but what does this tell us of ethical and spiritual interest? Very often the criticism that genetics is interfering with nature implies that the interference is going beyond acceptable limits; genetics goes too far. This may or may not be the case, but it is difficult to see how genetic technology by itself does this. Nature has given us genetic combinations that lead to Huntington's disease, diabetes and heart disease, but few would argue that these particular combinations constitute a good. Medicine has traditionally done its best to cope with genetic conditions, and these have not, in and of themselves, been regarded as transgressing the boundary of acceptable human endeavour. Humans have intruded into nature throughout recorded human history, whether it has been by draining swamps infested with malaria-bearing mosquitoes or by using antibiotics (Chapter 2). What is far more important to ask is whether the intrusions enhance or diminish the human condition.

Within a Christian context, we may also ask whether they enhance or diminish our ability to respond to God and to appreciate the world He has brought into existence and sustains. Nature is not to be worshipped as if it were some unchanging given; neither is the human genome to be elevated to some untouchable status as if it were fixed and immutable. Humans have been given stewardship of the created order, including the human genome. What is required is that we determine the sort of interference with nature and the genome that will advance human welfare, while respecting the dimensions of what it means to be human. This requires a great deal of enlightened ethical discernment, and an awareness of the tentative path along which we are travelling.

There are no black-and-white answers here, but there is the need for judgement and clear thinking. This has its problems, since all do not follow enlightened ethical paths, let alone ones with which most Christians will be happy. Judgement and discernment in a pluralistic community are qualities to be valued very highly, but they are not always present. These are exceedingly general comments, which become more poignant as the extent of the interference with natural processes increases. We have every reason to be cautious, but our caution has to be balanced against the destructive forces of nature out of control. Christians would do well to examine the effects of both, and then direct their efforts at seeing that the good of the interference outweighs the evil of both interference gone wrong and of nature unrestrained.

Going down a slippery slope

In spite of these points, another objection is frequently made: somatic-cell gene therapy is unethical since it represents the beginning of a slippery slope, the inevitable end result of which will be germ-line gene therapy and eugenics. This is an understandable objection, since one innocuous process has frequently led on to another, originally quite unintended, harmful process. But is this progression inevitable? Does this argument always have to hold? Implicit within the slippery slope argument is the assumption that permission to allow one kind of intervention holds for all kinds of intervention. However, this is not the case in moral reasoning, where there is an immense gulf between different sorts of measures. For instance, there is a considerable moral chasm between gene therapy to treat disease (such as cancer or heart disease) and gene manipulation to alter behaviour or morality. This is the boundary between the worlds of therapy and the alleviation of disease on the one hand, and eugenics and enhancement on the other; and it is a boundary where there is a logical and moral stop sign. Any ethical approach to gene therapy in general has to maintain that gulf and the moral world enshrined by it.

What this means is that once gene therapy has commenced, we have started on a progression governed by a therapeutic rationale. We can stop between somatic-cell gene therapy and germ-line gene therapy, since there are major ethical and biological issues of concern at this point. This does not mean we have to stop there, but we have to be utterly convinced before we move on to germ-line gene therapy. However, the additional move to genetic enhancement and eugenics is a move from the world of finding cures to diseases that kill and disfigure and that limit essential human capacities, to a world of idealistic attempts to perfect the human species and improve fundamental human attributes. Any move into this latter world places us on a slippery slope towards perfectibility and manipulation. But this is not where we are at the moment, and it is not where any serious geneticist or ethicist would wish us to be.

Inevitably, however, trust comes into play, since the slippery slope argument is based on a lack of trust. To deny individuals genetic treatments that are known to work (or will in the near future) on the ground that we are unwilling to distinguish between remedial gene therapy and eugenics indicates a lack of trust in the ability of societies to discriminate between quite different procedures. Perhaps this is right: we cannot trust humans to judge in this manner, since sinful humans cannot be trusted to act responsibly.

This is a stance that has to be taken seriously, because the Christian assessment of the human condition is a more pessimistic one than that of many others. Nevertheless, we demonstrate trust in many other dangerous areas, whether these be the use of motor vehicles, or of tranquillizers, or of nuclear power. In none of these areas can humans be trusted as much as we would like, but reflections of God's image still remain and these often restrain the more extreme actions of which humans are capable.

There is no easy answer, and reluctantly we have to accept this. What is important is that we do not allow the dangers to blind us to reaching responsible decisions. An easy way out is to oppose all developments in areas such as genetics, until they have become so common within society that we quietly change our minds and go along with the majority. In my estimate, this is sub-Christian, involving as it does an abrogation of our God-given responsibility to be leaders within society. If our minds are made new in Christ, we have to be prepared to chart new paths and take risks. We will sometimes be wrong, but if we are never prepared to make positive judgements on technological developments we will almost always be wrong.

The ambiguity of genetic knowledge

Nonetheless, the genetic realm is a potentially dangerous one, and this is a salutary reminder to all who would indulge in its possible excesses. Genetic knowledge confronts us in a poignant way with ambiguity. On the one hand, we want to know all; our curiosity drives us to search and to keep on searching. Genetics shows us much about why we are as we are, but it also enables us to know something about what we will be like in the future. And it is this ability to look into the future and control what may happen in the future that is so alluring. Is it too alluring? Or are we afraid of too much self-knowledge? Will this challenge our view of who we are? Will we lose control of our own lives?

Alongside this ambiguity goes another, and this is the prospect of greatly increased control over people's lives and all-pervasive intervention in their lives. Such control and intervention may be used exclusively for good, but there is always the prospect that this may not be the case, and we recoil from the prospect. Here then is ambiguity once more; we may be able to control others, but they equally will be able to control us and they may not do it with the best of intentions.

Alongside this perspective stands another: the tension between perfection and imperfection. Some grand genetic vistas allude to perfectibility, improving humans in some unspecified ways. I have already argued that such vistas are not on any current genetic agendas, and never should be, but they feed the imagination. Even in the imaginary realm there is ambiguity: do we really want perfection, with its message that challenges will be no more? Do we really want total genetic control? Isn't such a picture the complete antithesis of all that human existence means? Too much genetic control may lead to a loss of our self-identity. As we become increasingly able to change and control ourselves, it becomes more and more difficult to accept the wonder of what is given and cannot be made by us. The temptation is to think of the impossible as that which is not yet possible.

Such general considerations do not tell us whether or not we should go along the path of somatic-cell or germ-line gene

therapy. They remind us of our frailty. If it is true that as soon
as we are able to do something it must be done, we have limited the ethical possibilities open to us, since we have lost a
fundamental element of what we are, and of what we ought to
be. We must be able to say 'no' to possible future developments in genetics (or in anything else, for that matter). But this
only becomes possible when we accept that human value is not
dependent upon such developments. This is a serious matter
for Christians; it is also a challenge for them to show others
what it means to be human, as people in the image and likeness
of God.

Nine

Clones: Persons or Slaves?

To clone or not to clone, that was the question!

'Clone' is a term that comes from the Greek word *klon*, meaning 'twig', 'slip' or 'cutting'. One dictionary entry describes it as a 'group of organisms formed asexually from one ancestor'. To clone refers to reproduction by asexual means, with the result that the new individual or individuals are derived from a single parent and are genetically identical to that parent.

To produce a 'clone' of an organism which normally reproduces sexually, the nucleus of a mature unfertilized egg has to be removed and replaced with a nucleus which has the full complement of chromosomes, and this may be from a specialized body cell of an adult organism, or from an embryo or foetus. If this process is repeated with the transferred nucleus coming from the same source, the result is an unlimited number or clone of identical individuals. It results in the production of a number of individuals, all identical to the original individual from which they were derived. It should be noted that the word 'clone' is being treated like the word 'sheep', and is used interchangeably referring to both singular and plural entities but maintaining the concept that a clone is an offspring with an identical genetic constitution to its single parent.

The dominant picture of cloning used by the media is that of the xeroxing of human beings. In this manner, it is depicted as a means of obtaining 1, 20, 100 or 1000 copies of a human person, all genetically the same as the person from whom they were produced. Theoretically this process confers a form of genetic immortality on the original person, particularly if second-generation clones are subsequently made from first-generation clones, and so on, throughout the generations.

Bells should have rung when, in 1996, a research group reported that they had successfully cloned lambs from the cells of embryos. The title was on target: 'Sheep cloned by nuclear transfer from a cultured cell line'. Surprisingly, this paper elicited little debate in the public arena, even though it marked a very significant step scientifically on the path towards fully-fledged cloning, which uses nuclei from adult (as opposed to developing) cells. It was, therefore, a major advance in the cloning of mammals. Even prior to this 1996 paper there had been a very long history of attempts at cloning.

It has long been known that nuclei from very early embryonic frog tadpoles can be transplanted into egg cells to produce viable adults. On the other hand, nuclei from mature tadpoles or adult frogs have been less successful, with the cloned animals developing as far as the tadpole stage before dying. In mice, cloning has not worked with nuclei from embryos older than the eight-cell stage. Sheep and cows appear to be more amenable to cloning. From a technical angle the question of human cloning remains a tantalizing possibility.

The history of cloning has been a murky one since the fear and fascination of this procedure has led to some bizarre events. Perhaps the best-known occurred in 1978 when David Rorvick, a science journalist, wrote a book, *In His Image*, claiming to be an account of the events leading up to the first birth by cloning of a human being. According to this account, an American millionaire in his sixties wanted to leave posterity a clone – an identical replica – of himself. In order to do this he enlisted David Rorvick to find a biologist willing to work on the project in complete secrecy and with unlimited finances. Despite a chasm of unknowns, the work from the start utilized humans. Conveniently, the laboratory was situated in some undisclosed, idyllic-sounding paradise where there was little difficulty in obtaining women 'volunteers'. Conveniently, these 'volunteers' were not informed of the nature of the experiments and, during their dubious hospital stay, eggs were obtained from them. A few of the women acted as surrogate mothers to carry eggs cloned with cells from the donor millionaire. Eventually one of them carried a clone to term, and was apparently living with the millionaire and his one-year-old clone son towards the end of 1977.

This book was denounced as a fraud, and in 1982 one of the scientists mentioned in it won a legal suit against Rorvick and the publishers on the grounds that he had never engaged in or advocated the cloning of a human being. The publishers conceded that they believed the story to be untrue.

The world should, therefore, not have been taken by surprise when in February 1997 the article 'Viable offspring derived from foetal and adult mammalian cells' by an Edinburgh research group, headed by Ian Wilmut, appeared in the journal *Nature*. Strictly speaking, the epochal event happened three days earlier, when the findings were prematurely disclosed by a British newspaper, and Dolly (the cloned lamb) was presented to the public.

Wilmut and co-workers reported that they had transplanted the nucleus (C) from a somatic cell (the udder) of an adult sheep to an enucleated egg (E) of another sheep. During the process the egg (now E + C) was stimulated and responded just as if it had been fertilized. The resulting lamb was genetically identical to C. In spite of uncertainties at the time (it took 277 'E + Cs' to produce Dolly; it was doubted how long Dolly would survive, and whether she would age prematurely), what was far more significant was that a mature mammalian cell has the capacity to differentiate. For all intents and purposes this cell should have remained a sheep's udder cell. However, by appropriate manipulation, the nuclear material reprogrammed itself so that it could again differentiate.

As cloning in mammals such as sheep and calves has only just begun to produce living clones it is fair to say that at present the cloning of humans is far from reality. However, in order to have a clear view of the impact this technique will have on our society we have to project ourselves into the future when the birth of clones is as integral to society as is IVF today. In this way we shall confront the nebulous nature of our concerns, as well as our fears of the unknown.

Therefore, imagine a society in AD 2060, in which the cloning of humans is generally accepted.

Report: second thoughts from a cloning society

Did you know that of every 1000 babies born today, 20 will have been cloned? There are laws to govern cloning, because it is a complex process involving the manipulation of human embryos and sometimes surrogacy.

Animal cloning has had considerable effects on agriculture, and many products used in medical treatment are now manufactured via cloning in animals. The attraction of adult-cell cloning is that the outcome is known, whereas if you use an embryonic or foetal cell you do not know what the qualities or defects are. Once an animal with a desired trait has been produced, for example sheep genetically engineered to produce milk laced with enzymes and drugs, numerous copies of those animals can be produced. And so adult cell cloning has proved a highly effective biological means of producing pharmaceutical products. Some farmers have used cloning to propagate champion cows, and there have been feverish attempts to propagate endangered animal species by cloning.

Today, cystic fibrosis sufferers are able to minimize damage to their lungs and pancreas due to the availability of a substance produced in large quantities in sheep's milk. Clues are being provided as to the mechanisms that switch genes on and off during development, and could still provide further important insights into the lack of regeneration in the brain and spinal cord, and also into the way in which cancerous cells revert to the embryonic stage and start multiplying uncontrollably.

Cloning, therefore, has made its presence felt in this society, with three categories either in use or still being debated. Ego cloning is cloning for social reasons, whether these be public figures, or simply ordinary individuals ('another me'). Medical cloning is used for the treatment of various conditions, the principal ones being infertility (where the male partner is sterile) and certain genetic conditions. Research cloning could be used to produce tissues for other people, including organs and cell lines.

The first two have been approved by society, in spite of vigorous debate and intense controversy. Cloning procedures are controlled by a series of government committees, and all cloning centres are licensed.

Even those who disagree with cloning cannot say it is uncontrolled. Nevertheless, many feel that society is on a slippery slope, and consider that areas where cloning is currently forbidden will be allowed in future. This may or may not prove to be the case. All that can be said at present is that the regulations in force today have been in place for the past ten years without much modification. Time will tell.

Ego cloning

Ego cloning is controlled by legislation. For instance, no cloning is permitted over the age of sixty years, mainly because of grave doubts about how long the clone will live. This is because the cell from which the nucleus was taken is from a relatively old individual and we do not know yet what part the mitochondrial DNA of the oocyte cytoplasm plays in the aging process. Where minors are to be cloned, the legislation insists on the child having a legal guardian to act on his or her behalf to avoid exploitation by the parents. Any one person is allowed a maximum of three clones, in order to restrict the extent of genetic conformity. Consent is required of the person to be cloned (there are still difficulties with minors), the surrogate and those who will be the social parents. Of course, clones-to-be cannot consent, but neither can they with any other form of reproduction.

There are still technical problems, and cloning works best when the donor (the person to be cloned) is between ten and twenty years of age. Generally, however, ego cloning is requested only when a person has proved themselves, at least in their own eyes, and most of these are much older than twenty. There is an unexpected problem, though, and this is that clones are turning out to be far more variable than anticipated. Quite apart from the age difference they are not as similar in personality as are identical twins. Not only this, some clones have been positively disappointing.

Individuals are frustrated when 'my' clone has my failings, as well as my strengths. This should have been obvious to everyone, but perhaps those who want to have themselves cloned overlook the simple fact that they actually have failings. People who have had themselves cloned have been surprised when the clone has turned out to have totally different interests from themselves (the new 'me' is more unlike 'me' than I had thought possible). This is proving especially difficult when the clone of the self-made businessman-cum-philanthropist turns out to be a budding philosopher uninterested in money and abysmal at making any!

Ego cloning has proved something of a failure, especially in those families where the clones have been treated as slaves – created to do their masters' will. This was what the horror stories suggested would happen, and in some instances it has. The problem here is that clones have been treated as less than human. I am not suggesting that ego cloning is a good thing, but the major problems arise when clones are forced to behave as others expect them to behave. This is the crux of the issue. Why accept someone as different from you, when you brought them into the world to be like you? To rectify this situation a bill is before parliament, to ensure that before a cloning procedure is commenced the person providing the genetic material has the patent of that material, but does not own the resulting clone. This should be the end of the slavery dilemma, and of concerns that history will repeat itself by introducing a new form of slavery. The temptation to control and exert power over others remains as great as ever.

In some respects ego cloning has not turned out to be as bad as some of us had expected, but neither has it achieved much. Once individuals are given freedom and are allowed to develop as themselves, ego cloning becomes redundant. It is something of a farce, an all-too-obvious example of a tragic technical excess.

Medical cloning

For many years a host of reasons has been advanced in favour of human cloning. Generally at the top of the list is its role as a means of bypassing the risk of genetic disease. A couple, in which one partner has a genetic defect, can avoid the risk of passing on this defect to their children by having cloned children of the healthy partner. Where the male partner is unable to produce gametes, cloning of the woman is a means of bypassing his sterility, and it is at this point that it resembles more conventional practices ranging from adoption, to artificial insemination by a donor (DI), and to techniques such as intracytoplasmic sperm injection (ICSI).

However, it has been widely used outside a marital relationship, to enable single women, or lesbian couples to have children. Some gay men, and the occasional single man, have also used it, but they of course have had to employ women as surrogates. The problems in these cases are the ones we all expected. The practice has been difficult to control, because once a technique is available the drive to use it everywhere imaginable is very strong. Cloning has also become divorced (was it ever not divorced?) from any moral values. Its nature appears to be such that it is simply used as a way of enabling anyone at all to have children outside any conventional commitment relationship. Controls appear ineffective, stemming possibly from the technique itself, with its almost complete emphasis on the manufacturing side of reproduction. Children really are 'made' with this technique, hence, its biological potential and moral uncertainty.

Some people have cloned one of their children so that the clone could be the compatible bone marrow donor for a much-needed bone marrow transplantation. This has its problems, but the clone's life is not placed at risk, and in reality this differs little from those who years ago had another child (naturally) for the same reason. In fact one is assured of a compatible donor which is not the case if one has another child by the usual reproductive means. Before the transplantation is carried out a large range of ethical criteria have to be satisfied. Some of us think such people are misguided, but if the resulting child or clone is loved and cared for as an individual in its own right, the end result may be acceptable from an ethical standpoint.

Cloning seems to have proved beneficial for couples where infertility has been successfully bypassed. It is hard to condemn the couples who have used it in these instances, and the resulting clones (children) give the impression of being as well adjusted as any other children. This is because they were brought into existence to be themselves; the fact that they are genetically identical to their mothers was not the reason for resorting to cloning. They were created to be loved and to love. Just as the first IVF children turned out to be far more normal and unexceptional than some had supposed, the same can be said of these cloned children.

But what is the real cost of producing these children, not for the individuals concerned, but for society? The cost is in the price society may be paying for having accepted cloning into its midst. This is not the horror some imagined, it is far more subtle than that. It is in the changed expectations of children, the way we look at them, and at what we can do to ourselves and to them.

Should we be bringing into existence 'another me' even for good reasons? This is not ego cloning; it is serious medical treatment, just as the assisted reproductive technologies are serious medical treatment. But is cloning, even for the best of humanitarian reasons, bringing us unnervingly close to the disposable society? Medical cloning is quite different from ego cloning, but do I really want 'another me' even to overcome infertility or a genetic disease? It may be preferable to have no children rather than a cloned child, but neither way is easy. It also has to be remembered that many people have had to resort to unpalatable measures to overcome infertility – DI, IVF, ICSI or adoption. Cloning can now be added to this ever-lengthening and increasingly ambiguous list.

A society that accepts cloning in a few circumscribed situations finds it almost impossible to limit its use to just those situations. Perhaps all technologies are the same, but cloning by its nature seems to push society into an all-or-nothing corner.

Research clones

This has proved the most challenging of the three categories. Ethical discussion tends to centre on this category because it is closest to science fiction scenarios. After all, Aldous Huxley in *Brave New World* almost got it right, and the problems he foresaw are the same problems that have confronted our policymakers.

How is it possible to do research on human clones in an ethical manner, if the production of clones as the source of tissues and cell lines means that the clones themselves can have no say in what is done to them? What this amounts to is producing human beings (clones) in order to sacrifice them when organs or tissues are required.

We do not do this in any other area. Identical twins have been around throughout recorded history, and few societies have allowed one of them to be sacrificed in order to save the life of the other (the agonies experienced when Siamese twins have to be separated demonstrates this). If we do not do this with identical twins, why do it with clones?

The result is that there have been no moves to produce research clones. Experiments on animal clones have been extensively used, but not on human clones. That would be taking us back to the dark days of human experimentation, rather than into some glorious future. Although considerable pressures have been exerted by scientists to go in this direction, we have concluded as a society that the drawbacks are too great.

A clear moral line has been set, and there is no longer serious discussion about research clones. To destroy human clones so that others might live is considered outlandish even by those who normally think little about ethical matters. Such gross devaluation of human beings is not tolerated. Once clones have been born, they are to be treated in the same manner as any other human being.

However, cloning has also been used to produce cloned tissues and organs, rather than cloned individuals. These cloned tissues have been used extensively for research purposes, and have proved of enormous value in medical research. They have posed no ethical problems for most people. The cloning of human organs has proved more difficult, but some spectacular breakthroughs have taken place. What has intrigued some of us is whether these particular developments would ever have occurred apart from the more sinister aspects of the cloning of individuals. They may have, and on paper they could have, but some of us wonder.

Clones as people

A fascinating situation has arisen in a number of churches. A surprisingly large number of Christian groups have gone in for medical cloning – far more than ever predicted (before the legislation was passed they were vehemently opposed to it). Cloned individuals are far more human than frequently imagined. They stand before God as ordinary human individuals, and are just as responsible for their actions and motives as is anyone else. They can respond to God and have a personal relationship with him through Christ, in exactly the same way as their non-cloned counterparts.

However, just because they are genetic replicas of their faithful fathers (or mothers) does not mean they, too, will be faithful like them. There are no such people as cloned Christians; faith cannot be cloned, and we should all be thankful for that. The mistake some people have made is to think that God is limited by genetics. Just because there is genetic similarity between two individuals does not ensure there will be spiritual similarity. By the same token, evil cannot be cloned either. What astounds me is that it has taken cloning to teach our society some very basic lessons. Even clones reared in Christian families may walk away from faith; such an obvious lesson, and one that should have been known all along.

In the days before cloning, we failed to appreciate fully the uniqueness and individuality of each person. We thought we could mould likeness and conformity into people. Our goal was to have churches full of similar people, who believed the same things, had the same attitudes, and acted in the same ways. Some critics even used the term 'clones' in those days – metaphorically of course. Today our thinking has been revolutionized, Christians have begun to glimpse in a fresh way that God deals with each one of us separately because he views all of us as distinctly individual.

Even when clones turn out well as human beings, many are left with a nagging doubt, because the individuality and unpredictability of human life has gone. In view of this, Christians have begun to glimpse in a fresh way how God deals with us – as unique individuals. We dare not deal otherwise with each other, cloning or no cloning.

Once a new procedure has become established, one can see its good and bad features in a way not possible before its introduction. We learn from our mistakes. Human cloning has proved a two-edged sword; the pressures it has unleashed have been similar to those unleashed by all the other technologies used to control and manipulate human reproduction. Society has been changed for ever by them, and Christian standards have been placed under enormous pressure. Technologies like these have to be harnessed for good ends, but different agendas within society have made this exceedingly difficult, if not impossible. Life would certainly have been easier without cloning, just as it would be easier without many other things – both natural and technological. This is not as clear a story as I hoped it would be; it is more a cautionary tale about all scientific ventures into the reproductive unknown.

Clones and Christians

Our imaginary society in AD 2060 brings home to us our ability to conform to, and live with, the secular response to technological and medical developments. It teaches us that as Christians we have a role to play and that role is not a clear-cut, black-and-white one. We have to sift through the mire of doomsday predictions and narcissistic expectations and come up with a position which is faithful to biblical teaching and that will glorify God. We may not agree with the direction society has taken, yet we have to continue to be part of that society, to be a light for that society and to serve a prophetic role.

The temptation to close our eyes, and run away from hard decision-making has to be resisted. As indicated in this imaginary report, clones are people – to be valued as anyone else is valued. No matter what procedures were used to bring clones into existence, once in existence they are people created by God, with a God-bestowed dignity, with the gift of human life, and with the prospects and expectations of anyone round about them (see Chapter 3). Clones are far more like the rest of us than they are like the robots or androids of science fiction.

We tend to place great store by how people are brought into being, but I sometimes wonder whether God is as concerned about this as we are. This in no way justifies irresponsible actions (either in bed or in the laboratory), but once people *exist* we are to recognize their God-likeness. So it will be for clones (should human clones ever exist). They will stand before God, just as we do. And we shall stand before God to account for the ways we treated them, exactly as if they had come into being by natural sexual reproduction.

Cloning is an extreme technique. As such, it is to be analysed even more rigorously than are other technological procedures in the reproductive area. However, it fits at one end of a well-known continuum, that extends all the way to contraception at the other end. Like all other technological procedures, it confronts us with human responsibility and irresponsibility, with human wisdom and foolishness, and with the ever-present message that we are to look to God for guidance and direction. The danger in the end is that human beings think they are omnipotent and all-wise, able to do anything. Clones remind us that this is a dangerous and foolhardy illusion.

Ten

Saving Infants

Infanticide in history

The time has come to move away from embryos and foetuses into life after birth. However, even here, we will find that we are drawing on attitudes we have already developed towards embryos and foetuses. What this demonstrates is that the link between prenatal and postnatal human life is a very strong one. This should come as no surprise because, apart from the inevitable biological continuity between the two, we saw in Chapter 4 that the biblical writers were also aware of a personal continuity.

It is unfortunate that, as we turn to life shortly after birth – to neonates and infants – the issue we have to deal with is a negative one, namely, infanticide. Alongside abortion and euthanasia, it constitutes one of the most contentious medical procedures from a Christian perspective. An infant that has survived the rigours of foetal life is allowed to die (or is killed) for a variety of reasons and within a variety of social contexts. The world of infanticide covers both passive and active euthanasia. For some there is no significant ethical difference between denying an infant a life-saving operation and giving him or her a lethal injection. Others, however, may permit the withdrawal of medical treatment under certain, well-defined circumstances, but regard active euthanasia as morally wrong. The outspoken proponents of infanticide tend to support active euthanasia, whereas clinical debates revolve around the legitimacy of passive euthanasia.

The practice of infanticide is not a recent phenomenon, since in Greek and Roman times, sick or malformed babies were abandoned and left to die. Ritual infanticide, such as that practised in Canaan, may have served a number of purposes, including sacrifice to Baal in times of national danger, and regulation of the population. Infanticide may also have occurred under adverse social circumstances or when survival was at stake. Other reasons for infanticide through the centuries have included fear stemming from the shame or guilt associated with having an illegitimate child or extramarital pregnancy; mercy killing of a child believed to be facing inescapable doom; mental illness in the parent; or an attempt by one parent to take revenge on the other by killing their child.

The extent of infanticide in history has been a matter of controversy. Some have concluded that child murder was commonplace, and infanticide was the norm. For instance, the Netsilik Eskimo of Canada engaged in female infanticide in order to provide their society with sons, who in turn were needed as hunters and food gatherers. In other societies, including the Aborigines of Australia, several Polynesian tribes, the Yanomamo Indians of Venezuela and the Zhuntwasi bushmen of Africa, infanticide has been freely practised.

Infanticide or infant abandonment, has also been practised continuously, though episodically, throughout Western history. In medieval England, the most common means of infanticide was 'overlaying', where the child was taken to bed with the parent(s) and suffocated. Under ecclesiastical statute, overlaying was considered a crime, but the penance was generally light since the church recognized that this method of population control by the poor was in many cases necessary for survival. Infanticide became epidemic in England and western Europe in the eighteenth and nineteenth centuries. Many reasons have been offered, among them the socially accepted sexual exploitation of poor women by their male employers, in addition to unprecedented population growth and the migration of large numbers of the poor to cities.

However, the view that there have been substantial periods when parents despised their infants and commonly killed their newborn has been challenged, and it has been argued that the prolonged period of infant helplessness is indicative of the importance of caring rather than justification for destruction.

The contemporary debate

The one justification for infanticide that currently dominates debate is physical and mental abnormality, coupled with the prospect of a life of 'inadequate' quality. This debate occurs in the context of modern neonatal intensive care units where sophisticated paediatric surgery is available. Alongside this, increasing recognition is given to cognitive capacity as a means of determining infant (and foetal) worth, and to the continuum from foetal to infant life. The latter highlights the close relationship between attitudes towards abortion and infanticide. Shifts in ethical perceptions and world-views, as well as the increasingly complex technical and ethical decision-making entailed by technological advances, have had a profound impact on attitudes towards infanticide.

Today, it amounts to allowing severely disabled infants to die by withholding or withdrawing treatment or nutrition, but it was only in 1973 that the silence surrounding this controversial practice was broken. The most common targets for infanticide are infants suffering from Down's syndrome or spina bifida. Infants born with Down's syndrome are characterized by mental retardation and often suffer from life-threatening medical conditions, including heart defects and malformed digestive systems. Spina bifida is a spinal lesion, which occurs in two major forms: closed in which the spinal cord is covered by skin, and open in which the spinal cord is covered only by a membrane. The prognosis in closed spina bifida is good, but the open form is accompanied by a range of physical incapacities, including lack of bowel or bladder control and some lower limb paralysis. Approximately 70 per cent of those with the open condition have hydrocephaly, 50 per cent die by the age of two years, and 25 per cent are mentally retarded. Since the early 1970s paediatric practice has varied, with some devising specific criteria for the treatment or non-treatment of newborn babies with open spina bifida, whereas others have adopted a more conservative stance.

The current view of the medical mainstream is that it is right to allow an infant to die, but not actively to kill it. The circumstances under which many practitioners think it is permissible to leave defective newborns to die include an incompatibility with reasonable and independent life, and the presence of multiple severe congenital abnormalities (such as anencephaly, microcephaly, spina bifida, extreme prematurity, Down's syndrome with other anomalies, brain damage and mental retardation) which provide lifelong suffering for patients and family and an inevitable early death.

What is the attraction of infanticide?

For some writers this stems from the sharp distinction they draw between being a human being in the biological sense and being a person in the moral sense (see Chapter 5). From this they conclude that some human beings, such as infants, are not persons, since they are unable to recall past states, cannot envisage a future for themselves, and have personality traits that alter drastically over short periods of time. Consequently, they argue that even if it is wrong to kill innocent persons, infanticide is different. On the other hand, they think that the adult members of some animal species, including baboons, chimpanzees and dolphins, do qualify as persons.

But this is not the end of the story, since human foetuses and neonates may be thought of, not as non-persons, but as potential persons. For some, potential personhood allows us to confer a right to life on infants only if we also accept that it is wrong to refrain from producing additional persons. This argument ends up concluding that if we are under no obligation to produce children (that is, contraception is acceptable), the killing of a foetus, a potential person, is no worse than using contraceptives (see chapter 7). Some even consider that killing a neonate is no worse than killing a foetus.

Besides these possibilities, that infants are non-persons or potential persons, a third possibility asserts that human infants from three months of age onwards may be quasi-persons. The argument here is that quasi-persons differ morally from non-persons, and therefore qualify for the right to life. But there is a sting in the tail: this is a right that should also be recognized in adult animals from many species. What is more, if for some reason quasi-persons do not qualify for this protection, infanticide should be permitted up to one year of age. Consequently, it is worse to kill a baboon, in order to transplant its heart into a human infant, than it is to kill a normal two-month-old infant in order to use its body parts to save an adult baboon.

The approach I have just described has been most provocatively stated by the philosopher Michael Tooley (*Abortion and Infanticide*). He insists on the non-personhood of later foetuses, neonates and infants, since a very well-developed repertoire of behavioural patterns is necessary as a basis for personhood. He is comfortable with the conclusion that since newborn humans lack a capacity for thought, self-consciousness and rational deliberation, they are not persons.

Intriguing as this approach is, it takes no account of the commitments we have to the welfare and survival of infants and also, to varying degrees, even of foetuses. The newborn are totally dependent on the care and nurture of the mother, family and close friends, interactions that are essential for their survival and well-being. What this demonstrates is that, even when the neurological and behavioural features of the newborn (or foetus) are inadequate on a biological scale of values, our commitment to love and care for someone like us is basic to what we are as humans living in community (see chapter 7). In this we begin to see something of the Christian emphasis on our being made in the image of God. This emphasis on commitment is a powerful theological one, since it is commitment to God, to other images of God, and to the community of those created and sustained by God.

Tooley is not alone in his support for infanticide. For instance, Helge Kuhse and Peter Singer start from a rejection of speciesism, which they regard as indefensible as racism or sexism. From this basis, they conclude that killing a continuing self is of much greater moral significance than killing a being who is unable to recognize that it exists over time. According to these writers, a continuing self is a person (whether a human individual or animal), whereas any individual who lacks this (whether embryo, foetus or neonate, or an older individual with very severe retardation or brain damage) is not a person. Consequently, up until one year of age, no newborn human has a right to life, since it is only from this age onwards that the beginnings of self-awareness and a sense of the future make their appearance. For Kuhse and Singer (*Should the Baby Live?*), infanticide before the onset of self-awareness does not threaten anyone in a position to worry about it. On the other hand, killing a wanted newborn wrongs the baby's parents, suggesting there are limits to the defensible killing of an infant. In view of this, it becomes obvious that all postnatal human life is not of equal value. Even healthy and normal infants are not persons; in fact, they are only saved from death by the interests of those who love them and care for them.

These authors state quite categorically that some infants with severe disabilities should be killed. This is a step beyond that which states that normal infants may be killed. Handicapped infants lack even the limited interests afforded to normal infants, since their lack of quality tips the balance away from any possible benefits they may bring to others. As a result, what becomes determinative are the costs to the family and society; if the financial and emotional costs outweigh the relatively low moral status of infants, their lives can be terminated. What is all-pervading is cognitive capacity. Indeed, it is understanding (either in the present or the past) that emerges as the one feature possessed by disabled adults that protects them from being killed in the manner that imperilled infants may be killed.

The reliance of this position on brain development is all-important. While neurobiological features should not be ignored in difficult clinical assessments, there are some provisos. Biological data neither guarantee the presence of, nor constitute the definition of, a person. Scientific criteria play an important role in directing our moral gaze, but they do not by themselves constitute the whole of a moral perspective. Even in biological terms, human beings are more than their brains, and so to base moral judgements solely on neural parameters is to base them on a very narrow biological foundation. The use of neurobiological parameters to determine brain birth (when a 'brain' first appears), a concept with significant moral overtones, has major limitations due in part to the confusion inherent in definitions of brain death. This illustrates the problems associated with interweaving biological and moral aspirations, even in very specific and well-defined fields.

Christian philosopher, Robert Wennberg (*Terminal Choices*), has provided an alternative viewpoint on active euthanasia and its legalization. He fears that seriously handicapped infants will become more vulnerable within societies governed by a policy of active euthanasia, since they will be judged fit candidates for 'mercy'. He puts forward four reasons for these concerns. First, seriously handicapped infants already are objects of passive euthanasia. Second, there is confusion over whether infants have a right to life. Third, there is the temptation to view ending the lives of seriously handicapped infants as something that is being done for their sakes. Fourth, the emphasis placed on a dignified existence may deprive the seriously handicapped of their (undignified) existence. While these concerns reflect a profoundly different stance on the moral status of infants from that of Kuhse and Singer, they also throw the moral spotlight on the actions of people like us. The fact that a dog is not a person does not allow me to treat it in any way I choose. Killing dogs for no good reason is morally despicable because it throws doubt on the morality of my actions as a human being. Killing infants, even if they are not persons, and even if there is no one to love and care for them, seriously undermines the moral status of adults. In addition, infants are far more like us than unlike us; they are one of us, however limited their self-awareness and abilities at present.

Opposing viewpoints

The analysis carried out by Kuhse and Singer is strongly anti-Christian. They leave no place for any religious approach to ethical decision-making, and hence have no room for concepts such as human beings in the image of God. On the other side of the fence stands the leading American theologian Paul Ramsey, who was writing in a compelling fashion in the 1960s and 1970s (see futher reading). Ramsey's arguments were always grounded very firmly in the character of God, and particularly on the notion that his care for humans is based on need, and not on their capacity or merit. For Ramsey, infants' inability to do certain things and their lack of certain experiences is morally irrelevant. They should be cared for because life is a gift from God, to be accepted with gratitude and commitment. Such life should not be discarded whenever it fails to live up to arbitrary standards of quality. According to Ramsey, the duty of parents, doctors and the human community is to sustain the life of defective infants – and to ensure that their lives will be as free from disability as possible. Infants should be allowed to die only when they are already dying. As long as emphasis is placed on the inevitability of death, it allows one to dodge having to make judgements about the quality of life of these infants.

These ethical directives stemmed from Ramsey's stance that personhood is a theological notion grounded in the view that life is a gift in the image of God, and that it cannot be related to the capacities or incapacities of infants. Since all human life is a gift in this sense, all human life is of equal value. There is no doubt that this approach is successful in evading quality-of-life decisions, but it has its limitations when it comes to clinical decision-making, and a more nuanced approach then becomes necessary (see Chapter 5).

Ramsey's commitment to human life as a gift from God is an essential underpinning for any Christian approach, and this should be recognized. It says quite explicitly that all human life has value and dignity, and so infants become of concern to the whole moral community and not just to their parents. By the same token, communities are obliged to provide support for parents coping with infants and especially for those looking after severely damaged infants.

This is an excellent foundation for serious Christian thinking, but it is still necessary to ask what is the basis of Christian argument against active euthanasia of infants. In general, this tends to be the same as that against any form of active euthanasia: uncertainty in prognosis, the likely abuse of the procedure, the blurring of the distinction between medicine as a healing art and medicine as a killing profession, the slippery slope argument, and the increasing sophistication of pain management in deformed neonates. Sympathetic as I am towards reasons such as these, they are not entirely persuasive. They take us some of the way, but are too dependent upon extrapolation. They also inadvertently militate against any form of non-treatment (passive euthanasia), since whenever we move in this direction we impose our standards and expectations on those unable to speak for themselves. No neonate can ever request non-treatment, let alone active euthanasia, with the result that the parameters of the infant euthanasia debate are radically different from adult ones.

As defenceless members of a moral community, that community's bias should always be against actions that will terminate the lives of infants, just as it should be against actions to terminate the lives of embryos or foetuses. The underlying ethos is to be one of protection rather than destruction, and it is from this base that detailed clinical decision-making should spring.

Formulating a Christian perspective

Like embryos and foetuses, infants are weak and defenceless; they are in need of protection. They are due the profoundest of respect because they are partners with us in what it means to be human. We are called to place a wall of compassion and protection around them, even if this is limited when confronted by what appear to be insuperable physical and/or mental limitations. We are to be biased in favour of their protection, a directive that closes the door to active euthanasia.

Within Christian terms, life is a gift from God, to be enjoyed and lived out to its fullest expression. Human life is on loan from God to each one of us. Its value is derived from God, and is to be seen as coming from him and as being for his use. The gift also contains something of the giver, being the work of the giver's own hands, and containing within it the portrait of a loving parent. Consequently, to deface or destroy the likeness of the maker (the image and likeness of God) is a mark of the utmost disrespect. This provides a valuable framework when confronted by severe handicap in a neonate, since this severely damaged infant is a life-derived-from-God, even if the life will be tragically brief and seriously limited. This does not solve difficult ethical dilemmas, neither does it remove the heart-break and anguish, but it is a reminder of the framework within which we may map out the best way forward.

No human being is private property to possess or dispose of as we like; whether our own lives or the lives of others, healthy or damaged. As images of God, humans have been bestowed with responsibility under God to rule wisely over the remainder of creation, particularly over our fellow humans (and they over us). This responsibility reaches its zenith where the relationship is asymmetrical; where we have power over those entirely at our mercy. This is our relationship with infants, and notably with severely imperilled infants, where the parents are uncertain of the path to follow. It may seem that this degree of responsibility is beyond the capabilities of humans, with our tendency towards self-interest and towards displacing God from the centre of existence. Nevertheless, an intimate thread links the gift of responsibility with the gift of life, so that serious decision-making on how best to treat imperilled newborns is inescapable.

Built into our creation as images of God is a commitment to love and care for other members of the human community, who like us are images of God (see Chapter 3). They are our neighbours and are one with us in the human endeavour. Together we are exposed to human frailty, as well as to biological limitations and a host of diseases. As far as possible, all are to be valued as we value ourselves, regardless of the nature or circumstances of the groups. But there are inescapable limits, since not every appalling deficit or disease affecting infants can be rectified. Unsatisfactory solutions and tantalizing tensions cannot be avoided, but should be acknowledged and faced in a spirit of humility.

There is no escape from the brokenness, sadness and tragedy of our world. Whatever is done to help and heal infants will not eradicate the failure, heartache and suffering of human life. The Christian way is to acknowledge these realities, doing all possible to prevent them, but also being prepared to stare at them, and through them see the suffering of God, suffering that is capable of bringing healing to the whole person. In this way we can begin to see that God is with us in the midst of the suffering, that he is relevant in the depth of the tribulation, and that we learn to follow him as we wend our way through all the heartache and sorrow. Even as lives and hopes are precipitously interrupted, they have to be faced up to in the spirit of Christ, but as they are, progress has been made on the way to healing and wholeness.

Infanticide and the developing human

Far more discussion has occurred in both general ethical and theological circles on the status of the embryo and foetus, than on that of the infant. The reason is self-evident. The status of prenatal human life has been brought to the fore by abortion, and more recently by artificial reproductive technologies, and these have raised the most fundamental of issues regarding the meaning of the early stages of human existence (see Chapter 6). By contrast, in recent times it has been generally accepted that, once a baby is born, it is to be given all the protection afforded any other postnatal human. However, the philosophical and clinical developments already discussed have placed a question mark alongside this apparent certainty.

As we have already seen, there are three major views on embryos and foetuses, namely, they are persons, non-persons, or potential persons (see Chapter 7). Infanticide will be a non-issue for those adopting the stance that embryos are persons from fertilization onwards; from this perspective infants deserve complete protection. The practical issues raised previously still have to be tackled and this stance does not provide automatic solutions to some of the conflicts encountered in the nursery. The non-person position is clearly that adopted by those putting forward arguments in favour of infanticide. But where does the potential person position stand in relation to infanticide? This is a developmental perspective and it may not protect infants as much as some would like.

It is frequently stated that any laxity over abortion leads to infanticide, and so it is sometimes claimed that the potential person position leads inevitably to infanticide. This criticism is unfair, depending as it does on an exceedingly liberal interpretation of potential personhood, an interpretation much closer to the non-person than to the person position. According to a far more conservative interpretation of the potential person view, the foetus in the last trimester of pregnancy should be treated as a patient, since the death of a foetus at this stage is equivalent to the death of human life in the fullest sense. Consequently, imperilled newborns will be treated as patients, and every reasonable effort will be made to salvage their lives. The nature and extent of the clinical procedures undertaken will be determined by clinical criteria – in precisely the same way as when treating damaged adults.

One attempt to work through a developmental perspective, states that a developing individual's right to life increases as he or she approaches the threshold of personal life. Hence, if an imperilled newborn is reasonably expected to reach at least minimal personal capacity, treatment should be given. Using this approach three categories can be recognized: where newborns should receive no treatment (such as an anencephalic), where there should be mandatory treatment (Down's syndrome infants with, say, duodenal atresia), and marginal situations where treatment is optional (considerable mental retardation and/or severe physical handicap). In order to take this further, I shall refer to one case study, based on a well-known instance involving Down's syndrome.

Peter was born with Down's syndrome and oesophageal atresia. His parents refuse to consent to the surgical procedure necessary to correct the abnormality of the oesophagus. The obstetrician supports the parents in their decision, while the paediatrician disagrees. The ensuing conflict goes to court, the outcome of which is refusal to order the surgery necessary to correct the oesophageal malformation. As a result, Peter who was unable to feed, died five days after birth.

The obstetrician in this case considered that the chances for successful surgery were about even, that other physical defects such as congenital heart disease were probably present and would subsequently have to be surgically corrected, and that the child would be severely retarded. The paediatrician, on the other hand, considered that the likelihood of successful surgery was close to 90 per cent, that there was no evidence of congenital heart disease, and that it was impossible to determine the severity of the mental retardation. Substantial as the clinical conflict was, there was also moral conflict. Consider the birth of two other babies. Lela was born without Down's syndrome, but with oesophageal atresia. Consent to operate was given and Lela survived. The second baby, Gemma was born with Down's syndrome but without any life-threatening malformation of the oesophagus or any other organ. No operation was required and Gemma lived.

The only difference between Lela and Peter is that Peter had Down's syndrome, a difference that also signifies the boundary between life and death. The only distinction between Gemma and Peter is that Peter had oesophageal atresia in addition to Down's syndrome. Once again, this single difference is the critical factor between life and death. The crucial role is played by the Down's syndrome and not the malformed oesophagus. The issue, therefore, is what treatment is appropriate for Down's syndrome infants.

An infant with Down's syndrome can be deliberately neglected only if its loss will be of no moral consequence. The Tooley-Kuhse-Singer position states that its loss has no negative moral connotations, any more than would the loss of a stray dog. But this no longer holds once infants are recognized as part of the human community. For me, an infant with Down's syndrome is just as much part of this moral community as is a healthy infant. Very challenging ethical decisions will sometimes have to be taken regarding treatment options, but these should be on the basis of the legitimacy of treatment. This shifts the bias towards the welfare of the endangered infant, and away from its destruction. If intervention is justified in a normal infant, why should it be denied to a Down's syndrome infant?

A traditional medical model affirms human life, setting out to benefit the sick, to protect and nurture health, to maintain and restore a measure of physical well-being, to care for those in need, and to cure as far as is possible. Using this model all reasonable efforts will be expended on a Down's syndrome infant. We are to care for neonates and infants with deformities, doing everything possible to provide for their physical, emotional, moral and spiritual needs, for the simple reason that they are people like ourselves.

On the other hand, a market-place model, in which medicine embodies a set of technologies and skills, may or may not lead to treatment of the Down's syndrome infant. In the market-place environment, an operation is or is not performed depending on what the client demands, regardless of the consequences for the client or the client's offspring. The imperilled newborn is viewed as the property of parents to be disposed of as they wish, on the ground that infants exist for the parents' happiness. This perspective lends itself to demands for ideal children; normal, healthy infants who fit neatly into our ideal of the good life. Down's syndrome infants with congenital abnormalities fail this test, and are allowed to die because of their lack of perfection. In such situations, it may be considered preferable to start again.

Responses of this nature are understandable in societies where so much can be controlled and where so little assistance may be given to parents struggling with deformed children (and adults). An ethic of perfectionism stands against an ethic of trust, the latter incorporating hope, care and nurture. Perfection and sinlessness of this order have no place in an inherently imperfect and sinful world. Such goals are resolutely at odds with any Christian perspective, which is more at home with the ethos of integration and its overtones of welcoming children without celebrating or romanticizing their condition. Such an attitude is biased towards equal treatment for infants, no matter what their condition.

These pointers provide no easy answers to any ethical problems. Neither do they condemn those involved in the decision-making over Peter, or those who have made similar decisions over many other infants in similar predicaments. But they are reminders of a way that would seem to be more in accordance with the Christian way, with its tradition of accepting society's outcasts and caring for those in need, even though it does not provide easy answers.

Searching for guidelines

The Royal College of Paediatrics and Child Health in Britain has proposed some guidelines on withholding or withdrawing life-sustaining treatment in children ('Witholding or Withdrawing Life Saving Treatment in Children: A Framework for Practice', published in 1997). These guidelines recognize that technological advance has led to the situation that a life-sustaining treatment may be available even though that treatment is unable to produce real benefit to the patient or may cause prolonged suffering for children and their families. The College's report contains five general situations where withholding or withdrawal of curative medical treatment might be considered:

- In cases of brain death, where artificial ventilation and intensive care are futile.
- In cases of persistent vegetative state, where the child is unable to relate to the outside world.
- In cases of severe disease, where treatment may delay death but is unable to alleviate suffering (the 'no chance' situation).
- In cases where survival would leave the child with severe mental or physical impairment and he or she will never be capable of choice (the 'no purpose' situation).
- In cases of progressive and irreversible illness, where the child and family decide that further treatment is more than they can bear (the 'unbearable' situation).

Those who hold the extreme-equality, or sanctity-of-life, position would disagree with these guidelines, instead insisting on aggressive treatment even for dying infants. In my view, the use of treatment under such circumstances is akin to worshipping 'life', rather than serving the interests of severely debilitated infants. The hallmark of a Christian approach is love for one's neighbour, which translates into the care and protection of the dying infant; there is no room for exploitation, even with the best of intentions.

A less extreme sanctity-of-life position is that proposed by Ramsey. He views every child as possessing equal dignity and intrinsic worth, and therefore no child should be denied life-sustaining medical treatment, either because they are handicapped or because of their poor quality of life in future. Only under circumstances in which the infant is dying or the treatment is considered to be 'medically contraindicated' can a decision of non-treatment be supported. The force of this position is that it is non-discriminatory, focusing on possible treatments; it also emphasizes medical benefit, directing care-givers to provide medically beneficial treatment based on reasonable medical judgement.

The intentions of this position are excellent, but it is of limited assistance in practice. It is difficult to escape the use of some quality-of-life standards, ambiguous and unclear as they may be. One approach is that provided by seeking the 'best interests of the child', so that infants are treated unless they are dying, treatment is medically contraindicated, or continued life would be worse for the infant than an early death. It is the latter indication that opens the door to the possibility that an infant's best interests may lie in withholding or withdrawing medical treatment, resulting in death. The vagueness of this position disturbs many, and it can be interpreted in a variety of ways. One is to make it as child-centred as possible, attempting to make judgements from the infant's perspective and not from that of an unimpaired adult. An alternative approach is to stress the future potential of the infant for human relationships, leading to the conclusion that some severely neurologically impaired children have no future interests, and hence should not be treated. While there are problems with this approach, it has its usefulness, and if applied conservatively can, I believe, enhance a Christian perspective.

Quality-of-life considerations can only be avoided if treatment is always to be provided, or if we can be assured that the infant is dying. But even if there is agreement that the process of dying is not to be prolonged, we have to know with certainty that the infant is dying. There are no simple answers; all judgements will depend on a mixture of clinical (technical) considerations, clinical expertise, moral values, and theological stance. Even when the general thrust is in favour of treatment, difficult ethical decisions remain. Criteria based on the image of God can be of assistance, since they establish an overarching perspective of care and support, but specific technical criteria cannot be obtained, nor should they be expected to emanate, from a theological base.

The distinction between 'having a life' and merely 'being alive' may prove helpful here. This is the distinction between what James Rachels (*The End of Life*) calls 'life in the biographical sense' and 'life in the biological sense', or between personal life and non-personal life respectively. It may be that some lives are worth living, whereas others are not. If this is the case, there are different categories of imperilled people, those who are to be treated and those who are not. This appears to be perilously close to the Tooley-Kuhse-Singer school of thought, and the direct opposite of Ramsey's call for the equality of all human lives. It takes us into exceptionally dangerous territory, where we probably do not wish to go. But can we avoid it in some very tragic cases, where decisions have to be made about resources and priorities?

The Christian perspective I am putting forward is that our bias is to be in favour of continued existence, and of providing infants with as much of a quality future as possible – a future enshrined in love and warmth, a future with as many prospects as possible of interacting with others and of enjoying life as a gift from God. All these are possible even in the face of considerable deficiencies. However, there are limits. A grossly deformed infant may have no further potential for human relationships. Richard McCormick, the Roman Catholic ethicist, has suggested that if the infant's potential is non-existent and would be utterly submerged and underdeveloped in the mere struggle to survive, then that life has achieved its potential. This acknowledges that our technological wizardry has limits, and that caring for the dying is preferable to futile attempts at curing the incurable.

Some Christian and secular concepts overlap. What is profoundly different is the ethos within which they are interpreted. On a continuum, Tooley, Kuhse and Singer are located at one end, with Ramsey at the other; from infants as non-persons at one extreme to infants as our human equals at the other. A Christian stance is built upon a foundation provided by the humans-as-equals perspective, but in order to develop this stance technically based distinctions will sometimes have to be made, and this is where the 'biographical' and 'biological' approaches may have a role to play. Approaches such as these are attempting to provide a means of distinguishing between damaged infants worth treating and those perhaps not. Inevitably, considerable value judgements, as well as technical considerations are bound up in such decisions, and professionals as well as Christians will vary in their emphases.

Eleven

Human Value throughout Life

Confronting conflict

It would be possible to touch on a wide array of topics in the many intervening years between early postnatal life and old age, and any selection mirrors personal interests. My selection points clearly to my own interests in prenatal life and to damage, either occurring at the time of birth or becoming evident around this time. I am also especially interested in conflict situations, where the values and aspirations of one individual are pitted against the values and aspirations of another (see Chapter 1). So many of the ethical dilemmas facing us have conflict at their heart, and it is these dilemmas that force us to confront the hard questions: those messy and murky problems that prevent us finding solitude in definitive black-and-white answers. We detest such problems, and many refuse to face up to them.

I have to admit I relish these problems. They are the stuff of real decision-making, because they challenge us to think precisely and incisively. They also stop us hiding behind vague platitudes, hoping that one of the unpleasant possibilities will quietly disappear. Very often they don't, and we have to face them.

Maternal-foetal conflict

The first conflict is that between a woman and the foetus she is carrying. Dilemmas of this nature are becoming increasingly common in cases where a pregnant woman's intentions or actions do not coincide with the needs, interests or rights of her foetus as perceived by others – most often her obstetric caregivers. A current illustration of maternal-foetal conflict is the discovery that maternal transmission of HIV to newborns can be cut by 70 per cent when infected women are given the antiviral drug AZT during pregnancy. This poses the question whether the pregnant women can or should be forced to undergo HIV testing.

This is just one example of many that could be quoted of apparent conflict between mother and foetus. For instance, in the United States alone, a few hundred women have been criminally prosecuted for foetal drug delivery, *in vitro* child neglect or abuse. In addition, pregnant women have been forced to undergo Caesarean section delivery, maternal blood transfusion, invasive foetal monitoring for suspected foetal distress during labour, intravenous administration of agents to inhibit pre-term labour, and intrauterine foetal transfusion. Two American states have introduced foetal protection laws that allow courts to detain pregnant women who engage in conduct that may harm their foetus, such as drinking alcohol. In all these cases, foetuses are regarded as patients.

There are arguments on both sides of the fence. Either way, the value of one of the parties is being placed above that of the other. Critics of attempts to criminalize, restrict or regulate the behaviour of pregnant women in this manner argue that women are being relegated to the status of 'foetal containers' against their wishes. They are also being viewed as enemies of the foetus. What is happening here is that the medical needs of one person (the foetus) are overriding the rights of the woman to autonomy and physical integrity. Women are being forced to assume medical risks and forfeit their legal autonomy in a manner that is not required of competent non-pregnant female and competent male patients.

The most common justification for involuntary treatment of pregnant women is based on the assumption that forcing surgery or other medical interventions on women will do less harm to them than the harm that will be done to their foetuses if this treatment is not undertaken. Similarly, with the involuntary incarceration of pregnant women who are drug addicts;

the woman's loss of liberty for a period of months is justified because her continued use of drugs during pregnancy could impair the child.

Support of foetal protection policies in the workplace, and the compulsory medical treatment of pregnant women is often based on the assumption that the foetus is already a person, with rights and interests that require protection (see Chapter 7). In these terms, the interests of the foetus are exactly equal to those of the pregnant woman; both are to be valued in the same way. But this is not possible. If pregnant women are forced to undergo treatment they would not choose for themselves, or if they are prevented from acting in ways they would normally choose, they are being valued less than the foetus. It is impossible to treat both in precisely the same way when their interests come into head-on conflict. One or the other has to give way.

If the two have equal status, the interests of the foetus cannot automatically be placed ahead of the interests of the woman; they have to be assessed on their merits. We do not generally circumscribe the actions of a mother or a father on account of the interests of their children if, say, a father takes his family to work and live in an area with high levels of chemicals or radioactivity. These may damage his children's health, in the same way as a pregnant woman's lifestyle (drinking alcohol, smoking cigarettes) may damage her foetus's health. Such damage should be prevented if possible, but a foetus's dependence upon its mother is a major limiting factor if the mother's autonomy, dignity and responsibility (or irresponsibility) are given due weight. The conflicting interests of those made in the image of God bring us face to face with self-centredness and rebellion against God. It would be preferable for the interests of a foetus to be placed above those of the mother (if the potential damage to its future health and well-being is far greater than the discomfort or inconvenience to the mother), but coercion of the mother overrides her standing before God.

The tension becomes even greater when the major technological advances that allow open surgery on the foetus are considered. This can be undertaken for conditions such as congenital hydrocephalus, urinary obstruction, and the repair of a diaphragmatic hernia. Exciting as such advances are, this technique may only be possible by personalizing the foetus and depersonalizing the woman. Not only this, intervention of this sort may allow foetuses to be carried to term that would otherwise have been spontaneously aborted, or the resulting children may be left with a moderate or severe level of disease rather than be cured. Were *in utero* surgical techniques to become standard procedures, a situation may be reached where pregnant women who refused to undergo them may be criminally prosecuted for a failure to provide care. In these cases the mother may in no way be responsible for the foetal ill health, and so the gulf between the interests of the foetus and those of the mother will have widened alarmingly with implications not only for the mother but also for other members of the family.

When procedures like these become commonplace, there will have to be flexibility on both sides. The rescue scenario I used in the early part of Chapter 1 may have appeared irrelevant and highly academic, and yet as we contemplate the examples here on maternal-foetal conflict their relevance becomes obvious. There are no ready-made solutions, either for Christians or for anyone else. Foetuses, like every other human being, are to be valued as highly as possible, but in some circumstances, we shall have to work very hard indeed, to decide precisely how this manifests itself in practice. There is no escape from this, since pregnant women are also to be valued as highly as possible. What is required are altruism and self-sacrifice, grace and servanthood; the Christian virtues of hope and living for others will be urgently needed if destructive impasses are to be avoided.

Using the brains of aborted foetuses for good purposes

Up to this stage, we have looked at foetuses from their perspective. What is good for foetuses? What will promote their interests? There is another side to any discussion on foetuses: how they might be used in the hope of helping others within the human community. This introduces us to foetal neural transplantation or brain grafting, a procedure that emerged as a serious experimental tool in the 1970s. It has since burgeoned into one of the foremost research areas within biology.

> *Fred Smith is seventy years of age, and for the past few years has been suffering from Parkinson's disease. His symptoms have been well controlled for most of this time using the usual drugs, but of late some disturbing side-effects have been getting more noticeable. He is now very troubled by some of these, and his doctor has told him the drug regime will gradually become less effective from now on. However, since he lives near a large research and teaching hospital, his doctor advises him to consider undergoing assessment for a neural graft, in which a part of the brain from a human foetus will be placed in his brain in the region where some of his nerve cells have died. His doctor tells him this is still an experimental procedure, but that there is every chance it will improve his symptoms for a time. Fred goes home to think about this, because he only wants treatment that will give him long-lasting help, and he is also worried about the use of tissue from aborted foetuses.*

The thousands of laboratory studies demonstrate that transplants of developing central nervous system tissue (from foetuses) have a remarkable capacity to develop in their new environment, to integrate with host tissue, and to promote functional recovery after brain damage. Numerous questions still remain, and the clinical situation remains far from clear. Nevertheless, with further development of technical refinements, it is reasonable to anticipate that these approaches may eventually open up new possibilities for intervening in diseases of the nervous system, like Parkinson's disease.

The focus of the foetal transplantation debate is the use of tissue from foetuses made available by induced abortion. What are we to make of this? One of the predominant Christian positions is to condemn the procedure because of its link with abortion. Abortion is wrong; therefore, foetal transplantation is wrong. Indeed, the wrongness of the transplantation is so great that it is condemned in as strong terms as abortion is condemned. Not only this, it is another instance of the way-wardness of biomedical scientists and of the modern medical profession.

But can foetal neural transplantation be dismissed as readily as this analysis suggests, and is it as foreign to the Christian ethos as this denunciation would have us believe? In order to answer these questions with any degree of seriousness, we have to dig rather deeper, and to do this we have to come to terms with the notion of moral complicity. Let me illustrate what I mean. There are two viewpoints of particular interest to Christians, and these have to be assessed by reference to this notion.

The first stresses that foetal tissue transplants are wrong. The emphasis here is on the moral abhorrence of abortion. This is such that it is regarded as tainting beyond acceptability any possible beneficial uses of the resulting foetal material. No separation of the two acts is seen to be possible, with the result that the deliberate killing of the foetus in the act of induced abortion renders anyone using material from such a foetus an accessory to premeditated killing. Generally associated with this position are fears that such uses of aborted material will lead to an increase in the rate of induced abortion in the community, and to women becoming pregnant in order to serve as a source of foetal material. This is called the 'moral complicity' argument.

An alternative approach is that foetal tissue transplants are acceptable, even if abortion is considered morally wrong. A dead foetus is to be respected in the same manner as the body of a dead adult is respected. Consequently, following induced abortion foetal tissue can in principle be used in the same way as human organs are used for transplantation purposes following morally questionable or tragic circumstances. The thrust of this position depends entirely on the ability to view as morally acceptable a procedure (transplantation) that would not be possible apart from what many regard as a morally unacceptable procedure (induced abortion). Basic to this approach is a complete separation in practice between the two procedures, a separation made possible by a rejection of the moral complicity argument.

How are we to assess these two possibilities? The point I want to stress is that, whichever direction we take, it will be based on our view of the adequacy or otherwise of moral complicity, and not on our support of or opposition to abortion. In other words, this is not a discussion of abortion but of moral complicity, the Christian dimensions of which are far from clear, even if it has any Christian dimensions.

Moral complicity

Moral complicity asserts that the transplantation fails to disentangle itself from the moral evil of the underlying induced abortion. James Burtchael (*IRB: A Review of Human Subjects Research*) expresses it like this: 'Experimentation upon foetal tissue derived from elective abortion places the scientist in moral complicity with the abortionist . . . The researcher is a confederate by resorting to the abortionist as a ready supplier of tissue from unborn humans who have been purposely destroyed.'

Moral complicity appears frequently in arguments over the use or otherwise of data and material emanating from the Nazi era. One argument is that the use of material or data deriving from Nazi experiments implicates anyone who uses either of these as participating in the Nazi crimes themselves. According to this stance, we become one with the perpetrators of the original crimes, since our motives today cannot be isolated from the manner in which the material was obtained. Even to cite unethical work is to validate it, and to demonstrate that there is a continuing thread connecting respectable research today to ethically abhorrent work in the Nazi era.

Others argue that we should be prepared to use the material and data since they exist and cannot be denied. If the data are valid, they cannot be invalidated no matter how objectionable one may find the unethical behaviour used to obtain them. However, the horror should still be addressed, with no effort being made to cover it up. It has also been argued that data obtained unethically can be used since the scientific and clinical studies carried out today (which are carried out on the basis of clearly delineated and accepted ethical principles) have no link to studies carried out in the 1930s and 1940s on the basis of concepts like racial hygiene. While great care is required to ensure that such concepts never again become a part of medical thinking, this will be achieved by an understanding of ethical principles and not by a refusal to utilize any valid data from those earlier studies.

In my view, there are a number of problems with the moral complicity argument, because it is too strong and indiscriminate an argument. In practice it tends to be used selectively, when abortion or Nazi atrocities are involved. It could be used in many other cases, but it is not. For instance, if human tissue from any source is used, there is almost inevitably complicity in some moral evil. This may be complicity in the road toll when organs are used from the victims of automobile accidents, in homicide when organs are used from murder victims, in suicide when organs are used from those who have committed suicide, or in poverty when the cadavers of the destitute are used for dissection. To suggest that the surgeon or anatomist is in a supportive alliance with intoxicated car drivers, murderers, those who commit suicide, or an inequitable social system bears little relationship to moral reality. They are not accomplices in the prior evil by seeking to achieve some good from a contingent event over which they had no control. In all these instances, there is a moral distance between the evil and the intended good, a moral distance that emerges repeatedly in society's use of human material. Admittedly, the moral distance can readily be eroded, but if the significance of this distance is rejected, most uses of human material become unethical and most medically related disciplines automatically become tainted with moral evil.

We routinely act on the assumption that good can come from evil. We are prepared to benefit from tragedies as long as we are in no way responsible for them and if we would have prevented them had we been in a position to do so. For instance, many studies of malnourished children have thrown a great deal of light on the effects of malnutrition on the developing brain, while studies of the after-effects of the atom bomb explosions at Hiroshima and Nagasaki have proved of enormous value in understanding the long-term effects of radiation on human populations. Moreover, Jewish doctors in the Warsaw ghetto made systematic studies of their starving compatriots in order to reap some scientific good from the evil that was destroying everyone involved. More recently, there have been studies on the brains of suicide victims in order to throw light on the causes of depression, and on foetuses aborted for suspected foetal abnormality in order to determine the accuracy of mid-trimester diagnosis of foetal abnormality. These illustrations show very clearly that, as societies, we are prepared to benefit from tragedies, as long as the killing and maiming are not undertaken in order to yield scientific data.

The challenge for us is to decide what we make of moral complicity in these cases, and then in the light of them the use of brain material from aborted foetuses as treatment for Parkinson's disease (and possibly also for Huntington's disease and Alzheimer's disease). My conclusion is that the use of foetal material for transplantation purposes is in accordance with our use of human material in many other situations. To object to its use on ethical grounds is to object to the use of human material in most other areas. Its use in the foetal transplantation area in countries such as Britain and the United States accords with the highest ethical standards found in traditional medical practice, and has nothing in common with the examples of lamentable medical practice that unfortunately have occurred all too frequently in the past.

In the case of foetal transplants it is essential to ensure that there is no connection whatsoever between the abortion and the transplantation, and that the manner of foetal death is not modified in any way in order to facilitate subsequent use of the foetal tissue. Under these conditions I am prepared to affirm that foetal transplantation is acceptable, even if abortion is considered morally wrong. This is because respect for the dead foetus is not demonstrated solely by its immediate disposal. It may also emanate from its subsequent use to provide the gift of life to another person.

I am prepared to admit that I may be able to accept this practice more readily than some other Christians because I am used to dealing with dead human material in my profession. I have to face up to the possibilities of moral complicity each week, and one has to be vigilant to ensure that high ethical standards are not flouted. Any use of human material for research or teaching purposes is something ordinary people are not exposed to, and its use from foetuses is even more open to abuse. What is required is integrity and stringent ethical guidelines, without which this would rapidly become an ethical wasteland.

Valuing three individuals

In spite of what I have just written, I admit that none of the arguments takes us completely out of the abortion domain. What, then, are the inter-relationships between those involved in this sort of decision-making?

Since three individuals have to be considered – mother, foetus and patient – we have to ask three questions. What value is to be placed on the mother? What value should we place on the 8–11-week-old foetus? What value should the patient have?

The value placed on the *mother* is of significance when debating the legitimacy or otherwise of the abortion decision, but since this is not the focus of the transplantation debate, I shall omit this consideration. A decision to abort has been taken, and so this is a *fait accompli*.

What about the value of the *foetus*? The mother has decided to end the life of the foetus. If this is for an insubstantial reason, she does not have the welfare of the foetus (and the life that represents) at heart. She has acted against the interests of that individual, whatever her motives and however laudable or otherwise we may consider these to be. The interests of an individual, the foetus, have been contravened, and we must now ask what action will best uphold human dignity?

In this case, whatever value the mother may have placed on the foetus has not prevented its life being taken. Clearly, the value of the foetus was regarded as subsidiary to the value and interests of the mother. We ourselves may have placed far greater value on the foetus, but it was not within our scope of concern to value *that particular* foetus, since we were not in a position to act on its behalf. The foetus is now dead through no evil actions on *our* part. How do we best demonstrate the value of that dead foetus?

We may decide that it is to oppose the evil of abortion, but even such actions will not help *that* foetus which is now dead. How can *that* dead foetus best be valued? It may be to bury it as a dead human person; it may be to dispose of it; it may be to act in either of these ways, but also to place it in the context of human suffering and illness recognizing that it could contribute to the task of bringing wholeness and hope to other human beings in need of healing. In other words, it could (with appropriate safeguards) be used to give new life to another.

Arguments such as these bypass the value to be placed on the *patient* in need of something that can be 'given' by a dead foetus. The patient is in need of health and care, and possibly of healing and a cure. These are good ends and constitute basic obligations placed upon the medical profession. If it is feasible to give these, should they be withheld? Any answer to this question will have to enquire about the costs – financial, social, medical and moral.

The first three costs are pragmatic ones, and have to be determined by society and by the health professions. The fourth, the moral cost, is a mixed one. For me, the interests of the patient are to be of paramount significance. They cannot be sidetracked by concentrating entirely on the dead foetus, tragic as that death may be; as long, that is, as the death was in no way orchestrated by those looking after the patient.

Whatever conclusion we reach in practice will involve some moral compromise, and will be based on valuing one of the three participants more highly than the other two. If greatest value is placed on the dead *foetus*, this may be at the expense of the value placed on the mother (although this is problematic and highly contentious, and is basic to the abortion decision itself) and in the long term will almost definitely be at the expense of the patient; strictly speaking, at the expense of prospective patients in the future. If greatest value is placed on the *mother* (in the abortion decision), this may well be at the expense of the foetus (since the mother's wishes could always be placed above the interests of foetuses); this may or may not have consequences for the patients' interests. If greatest value is placed on the *patient*, this may be at the expense of the foetus (in terms of what is done with the remains of a dead foetus); it could place the mother's interests at stake if a mother was coerced into having an abortion in order to make tissue available for a patient (if this is outlawed, it has no relevance for the mother's interests).

What we see here is the interrelatedness of members of the human community. Protection of one member has implications for the other members. We may wish to protect this member, but if we do we should realize the implications. Any serious ethical perspective will take account of these implications and assess them in terms of the value we aim to place on all members of the human community.

Which course of action is the more likely to advance the value of human individuals, to uphold and advance human dignity, to show love and concern for all within the human community, to combat ill health, and to improve the welfare of human beings? Perhaps there is no one categorical answer; there may be different answers in different social and clinical situations. The answer we give may also depend to some extent on the success of the grafting technology.

What has become clear is that the interests of foetuses are closely intertwined with the interests of other human beings, yet this should not surprise us. We are all interrelated, and as we have seen previously our interrelatedness is fundamental to our lives as God's images (see Chapters 3 and 7). What is called for is clear thinking, a high sense of responsibility, and a longing to be led by Christ himself.

At the edges of human life

For the remainder of this chapter, I am moving away from foetal life but I am not moving away from conflict and tension. My concern turns to situations where the continuation of human life is perplexing, as a result of massive medical problems and imponderable perplexities. I am not looking at old age, nor at the final stages of a terminal illness; these will come to prominence in Chapter 12. The question I am asking is what we can learn about the breadth and depth of a Christian perspective of human value when faced by deep dilemmas at these immensely challenging edges of human life.

This exploration is an attempt to delineate some of the factors that need to be taken account of in this difficult, and frequently encountered, territory. No easy answers are suggested, and even some of the idealistic pointers may need to be tempered by the pragmatic realities of barely discerned clinical and social pressures. The perplexities are theological, as well as medical and ethical, and coming to terms with the theological ones may prove as taxing as coming to terms with the ethical dilemmas.

In the last chapter I referred to Peter who was born with Down's syndrome, but who also had congenital abnormalities of his oesophagus. There we saw how the existence of Down's syndrome may have a crucial impact on whether other abnormalities are or are not treated. In discussing this case, we saw that a distinction has to be made between different models of medicine, and also between an ethic of perfectionism and an ethic of trust. In this chapter I shall take discussion of this latter point a little further, since it is important for an approach to children like this who exist at one of these edges of human life.

One approach is to ask what is meant by parenting. When presented with newborn infants and particularly infants with problems, there are two options. One is to insist on caring for children, and tending for their physical, emotional, moral and spiritual needs, simply because they are people like ourselves. The other is to view children as the property of parents to be disposed of as they wish. According to this view, children exist for the happiness of their parents. Once this is accepted, some parents will demand that their children be biologically 'perfect', to fit in with their ideal of the good life. The Down's syndrome infant with congenital abnormalities is allowed to die because he or she is not perfect; by implication, a dead child may be preferable. If perfectionism like this becomes established, no room will remain for the alternative ethic, that of trust and hope, with its implicit emphasis on care and nurture. Theologically, an attitude based on perfectionism has no place in the far more realistic world of fallenness, selfishness and limited ambitions, nor even within a world of biological limitations and inevitable mortality. Acceptance of the latter are far more amenable to a Christian perspective, and need to be taken into account in any Christian assessment.

A related ethos is that of *integration* with its overtones of welcoming children without celebrating or romanticizing their condition. Such an attitude ensures equal treatment for these children, whatever their condition, while it contends that attempts to cut off human and emotional relations with them are self-deceptive. We are to practise hospitality towards them, accepting that the community has obligations towards them. They are one of us, regardless of their impoverishment and limitations. These pointers are reminders that there is a 'better way'; not of an easy answer, not even of a correct way, but of a way that is at least in touch with Christian aspirations and expectations.

Spina bifida and unwarranted medical treatment

Joanna was born with multiple defects including spina bifida, hydrocephaly, and microencephaly. A CT scan indicates that part of her cerebral cortex is absent. Her parents are told that without surgery she will die within two years; with surgery she may have a 50–50 chance of surviving into her twenties. If she does survive, she will be severely mentally retarded and physically impaired, paralyzed, and at constant risk of contracting meningitis. Confronted with these data and this prognosis the parents decided against surgery.

A third party persistently intervenes and successfully petitions a district court, which orders that surgery be performed on Joanna. Subsequently, the Higher Courts overturn this order, while the Supreme Court declines to hear the case. Alongside this, a new set of guidelines to govern hospitals in dealing with such cases is formulated; and new legislation is passed.

Is it possible to conclude that an individual, whether infant or adult, *can ever be so badly damaged as not to warrant medical treatment?* Another way of putting this is to ask whether a badly damaged individual merits the same moral protection as one would give a normal individual.

This raises some exceedingly contentious points. In the last chapter we touched on the distinction between 'having a life' and merely 'being alive': 'life in the biographical sense' and 'life in the biological sense'; between personal life and non-personal life respectively. Are there different categories of people in the sense that the lives of some are of value whereas the lives of others are not of value?

Sometimes we do make this distinction, especially when confronted by diverting medical resources to one or the other. Take the case of a choice between someone who has been comatose for years and a celebrity who is dying. Most people would take account of the quality of these lives and the contributions they can make to others. This is an extreme contrast, and its extremity is the key.

In more direct clinical terms, there is the very common decision faced by neurosurgeons about initiating or not initiating, or alternatively continuing or discontinuing, the treatment of patients with severe brain damage. Let us imagine a young woman admitted to hospital after a serious road accident (see Chapter 2). She reaches hospital an hour after the accident, is in a coma, and has disordered brain stem reflexes. Her vital signs suggest brain-stem damage. The diagnosis is multifocal brain injury, and this is confirmed with a CT scan. The prognosis is grave, with a high chance of progression to brain death. What is to be done in the case of such a patient who is not brain dead, but is severely brain damaged?

The patient may progress into a state in which brain stem, but not higher cerebral function is preserved. The classic persistent vegetative state may not have developed at the time a decision has to be taken, but it is a possible outcome. On the other hand, there may be recovery to a dependent existence with major mental and neurological deficits, and a doubtful level of conscious mental life. With these possibilities in mind, what is to be done *now*, at the time of the emergency? Should an intensive resuscitation and support regime be offered to this patient, or should it simply be commenced and then discussed later with the patient's relatives? In other words, it has to be decided whether normal efforts should be employed to sustain life and combat illness, regardless of the outcome in human and personal terms. If the outlook for this patient is life with major irreversible brain damage, it may well be decided that this human life is not of sufficient value to justify active medical intervention.

I have strayed some distance from Joanna, and there are differences between a subnormal infant and a severely brain damaged adult, but there is a common underlying theme. This is that a badly damaged individual may lack the marks of what we take to characterize ordinary human life. Indeed, they may veer so much from it, that we wonder whether major efforts should be devoted to prolonging that life. This will be a matter of clinical judgement, although this judgement may well have moral overtones.

What underlies this decision is whether the individual in question has, or retains, the ability (or potential ability) to interact with others and with the world around us. If an individual's brain is no longer working and has no prospect of returning to an adequate level of function, then that individual's identity as an embodied person has been destroyed. In other words, Tom who was once with us, and whom we knew as Tom, with all his personal characteristics, foibles, likes and dislikes, good points and bad points – that person is no longer with us. He can no longer influence either his world or ours, except in so far as he has to be totally looked after and cared for in his grossly debilitated and limited condition. May it be that a grossly deformed infant has so little further potential as a human, that the little that will ever be achieved has already been achieved?

Possibilities like this are not intended to devalue or denigrate the damaged individual, but are seeking to base difficult decisions on whether that individual seems to be 'one of us', one of the human community in any meaningful sense. They are still human beings, they still belong to the human community, and yet when decisions over treatment and sustenance have to be taken, the severity of the brain damage (remember it is massive and exceedingly severe damage that I have in mind) is not an inconsequential factor to be taken into account.

The second feature we look for in a person is the quality of that person's life. When confronted by a patient in a persistent vegetative state, we realize that none of the qualities we normally associate with 'being alive' and 'enjoying life' are present. While we still have no doubt about such an individual's physical and legal identity, we would be hard pressed to demonstrate that there is any meaning to their living on as a person. The inability to breathe fresh air, to do the sorts of things they like doing, to enjoy a good meal or a concert or a game of tennis, or in fact anything we associate with human existence denies to them even the hint of that quality of life we deem essential to being human. It is not a question of lacking *certain* of these qualities, but of lacking *all* of them.

A third constituent is responsibility for one's own life and one's own actions, which as we saw in Chapter 3 is one of the supreme marks of being in the image of God. In this way we are recognized as the individuals we are, what we are known as, what we stand for, our beliefs and our moral sense. We are recognized as being different from other people, so that we have an individual and recognizable identity. When this has gone for good, it has to be very seriously questioned whether we can still be said to be responsible for our own lives. Such lack of responsibility is generally relative, except perhaps in the persistent vegetative state, and it is just one factor to be entered into in any decision-making calculus.

Many Christians will be intensely uneasy with these possibilities, and they are not put forward lightly. Like so many other considerations, they do not lead automatically to any particular way of acting. Some will think that I am acting outside a Christian consensus and that I am arguing within the realm of the silences of Scripture. This may be the case, and therefore my suggestions should be treated with caution. I have no problem with this, and I would not want anyone to take these tentative conclusions and treat them as more assured than they are. They are simply possible ways forward, based on a general Christian understanding of the human condition, neurobiological realities, and the necessity of having to make hard clinical decisions even when the level of understanding of the factors involved is less assured than one would like.

Cerebral palsy and dependence on others

At the age of twenty-six Ellen has an Honour's degree in psychology, is estranged from her husband of one year and is disappointed she is unable to have a baby. This is not so remarkable, except that Ellen was born with severe cerebral palsy which means her motor-function control is limited to movement of her right hand (sufficient to operate an electrically powered wheelchair); eating when fed, and speaking. To date she has been able to live a reasonably independent life with the help of family and friends. However, she has just learned that the government assistance for her transportation costs have been withdrawn. All in all her chances of securing any employment are virtually none and she does not want to go on living a life totally reliant on other people.

Ellen asks her older sister to drive her to a hospital a considerable distance from her family and friends and arranges for a voluntary psychiatric admission on the grounds that she is suicidal. She figures that here she will be left alone and can starve herself to death. Once at this hospital she refuses to eat solid food. Her attending doctor threatens to have her certified as mentally ill and dangerous to herself so that she can be force-fed. Consequently, she phones the local newspapers with her story in an attempt to get legal assistance. As a result, she is provided with a lawyer who persuades her to continue to eat while he applies for a court order restraining the hospital from either discharging or force-feeding her.

At the hearing, Ellen testifies that she is no longer willing to live completely dependent on other people, and so is choosing this course of action due to her physical limitation and disability. The chief of psychiatry at the hospital

*testifies that he will force-feed her with a nasogastric tube
even if the court orders him not to. Her lawyer argues that
her decision is medically and morally analogous to a
patient deciding against further kidney dialysis. On the
other hand, the state questions whether an individual has a
right to commit suicide in a public hospital.*

*The judge declares that Ellen is fully competent, and that
her decision is 'rational' and 'sincere', stemming from her
physical disability and dependence on others. He also
believes, however, that permitting her to starve to death in a
hospital will have a devastating effect on other patients,
especially the physically handicapped. The decisive point
for the judge is that Ellen has a life expectancy of a further
20 years, and she is not terminally ill. He rules that she
should be kept alive by forced feeding.*

In this case, Ellen sought painkilling drugs and palliative care
while she starved herself to death. In other words, she sought
medical support for her suicide. Since she is a person, the hospital staff would be co-operating in the death of someone who
unquestionably is a person. There are differences between this
situation and that of those patients who refuse kidney dialysis,
or Jehovah's Witnesses who refuse blood transfusions, and yet
continue to be cared for by hospital staff. This is because she is
not so much refusing treatment as demanding administration
of pain killers, nor was she objecting to costly or painful treatment, like dialysis. She was objecting to life itself – she wanted
to die.

This request is not a frivolous one: the ability to make one's
own decisions is an important one. However, in this instance,
other people would have to be involved in assisting her to commit suicide. This entails an assault on their liberty. If Ellen's
claim rests ultimately on the importance of her own freedom,
she can hardly insist that the freedom of others is violated.
What is of ultimate significance for the community is not
simply individual freedom, but the common good of that community. Society needs a common fabric of belief, however
vague this may be, since it signifies a special commitment to
one another and to our common life together.

In Ellen's eyes, her life is worthless. If she is helped to die, society is agreeing that some human lives are of *no* value. This is a crucial issue, and in my view it is important for society's bias to be the preservation of life.

A very fine line is being trod here, since what is being juggled is respect for life, the quality of life over the mere value of life, and the rational desire of some people to end their lives. Argument will continue to rage on which of these values society should stress, and which of these values are most conducive to building a caring and humane society. If the quality of an individual's life is stressed, as I have done, it has to be balanced against the significance of every handicapped person's life. A society which accepts quality-of-life arguments must also provide major support for the handicapped, that is, those with a questionable quality of life.

From a Christian angle, what a patient requires is not freedom, but humility (see Chapter 3) since this recognizes our dependence on God. When we begin to learn this, we begin to see that we have to cast ourselves upon his grace and mercy (see Chapter 10). This Christian perspective is not accepted by society at large, neither is it understood in practice by many within the Christian community itself. It would, therefore, be harsh in the extreme and also unwarranted to castigate someone like Ellen for her response. For me it is less than an ideal response, and yet we have to empathize with her in the tragedy of her situation.

It is no condemnation of her or of her strivings to end her life, to say that what is required is a 'better way'. Nevertheless, there are no ready solutions or trite answers, since Christians have to begin to work out how her story relates to Christ's story. As we concentrate on the latter, we begin to learn that the God we worship suffers with us, and that our sufferings are also his sufferings (see Chapter 3). And so, what Ellen presents us with is a challenge to our theology of suffering and anguish, forcing us to ask what the suffering of Christ has to teach us in the area of medical tragedy, worthless lives, and rational suicide. We also begin to learn that humility has to become part of life lived in the midst of overwhelming pain, loss and hopelessness. Such a response can only eventuate when the suffering and sacrifice of Christ are recognized as the way forward for people confronted by grotesque tragedy. This is not a facile intellectual response to loss, neither can it be made by those who emphasize only the biological perfectibility of humankind. The holism this demands is only learned as we mature in Christian thinking and acting.

Twelve

Human Value at the End of Life

Respecting the elderly

Across the world life expectancy is increasing due to the success of public health programmes, improved nutrition, better sanitation and, in the industrialized nations, the advances of sophisticated medical technology. In Europe and the United States over the years 1890 to 1993, the life expectancy from birth has risen by 28.5 years, that is, from 47 years to 75.5 years. Recently, this trend has surfaced in the developing countries where in 1990 the life expectancy was 62 years, 22 years more than the 40 years expected in the 1950s.

With this increase in life expectancy, the proportion of those sixty-five years and older in the population is steadily increasing, with the prediction that in the United States they will make up 20 per cent of the population in 2030; this compares with 12.5 per cent in 1990. As the proportion of older people increases, the proportion of those in the workforce decreases, with the result that the resources needed to sustain society, particularly in health care, also increase. Matters are actually more serious than this, since around 56 per cent of the world's over-65-year-olds live in developing countries, a proportion that is increasing. For these countries, which are already struggling with the demands of large populations, an aging population simply adds to this burden.

My task in this chapter is not to grapple with the problems of overpopulation, but to take seriously the consequences of increasing proportions of elderly people on the health services that societies can offer to the elderly themselves, let alone anyone else. Is there enough money to go around, particularly since the elderly demand a greater proportion of the health budget? Can this be allowed to continue, or should restrictions be imposed on the money spent on the elderly? Perhaps there should actually be an age limit beyond which no money is spent on them. One writer has placed this limit at seventy years.

Any approach along these lines is highly divisive, based as it is on overt ageism: the under-seventies (or whatever age one chooses) are to be treated, the over-seventies are to be allowed to die. Here we have two groups of people: the under-seventies who are to be valued and cared for, and the over-seventies who are not. No matter how this distinction is phrased, it is diametrically opposed to any of the value systems I have been developing in this book. It runs counter to any Christian ethos, and it is unethical.

That is the easy part of the analysis, and it is acceptable as far as it goes. But it doesn't go far enough. There are resource problems, and these cannot be ignored. Where do we start?

Old age isn't merely a transitional stage between life and death. Those who are old are one with the rest of humanity. What this emphasizes is the importance of *each individual old person*, whatever their circumstances. This is an individual-centred approach, that seeks to take each old person seriously and to bestow upon each person honour and respect. But this is no easy task in societies dominated by the allure to be healthy, fit and young.

Beyond this, a Christian approach also stresses the *whole person*, so that elderly people are seen not just as individuals, but as sets of relationships. Unfortunately, it is these that are so rapidly broken down in old age, as one friend and relation after another die, and as physical weakness limits the range of contacts the person would once have enjoyed. A further problem is that with changes in society and within the church, the old person may come to feel more and more estranged from once-familiar landmarks and institutions. All too readily, the old person may become a stranger – physically, socially and even spiritually, as even the most basic of relationships with family, and with one's own past, break down. This estrangement is markedly accentuated when dementia sets in.

Biblical directions and themes

The first direction we can discern from Scripture is that old age is *integral to the human lifespan*. In this regard, it is sometimes viewed negatively. For instance, in 2 Samuel 19:35, Barzillai is recognized as showing declining discernment, taste and hearing, while the preacher in Ecclesiastes graphically describes losses of sight, teeth and physical strength (Eccl. 12:2ff.). Along similar lines, the psalmist viewed our span of years as nothing but trouble and sorrow (Ps. 90:10). This is the pessimistic aspect, but alongside it there is also recognition that old age is a blessing from God within the covenant relationship. In Proverbs 16:31, grey hair is seen as a crown of splendour that is attained by a righteous life. In Ruth 4:15, God is viewed as renewing life and sustaining people in old age. One may even argue that the extremely long lives lived by the patriarchs, whatever they precisely signify, are symbolic of the blessing of old age. In other words, old age may be a time in which God is found as powerfully as at any other stage of life.

A second direction is that of the wisdom of the elderly. Although the elderly are by no means the only ones who are wise (Job 32:6ff.), wisdom and old age have a special relationship. In this way, a corporate tradition was established and was brought to life for succeeding generations, who were to remember the days of old. This would be explained to them by their elders (Deut. 32:7), who had a special role to play in maintaining the nation's faith by recalling God's activity in the past.

A third emphasis is that of *respect for the elderly*, itself the mark of a well-ordered society. In Israelite law, provision was made for widows, while adults were to honour their parents. On the negative side, disrespect for the elderly was a sign of chaos within society. For instance, one particular judgement on Judah and Jerusalem was insolence on the part of the young towards the elderly (Is. 3:5), while a disobedient Israel was threatened with attack by a nation lacking respect for the old (Deut. 28:50).

Then again, the elderly played an important part through-out the history of salvation. On the one hand, the patriarchs were regarded as the epitome of wisdom in old age; while on the other hand, Ruth assisted Naomi to help her cope with the bitterness of loss and aging. Also of interest were the aging Simeon and Anna who greeted and proclaimed the Saviour (Lk. 2), while the Spirit was promised to old as well as young (Joel 2).

Against a background of these directions, we can elicit a number of themes. The first of these is *hope*. Hope gives confidence no matter what changes occur throughout life, since there is a continuity of identity regardless of what happens to an individual's body. Under some circumstances, the loss may be catastrophic, and the continuity may be confined to what is retained in the memory and, therefore, belongs to the past. Nevertheless, there is still continuity, however tenuous, and this provides hope for bystanders if not for the person concerned.

This continuity of identity emphasizes a broader continuity, from the past, through the present and into the future. The 'real me' that has been created by God and that relates to God continues. Not only this, but whatever God has promised to his people in the past applies equally strongly today. His faithfulness never ends, no matter how frail or limited we may be today. As Jesus is the same yesterday, today, and forever, so his relationship with the elderly is the same as it has ever been. The relationship that believers have with God will never be destroyed, no matter how feeble the body or brain may become. Nothing can separate us from God and his loving concern, not even frailty, dementia or death (Rom. 8).

A second theme is the *incarnation*. Look at Jesus who, although young, experienced loss of status, insecurity, the necessity of depending upon others, and suffering; experiences frequently associated with getting old. In other words, old age should not be viewed as an aberration of the human condition, but as a fitting end of what we are as humans made in the image of God, living in a fallen world. The incarnation also demon-strates that these experiences can be redeemed and redirected, serving as powerful reminders of God's concern for his people.

They are also reminders that security and status based on material well-being are ephemeral, since human living is then reduced to an experience owing more to chance than to any-thing else. The chances of becoming demented are far from evenly distributed across a community, and in general do not depend upon lifestyle, belief or faithfulness as a Christian. They increase with increasing age (especially over eighty years), hence the disturbing sight of once stalwart Christians now reduced to frail, dependent, incoherent patients. In such situations, it is only the continuing, unchanging status of God's love and care that provide a modicum of security in the midst of a tragic degree of insecurity.

The relationships so vital to human community come to the fore when the elderly have to rely increasingly upon others. The vulnerability of the elderly reflects the way in which we are to make ourselves vulnerable to others as we become more like Jesus.

A related theme is that of *weakness and equality*. Our temp-tation is to value most highly those who appear to be powerful and capable, the successful ones in society. And yet the heart of the Christian gospel is the very opposite, characterized as it is by God's self-emptying and by the way in which he became vulnerable and weak in Jesus. Within a Christian framework, weakness becomes acceptable, becoming the norm and even the new way. The result is that the weak, including the aging, are to be highly valued within society. This does not automati-cally solve specific ethical dilemmas, but it brings us back to the foundational ethical principle of equality.

For Christians, equality is not only a matter of equality among individuals, but of equality of membership of the com-munity of faith. We are all part of the body of Christ, and if one part suffers so do all other parts. We cannot escape from the aging, who are with us as members of Christ's body. All are inextricably part of a whole. Once we realize this, we are caught in the web of faith, a web with problems and challenges, but a web in which we should rejoice and grow.

Living as mortals

All human beings are dust, and to dust we shall return (Gen. 31:19–20). If we learn to accept that our days are numbered, we have an important starting point for aspiring to wisdom (Ps. 90:12). It is not unreasonable, therefore, that we learn to accept that a life of three score years and ten is not a totally misleading guide when confronted by the ethical, social and spiritual dilemmas of aging. At the very least it forces us to face up to the reality of our mortality. Our lives as human beings are limited in time. We are neither timeless nor eternal. This is such an obvious statement, and yet on closer inspection it is far from obvious. It is not obvious because it explicitly accepts an end to each human life. We will all die, and if this is accepted, it has repercussions for how we all live: we live with the expectation of an end to life. We cast aside the illusion that we will go on living endlessly, more or less unchanged. We cast aside the attachment to life as we know it.

However, many want to go on living endlessly; they refuse to accept that they will wither and die. They reject the reality of human mortality. Or, if not this, they look to a time when all who are alive will know increased health, increased vigour, and an absence of decay or dementia, until the day of one's death. Life will end, but life will be healthy up to the point of death. And yet even here there may be a problem. Given that such a state ever does become attainable, can we really conceive of a situation where this illness-free condition will not lull us into a longing for everlasting life in an illness-free body? Within such a scenario, death would seem even more shocking than it does now.

These approaches are misleading, because they fail to acknowledge what Christians call the 'fall'. In their different ways, these approaches attempt to escape from the all-pervading effects of sin and the evil that permeates everything we touch or experience. Both are idealistic and, in the long term, unhelpful. They are of little help in sorting out ethical issues of significance in coping with the aged, since they are attempting to escape from aging and its consequences. Mortality is inevitable; it may even be a blessing. Once we accept that our days are limited, we can begin to take life seriously; we can redeem the time, and we can live with intensity and enthusiasm. In this way, we can begin to appreciate what life is for, and how we can make the most of it in the limited time available. This is hardly a surprising conclusion for Christians, since we are constantly urged to redeem the time, to be holy, to devote ourselves to the service of others, and to live as though we will meet Christ today. We are to be constantly vigilant, responding to the call of Christ and to the message of the gospel, since the time is short and our days are few.

A longing for some sort of human immortality is a longing for more of the same. This is not the Christian view, which seeks to redirect our goals and longings, our worship and our meaning, towards God and away from ourselves. Eternal life is a transformation of all we have ever been, although it builds on our responses and priorities during this life. It heals our present estrangement from God in a radical, lasting way, bringing fulfilment, wholeness and completeness of a sort only barely discernible now. Such immortality has no connection with the longing for a prolonged earthly life, which cannot possibly begin to satisfy our deepest aspirations.

Mortality and aging are inseparable. If we accept mortality, we have to accept one of its consequences for an increasing number of people, namely, aging. From this there is no escape, either for ourselves as individuals or for our communities. Not only this, but we have to link our concern for the unborn and for children with our concern for the aging. We cannot have one without the others, since all are inextricably intertwined within our experience of what it means to be human and mortal. In Christian terms, all image God and all must, therefore, be taken seriously as moral beings.

But what about the specific issues of limited resources, or of appalling limitations due to dementia or other chronic medical problems, or of the lack of support younger family members are given in order to cope with long-term illness and incapacity? What I have argued so far is that those who are aging are to be valued and respected as one of us, since aging is an integral part of what it means to be human and mortal. Those who are aging remind us of the importance of our interdependence within the human and Christian communities, and they confront us with our treatment of those who are our equals and yet who are weaker than we are and are dependent upon us for care and protection. From this there is no escape, and we cannot expect any escape.

Making choices

These thoughts do not shield us from having to face major dilemmas in weighing up the resources to be placed at the disposal of the aged compared with the resources to be directed towards other groups within any community. Consider the following

> *Brendon is thirty, Tony is seventy, and Jim is eighty. All are in hospital for the same reason, they have appendicitis. All are operated on, and all leave hospital fitter than when they came in. Apart from the appendicitis which is an aberration, Brendon is in very good health. Tony is in reasonably good health, apart from what he describes as the usual aches and pains of a seventy-year-old. Jim has Alzheimer's disease, and while his appendicitis has been sorted out, his dementia is as bad as ever – in fact, it may be a little worse after the general anaesthetic.*

This scenario is, in many ways, a straightforward one. Surgery for appendicitis is usually an uneventful operation. It is an acute operation that has to be carried out, since if this is not done the patient may eventually end up with a serious and even life-threatening condition. By today's standards there is nothing heroic about the operation, and it is as essential to carry it out on an eighty-year-old as on a thirty-year-old. If society decided that it was not worth carrying it out on eighty-year-olds, it would be seriously undervaluing the lives of eighty-year-olds. It would be treating them dramatically differently from the way it treats thirty-year-olds, regardless of the reasoning behind such a decision. In some instances it would be condemning these eighty-year-olds to death, since they could be saved from death by a simple, relatively inexpensive operation. Now consider the following:

> *Natalie is thirty and is on renal dialysis; she needs a kidney transplant and is on a waiting list. Apart from her kidney problems she has no other major health problems. She is married with a young son. Miriam is seventy and is also on dialysis. She too is reasonably healthy apart from her kidney problems, and she too would like a kidney transplant. Discussion is taking place about the justification of this and whether she should be put on a waiting list. Some people think the doubt surrounding this stems from her age. Catriona is eighty and is in similar circumstances, suffering from kidney failure. She has just been put on dialysis but there is considerable discussion about whether this is justified, since she has moderate dementia and various heart problems, and she also finds it difficult to understand what is going on. Under no circumstances would anyone contemplate a kidney transplant.*

Here we have three patients, all of whom are suffering from a similar medical condition, but they are distinguished by their vastly different ages. In addition, some have other health problems as well. The question we have to face is whether their ages make any difference to the treatment they receive. This scenario is not as simple as the earlier one, since the treatment in this instance will not remove the diseased state. Apart from the expense of the treatments, dialysis is a demanding regime, and there are not enough kidneys to supply the demand across many groups within society. In other words, there is now competition for resources, both financial and in terms of kidneys themselves.

In the first set of cases there was no question about providing everything possible for the older patients, nor whether the presence of dementia in the one case was a relevant factor to take into account. This is probably not so for the second series, because here there is competition for resources while the procedures are complex and make considerable demands on the patients and their caregivers. The age of patients is beginning to intrude, although the critical factor is probably associated issues rather than age itself.

Limited life expectancy

Our mortal life begins at one point and ends at another, often much later in time. For the aged this means that much of that finite life has already been lived; they have had their opportunities to experience what human life means, and to contribute to the welfare of others. They have participated in the human community and in the relationships making up that community. They are still one with the rest of us, and they continue to image the God who made them. We continue to have responsibilities for them, since they mirror so much of what we too are as images in the likeness of God. As people age they become more dependent on others within the human community, placing on others the moral obligation to care and protect them in ways not required since their childhood.

They are, therefore, to be valued as we would value anyone else within the human community. However, as we saw in the second of the scenario series, this may not entail equal resources to those who are younger when there is competition for those resources. Nevertheless, care and provision of the basic necessities of existence are unaffected. Since resources are limited, and our life expectancy is also limited, it can be argued that whenever there is competition for resources, the needs of the younger should be placed first. This will generally have little repercussion for most clinical procedures, and in no way does this undervalue the significance of the elderly. What it does do is come to terms with our mortality and with the fact that our lives as earthly beings will one day cease. This is a deeply Christian emphasis, with its many overtones of our createdness and fall, and its reminder of the need of redemption and rebirth. After all, Christians look forward to a new body, a new heaven and a new earth.

Daniel Callahan, in his book *Setting Limits*, argued that we should accept aging as a part of life, rather than as another medical obstacle to be overcome. We should also find a meaningful place for suffering and decline in life, and should not pretend that old age can be turned into some form of endless middle age. And so, while the aging have a substantial claim upon public funds for health care, this is not an unlimited claim.

Callahan's position is that the interests and claims of elderly individuals are to be protected, but that this in itself does not entail measures such as directing unlimited resources in their direction, pursuing unlimited life extension, or failing to balance the needs of different age groups. Based on this approach, the old may have a duty to the young not to make demands that will harm the young, but at the same time the young have duties to sustain the welfare of the old. Society has an obligation to help people make it from youth to old age, but by the same token it does not have an unlimited obligation to continue the extension of life in old age.

Central to this notion are two interrelated ideas: a 'natural lifespan' and a 'tolerable death'. According to Callahan, a *natural life span* is 'one in which life's possibilities have on the whole been achieved and after which death may be understood as a sad, but nonetheless relatively acceptable event.' A *tolerable death* is when 'one's life possibilities have on the whole been accomplished; one's moral obligations to those for whom one has had responsibility have been discharged; and one's death will not seem to others an offence . . .'

Death is the final part of living, and dying is the end stage of a normal course of biological events. Consequently, dying should not be viewed as a medical event, or simply a failure of medical diagnosis and treatment. This view in no way leads to euthanasia for the elderly, simply because their dignity is to be maintained and substantiated, and their lives are to be filled with meaning and significance.

However, for some writers, setting limits on the elderly is morally wrong, and treatment decisions should be based on individual need with no reference to age. Nevertheless, in practice, limits on medical treatment are implicitly, if not explicitly, set on most age and treatment groups in public health care systems. What is of crucial importance is that the elderly are freed from unnecessary burdens imposed by excessive life-sustaining treatment. Compare the following:

Stephanie is a vigorous 75-year-old, who requires a hip replacement. This is done, and within a short time she is on her feet with the help of crutches. She feels renewed, and as soon as she can she is back tending her garden, showing hospitality at home, visiting the 'elderly' and leading her Bible study group. Anne is also a 75-year-old, but she has been going downhill for the last ten years, and now has heart problems, high blood pressure and diabetes. She is confined to bed, and tends to be confused for much of the time. After a heart attack, there is discussion about whether she should have coronary bypass surgery since there is the possibility that will prolong her life for a few weeks or possibly months. Her family think this would simply prolong her dying.

Stephanie and Anne are the same age. For most people Stephanie should receive the operation she needs, whereas Anne's needs are not as self-evident. In the former instance, the operation will enable Stephanie to function well; she will return to meaningful life. Anne, though, will not be able to return to anything remotely resembling normality, since no operation will bring this about. Hence, in Anne's case the high-technology medicine is just that, and it is this approach that I am questioning, since Anne as a person and human individual will not benefit from it. If that is the case, why do it? Limits are being set, but they are carefully thought out limits, and not simplistic ones based on age alone. They stem from serious reflection on what is best for the individual patient, and as such are precisely what one would expect of a Christian assessment.

For the elderly, as for other age groups, personal relationships play a crucial role in making them what they are. It is these that make the difference between achieving significance as 'one of us' and losing that significance altogether. In this sense, the elderly are 'one of us' and this is to be acknowledged in matters of privacy, considering their wishes, welcoming them as equal partners, and advocating their cause. Nevertheless, their time as 'one of us' is limited, and while this in no way invalidates basic values, it restricts the measures that are appropriate for extending this time span.

Once more, we arrive at the conclusion that no human life can be given ultimate value. That belongs to God alone. We are to do our best to bestow as much value as we can upon all humans, whatever their circumstances, but this is always limited. In some conditions it is more limited than in others. To some extent this is true of those who are aging, although enormous care is required here since growing old is not an inevitable downward spiral. Each older person is to be assessed on merit, the bias always being in favour of bestowing as much value as possible on them.

The experience of dementia

We are living in aging societies. Obvious as this statement may sound, its innumerable ramifications cannot be readily overlooked. The revolution through which we are living stems from the well-known fact that aging is accompanied not only by a limitation of abilities in general, but by dementia in particular. The accompanying problems, which are legion, bring into focus the value we seek to ascribe to those who are growing old, and in particular to those unable to cope in any meaningful way with the normal exigencies of daily living.

The behavioural and personality changes associated with Alzheimer's disease raise fundamental questions about human personhood – just as fundamental as any similar questions surrounding the status of the human embryo. How does the patient respond to personality and behavioural changes of which he or she is aware? What consequences may this have for his or her self-image? What is the nature of the demands being made on others, when the normal relationship between them has been shattered? How are caregivers to respond to the increasing dependence of the patient upon them, and how can this be coped with in the midst of the grief at the 'loss' of a loved one? Even if these are seen as primarily social questions, specific ethical ones are not difficult to find. Does the loss of the personality traits that once characterized a person have consequences for the value a society ascribes to that person? Is such a person to be valued as highly as, for instance, a thirty-year-old in good mental health, in that equal resources are to be devoted to each? If the answer is 'no', how far is this argument to be taken? Is the life of a person with severe dementia worth maintaining, let alone saving?

Dementia, more than any other illness confronts us with realities that affect our view of ourselves as human beings. How do I respond to the knowledge that my brain is dying? How do I cope with the knowledge that I as a person am changing, and that the changes are for the worse? How do I learn to live with the knowledge that I am slowly dying as the person I know myself to be, and as the person everyone else knows me to be? It is one thing to be aware that I have a terminal illness and that I have a very limited time left on this earth, but it is something quite different to know that I will, in all probability, continue to live for some years, but will no longer be 'me' and that I will make increasingly unreasonable demands on those very close to me. Instead of caring for others as I am used to doing, I will have to be cared for in a way that has not occurred since my early childhood. Instead of being a leader of others, I will have to be both led and upheld at all points of my existence.

How does the demented person think and feel? Some have a full awareness that something is wrong with their intellectual capacities, and this awareness is preserved to some extent throughout the course of the disease. But the opposite is also found when there is no awareness of any deficiency, a situation that may persist even while the patient's world disintegrates. In between these two extremes are those who are aware that something is wrong, but actively deny it; yet others have good insight initially but lose it as the disease progresses, denying it or appearing to be totally unaware of their predicament later on.

A graphic and intensely personal account of Alzheimer's disease is provided by Robert Davis in his autobiography *My Journey into Alzheimer's Disease*. Following a highly success-ful ministry in a large American church, at the age of fifty-three he was diagnosed as suffering from Alzheimer's disease. With assistance, he recorded his thoughts as the dementia progressed, as he retired from the ministry, and as he came to terms with what was happening to him.

Davis did not drift into dementia; rather, he worked through it and strove to control it as his own brain mechanisms were failing. In doing this, his cries are the cries of all with dementia; he spoke for them as a protagonist and sage. With muted and tragic eloquence, he sums up the predicament of this condition:

> I am still human. I laugh at the ridiculous disease that steals the most obvious things from my thoughts and leaves me spouting some of the most obscure, irrelevant information when the right button is pushed. I want to participate in life to my utmost limit. The reduced capacity, however, leaves me barely able to take care of my basic living needs, and there is nothing left over for being a productive member of society. This leaves me in a terrible dilemma. When I go out into society I look whole. There is no wheelchair, no bandage, or missing part to remind people of my loss. It is difficult to meet the question, 'What do you do?' When I answer, 'I am a retired minister'.
>
> In Alzheimer's disease there is the loss of the personality, a diminished sense of self-worth. A highly productive person has to wonder why he is still alive and what purpose the Lord has in keeping him on this earth. As I struggle with the indignities that accompany daily living, I am losing my sense of humanity and self-worth. Blessed is the person who can take the Alzheimer's patient back to that happier time when they were worthwhile and allow them to see the situation in which they were of some use (pp. 114 & 117).[1]

How did Davis handle the appalling losses of his present state, and the even more devastating destruction which he knew awaited him in the near future? In the early stages he did not come to terms with a daily experience of his own slow disintegration as a person. He raged against it, and this continued until he had a spiritual crisis, following which he came to the conclusion that:

---

[1] Extracts from this book are used by permission of Tyndale House Publishers, Inc. All rights reserved.

I have a life that can be either frustrating and frightening or peaceful and submissive. The choice is mine. I choose to take things moment by moment, thankful for everything that I have, instead of raging wildly at the things that I have lost. I must thank God for the ability to do this . . . In accepting this progressive handicap as from the Lord, I am coming to a fuller understanding of that phrase from the Lord's Prayer, 'Thy will be done' (pp. 65–66).

In another place, Davis expresses the same sentiment in different words, as he recognizes the two options confronting him. He writes:

We can either be bitter and groan and be miserable and curse God, or else we can thank God for what he has done, especially for giving us his great healing power when it was so critical in our lives . . . In the most helpless, hopeless, and extreme part of my life, Christ is here comforting and giving life meaning, even when all I have to look forward to in this life is becoming a mindless vegetable (p. 77).

It was this acceptance that enabled Robert Davis to come to terms with his continued inability to preach or teach. He recognized that all he would be able to do in the future would be limited to listening and praying.

Davis's account of his existence with Alzheimer's disease is not confined to generalities. He outlines how he attempted to establish routines to cope with the ever-decreasing world within which he had to live, how he lived with paranoia and with the awful fear of failure as an Alzheimer sufferer. He deals with his inability to go into crowds and the subsequent disorganization of his coping mechanisms whenever he did, with his forgetfulness and the reasons for his wandering, and also with the terror of the sleeplessness associated with Alzheimer's disease. We are left with all the perplexities and uncertainties of human existence, since there are no slick answers to the tragedy and horror of dementia.

Overshadowing every aspect of dementia is an awareness of vulnerability and isolation, as the most basic of life skills are lost, and as normal relationships deteriorate and eventually disappear. Dementia is closely associated with a loss of dignity in the eyes of others, as these others adapt to the situation, become accustomed to the patient's incompetence, and finally consider the patient less than a person. The dementia victim may be likened to an infrahuman being who lives among human beings but is no longer able to share their world. As human relationships break down, those close to the sufferer may make valiant efforts to act as though everything is normal in an effort to preserve that which is being violently disrupted.

From here it is but a short step to the place of caring in dementia, since in dementia the body organ for which compensation is required is not an arm or leg, but the brain. As a result, the caregiver with responsibility for another's brain is in a position of great power, performing functions of judgement and self-control, besides those of memory and language. The difficulties are immense in view of the lack of reciprocity in the relationship with the patient, so that success is marked by criteria such as the accident prevented, the nutrition maintained, and the cleanliness obtained.

Dementia and dignity

How much do demented people matter? Some start from the premise that Alzheimer patients are not persons. However, this viewpoint has enormous problems, since it may lead to a great deal of insensitivity. This approach means that patients with Alzheimer's disease count for less than do the rest of us as the dementia advances. When someone cannot be praised or blamed for their actions, they do not make the same moral claim on us. This may mean that, at some point, such a patient may no longer claim our respect, our love, or our resources.

This conclusion is unsatisfactory, since Alzheimer's disease sufferers have not completely lost their human dignity. Consider an Alzheimer's disease patient whose name is Deidre; she will always be Deidre, regardless of the changes that have taken place over the years and especially since the onset of the dementia. She is still a wife, mother and grandmother, no matter how frail some of these realities have become. The demented continue to be part of our family and community.

This is fine as far as it goes, but severe dementia may lead to loss of a recognizable personality and of all that we considered inseparable from that person as the person we knew. Even though Deidre's body is still here, Deidre may no longer be with us as Deidre, even bearing in mind that she makes a plethora of demands on her caregivers. This brings us face to face with the tragedy of the human condition, in which someone we knew and loved has to all appearances died and gone. The tragedy is that the death is a prolonged one, perhaps a very prolonged one, and the interregnum may be devastating for those left behind who have the onerous task of caring for the personality-depleted person. In one sense, of course, Deidre remains a wife, mother and grandmother, but this is true *for our memories* and not for hers. It is we who remember what she has been; she herself is unable to live out these relationships in the present, and she may even be unable to ascertain what they mean.

We are to do our best to bestow as much value as we can upon everyone, whatever their circumstances, but this is always limited. In some conditions it is more restricted than others, and in aging it gradually becomes narrower, although since chronological aging frequently bears little relationship to psychological aging this principle has to be used very judiciously. When there is very severe brain damage the value we are able to place on human beings becomes ever more circumscribed, although it never ceases to exist, not even at death.

If the severely demented have lost the capacity to envisage a future for themselves, they have lost an interest in any treatment aimed at prolonging or sustaining their lives. However, their limited capacity for experiences leads to an interest in receiving whatever health-care treatment may relieve pain or suffering, even if life-sustaining care is beyond their interests. These measures include anything that ensures these persons are treated with dignity for what they still are, and for what they used to be.

Rod has severe Alzheimer's disease and has been looked after by his wife for the past five years. She has been worn down by this, but has valiantly continued to provide for his every need. However much she may complain, she loves him dearly and has done everything she possibly can to maintain his cleanliness and dignity, whether in his eating or coping with his incontinence. His interests in spiritual matters have long since disappeared, but she does her best to remember him as he was in his prime. The one thing his wife would detest would be for him to be in an impersonal environment where no one knew what he once was, and where all he had stood for disappeared beneath his confusion and general incompetence.

Rod's wife's concern for him in the little things of his life are important. She wants him to live as dignified an existence as possible even when the pressures to lose his dignity are extremely powerful. For her, his loss of dignity is a loss of something that is central to what he is as a human being. With progressive Alzheimer's disease it is a losing battle, but it is a battle worth fighting for as long as possible. The little things in life become central, and it is these that are crucial in ethical decision-making. This fits in with Christian concerns where what we are, and how we live, become more important than what we say. It was in this spirit that Paul repeatedly instructed the Christians in the early church to imitate him as he sought to imitate Christ (Phil. 3:17; 4:9; 2 Thes. 3:6–9).

From this it follows that in old age, and especially in demented old age, our bias should be in favour of caring, as opposed to acute-treatment, life-extending medicine. The latter has as its goal extending the life of patients and enhancing their appreciation of their circumstances. However, in the case of patients with advanced Alzheimer's disease, this is inappropriate, since the only goal of such treatment is maintenance of bodily organs. What this accomplishes is little more than additional time to live out a demented existence. It would seem that the preferred option would be to die from an acute illness rather than continued existence in a demented state.

Once emphasis is placed on care rather than cure, the patient is protected by the dimensions of caring medicine, including comfort and palliation. This is not a short cut or cheap option, but is appropriate for patients suffering in these ways. In no sense does this lessen the value placed on demented patients: they can still be treated with dignity, even while acknowledging that high-technology acute care is out of place. This, it seems to me, is an appropriate response to patients facing not only inevitable decline and death, but also a diminished sense of self, an inability to compare the present with the past, a lack of memory, and a failure to understand their predicament.

Demented patients should be cared for as persons, even if the individual does not meet our usual expectations of what constitutes the full repertoire of human behaviour and responsibility. Their values as demonstrated by a lifetime of memories and interests, are to be honoured as far as possible, even when we judge that the usual marks of personhood have almost entirely vanished.

This is the position at which I have arrived: the severely demented elderly are to be provided with basic care, but seldom with life-sustaining technologies such as respirators, cardiopulmonary resuscitation, dialysis or artificial feeding. On the other hand, custodial care, minimization of anxiety and distress, and emotional support are always to be provided, with the aim of ensuring that the severely demented do not suffer from indignities. No matter how severe the dementia, those with Alzheimer's disease are never a 'nothing'. Their 'something' derives from what they once were. The values demonstrated prior to the onset of Alzheimer's disease (the 'then' self) should shape how the 'now' self of that person (when there is little, if any, memory of the past remaining) is to be treated. The lives of such sufferers may even contain redeeming experiences.

Looking ahead

We have so far looked at the sufferers themselves, but what about those who look after them? The interrelatedness of the human community forces us to deflect some of our attention away from the demented person to those who are left behind, to those who are suffering and caring and perhaps being destroyed in the process. It is they who are now our neighbours in the foremost sense, and it is them that we should look to help and support. They tend to get forgotten, but they are humans whose value we are to undergird and protect. Perhaps we can can even say that it is their image in God's likeness that should be our principal concern, as God's image in the severely demented gradually ebbs away. However, it never ceases to exist, not even at death.

In considering the question of whether it is ever right to let someone die, we look at the sometimes conflicting principles that while life should be regarded as a gift, it is not the most critical reality we have to deal with. Life is a gift of God to a living individual, and yet that gift can be turned back to God as a mark of good stewardship. For instance, 'Greater love has no person than this, that they trade their [gift of] life for the life of a friend' (Jn. 15:13). Neither should we be worshippers of vitality. Rather, we should be respecters of persons, and whenever confronted by the question of letting someone die we are confronted by an actual person and not by life in general. We cannot, therefore, escape from the question of whether the life before us is personal life, or whether it has a future as personal life.

We may allow a demented patient to die, when in our judgement, there is a body without a person. Lewis Smedes (*Mere Morality*) notes that 'a living corpse is not a living person', and this enshrines a permanent absence of adequate cerebral function. We may allow a dying person to die, when it is clear that treatment will only prolong the demented state rather than reverse it. Then again, we may allow people without a personal future to die, including the severely demented who, as far as one can discern, will never again respond in any adequate terms to another person, never again convey a meaningful message, and never again enter into a dialogue. Many situations are not this clear-cut, and then delicate clinical and moral judgements have to be taken.

In acting in ways such as these, doctors are not 'playing God' in an unwarranted fashion (see Chapter 8). Rational human beings are meant to act as God's stewards on this earth, and we cannot run away from the responsibility of acting as God's agents even when this may entail withholding life-prolonging treatment (see Chapter 3). When we give life we believe we are co-operating with God. But what if medical technology is forcing someone to live whom God wants to die, and who would die if we let him or her alone? Might not this be 'playing God' in an unwarranted manner? Decisions can only be made in the light of the circumstances, and care needs to be taken that we do not overstep the bounds of our dominion in both directions. To kill prematurely is arrogance; but to keep a body respiring endlessly may also be arrogance. There are no simple, absolute rules when confronted by life-and-death decisions. There are useful principles available, there are complex decisions to be made and there are needy patients to be cared for.

Final remarks

My hope is that anyone who has accompanied me this far will have been informed and challenged about the status of ordinary people. That journey from non-existence through to our lives at the end of human life has been an exciting and sobering one. The purpose of this voyage has been to share my conviction that we have immense responsibility to value all human life, and yet at the same time to be aware that in practical terms not all people are accorded precisely the same worth. As we live with this dichotomy, we are faced with the challenge of redeeming each situation we encounter, bringing to it healing and redirecting it as Christ would have done. What is done at the individual level should serve as a model of what is to be done at the level of society. The pressures towards depersonalization are ever present, and can only be combated by those whose priorities are directed at valuing people where they are generally undervalued. This is no easy task, and those embarking on it have to learn to wait patiently for that time when all will unequivocally be of equal value.

Glossary

AIH: artificial insemination with the sperm of the husband (or partner) into the vagina or cervix.

Alzheimer's disease: the most common cause of dementia, characterized initially by disturbances of memory, and eventually by severe changes in personality. Named after Alois Alzheimer, who first described the characteristic brain features of this disease.

Amniocentesis: a test in which some of the amniotic fluid surrounding the foetus is withdrawn from the amniotic sac and analysed for abnormal genes or chromosomes; carried out at around 14–18 weeks gestation. Frequently conducted to test for chromosomal abnormalities, such as Down's syndrome.

Amyotrophic lateral sclerosis: a disease causing muscle weakness and wasting; results from the death of nerve cells in the brain and spinal cord responsible for movement (also known as motor neuron disease).

Anencephaly: a severe congenital abnormality in which the vault of the skull is absent, with the cerebral hemispheres of the brain completely missing, or reduced to small masses attached to the base of the skull.

Blastocyst: name given to an early embryo at 4–5 days gestation after it reaches the cavity of the uterus; consists of a sphere of cells, with a fluid-filled cavity.

Brain birth: a controversial attempt to define a time during early human development at which a 'brain' first appears. Also referred to as 'brain life'; based on the notion of brain death at the end of human life.

Brain death: an attempt by philosophers, ethicists and physicians to define a point when the brain can be said to have ceased to function; includes 'whole brain' and 'higher brain' definitions. Once brain death has occurred, organs can be removed for organ transplantation.

Chorion villus biopsy: a test in which cells are removed from the embryo's chorionic villi which help it implant in the wall of the uterus; the cells are analysed for abnormal genes or chromosomes, at 8–10 weeks gestation. Used to detect genetic defects underlying conditions such as cystic fibrosis and haemophilia.

Cloning: asexual reproduction, in which the nucleus (and chromosomes) of an ovum is replaced with the nucleus of a somatic (body) cell of an adult. This fertilizes the ovum, without the involvement of sperm.

Congenital abnormality: a structural or chemical imperfection present at birth.

Congenital hydrocephalus: a condition present at birth in which there is an abnormal accumulation of fluid in the cranial vault causing an enlargement of the head, prominence of the forehead, and atrophy of the brain.

CT scan: computed tomography scan; imaging technique capable of showing cross-sectional pictures of regions of the body; particularly useful for investigating the brain and abdomen.

Dementia: irreversible and progressive impairment of mental functions; including intellectual deterioration, disordered personality and an inability to carry out the tasks of daily living.

DI: donor insemination; artificial insemination with the sperm from a donor.

Dialysis: common treatment for kidney failure, involving the use of a machine to cleanse the blood of waste products, a function usually performed by the kidney.

Duodenal atresia: a condition in which the duodenum (the first part of the small intestine) fails to close properly.

Egg: the female gamete, also referred to as an oocyte or ovum, from a woman's ovary.

Embryo: the stage of development up to 8 weeks gestation in humans, by which point all the major organs have been laid down. The first two weeks after fertilization are variously referred to as pre-embryo or preimplantation embryo.

Embryo biopsy: removal of one cell at the 4 or 8 cell stage, in order to test it for genetic and chromosomal abnormalities; a whole individual can develop from the remaining cells.

Enhancement genetic engineering: use of techniques to manipulate the genetic information of an organism in order to improve its characteristics, rather than to correct deficiencies.

Enucleated egg: removal of the nucleus from an egg (oocyte), as the prelude to cloning.

Eugenics: study of methods of improving the quality of the human race by breeding and genetic manipulation; the subject of intense debate since the late nineteenth century.

Euthanasia: the act of killing someone painlessly; usually to relieve the suffering of a patient with an incurable illness. Of the two main varieties, voluntary and involuntary, most discussion centres on voluntary euthanasia.

Fallopian tubes: equivalent to the uterine tubes, which pass between the ovaries and the cavity of the uterus; fertilization takes place in them.

Fertilization: the act of rendering gametes fertile or capable of further development; begins with contact between spermatozoon and ovum, leading to their fusion, which stimulates the completion of ovum maturation.

Foetus: the developing human being from the end of the eighth week of gestation until birth.

Gamete: the mature male or female sex cell.

Gene: the biological unit of heredity; a unit of DNA in a chromosome, controlling the formation of a single protein.

Gene therapy: the replacement of a gene responsible for a disease like cystic fibrosis, by a (normal) gene in an attempt to remove that disease from the individual; this may be carried out in the embryo or individual after birth.

Genetic engineering: the manipulation of genetic information in an embryo in order to control the characteristics of the future individual; the term is frequently used in a negative, critical sense.

Genetic screening: the assessment of a population in order to detect embryos or foetuses carrying genes responsible for certain diseases.

Germ line cells: a sexual reproductive cell (or gamete) such as sperm and eggs.

Germ line gene therapy: the process of inserting a gene into a germ cell in order to remove a disease from the modified individual. When the latter reproduces, the modification is also present in the offspring.

Gestation: the period of development from the time of fertilization of the ovum until birth.

GIFT: gamete intrafallopian transfer, in which sperm and up to three eggs are mixed together and transferred to one or both of a woman's uterine tubes. This is not strictly IVF, since fertilization occurs in the woman's body and not in the laboratory.

Human genome project: a major scientific project with the aim of producing a complete nucleotide sequence of the human genome.

Hydrocephaly: a disorder caused by an accumulation of cerebrospinal fluid (the fluid surrounding the brain) which exerts pressure on the brain.

Implantation: the embedding of the early embryo (between 6–14 days gestation) in the lining of the uterus (womb), so that further development of the embryo can take place.

Infanticide: the killing of an infant.

ICSI: intracytoplasmic sperm injection, where the male partner has very few sperm; a single sperm is injected directly into the egg previously retrieved from the woman. If the egg fertilizes, it can be transferred to the uterus in the usual way. This is now viewed as the treatment of choice for severe male infertility.

IVF: in vitro fertilization; the process of fertilizing a (human) egg with a (human) sperm in vitro in the laboratory and therefore outside the body of the woman. Embryo transfer may follow, and the term 'IVF' is used to cover both the fertilization and the embryo transfer.

Microcephaly: a condition present at birth in which the brain is abnormally small, as evidenced by reduced skull size.

Non-therapeutic research: clinical research which has, as its primary goal, the acquisition of knowledge rather than the benefit of the patient (therapeutic research).

Oesophageal atresia: a condition in which the oesophagus (the muscular tube that carries food from the mouth to the stomach) fails to form properly during development.

Oocyte: precursor of a woman's egg; often used loosely to refer to the egg.

Persistent vegetative state (PVS): a condition resulting from severe damage to the higher centres of the brain; after a few months most authorities consider the condition to be permanent. The patient is unable to engage in any mental activity but retains the ability to swallow, breath and blink, and can absorb nutrients supplied through a nasogastric tube.

Person: sometimes used as a synonym for 'human being', but increasingly used to mean a sentient being that has a concept of itself, and is capable of reflective, rational thought.

Somatic cells: the ordinary cells in an organism (that is, not a reproductive cell).

Surrogacy: one woman bearing a child for another woman, where generally the surrogate is artificially inseminated with sperm from the partner of the second woman. In its simplest form it does not involve IVF. It generally involves a fee being paid to the surrogate.

Therapeutic research: a scientific project which has the aim of directly benefiting the person on whom the research is being conducted.

Uterus: hollow muscular organ in the female body, in which the fertilized ovum normally becomes embedded, and in which the developing embryo and fetus is nourished.

Further Reading

Berry, C., *The Rites of Life* (London: Hodder and Stoughton, 1987)

Berry, R.J., *God and the Biologist* (Leicester: IVP, 1996)

Binstock, R.H., S.G. Post and P.J. Whitehouse, *Dementia and Aging: Ethics, Values, and Policy Choices* (Baltimore: The Johns Hopkins University Press, 1992)

Bouma, H., D. Diekema, E. Langerak, T. Rottman and A. Verhey, *Christian Faith, Health, and Medical Practice* (Grand Rapids, MI: Eerdmans, 1989)

Burtchael, J., 'University Policy on Experimental Use of Aborted Foetal Tissue', *IRB: A Review of Human Subjects Research* 10(4), 7–11 (1988)

Callahan, D., *Setting Limits: Medical Goals in an Aging Society* (New York: Touchstone, 1987)

Cameron, N.M. de S. (ed.), *Embryos and Ethics* (Edinburgh: Rutherford House, 1987)

Campbell, A., M. Charlesworth, G. Gillett and G. Jones, *Medical Ethics* (Auckland: Oxford University Press, 1997)

Cole-Turner, R., *The New Genesis* (Louisville, KY: Westminster/John Knox Press, 1993)

Cook, D., *The Moral Maze* (London: SPCK, 1983)

—, *Dilemmas of Life* (Leicester: IVP, 1990)

Davis, R., *My Journey into Alzheimer's Disease* (Wheaton, Illinois: Tyndale House, 1989)

Ford, N.M., *When Did I Begin?* (Cambridge: Cambridge University Press, 1988)

Higginson, R., *Dilemmas* (London: Hodder and Stoughton, 1988)

Jonas, H., 'The burden and blessing of mortality', *Hastings Center Report*, 22(1) (1992), 34–40

Jones, D.G., *Brave New People* (Leicester: IVP, 1984)

—, *Manufacturing Humans* (Leicester: IVP, 1987)

—, 'The human embryo: Between oblivion and meaningful life', *Science and Christian Belief* 6 (1994), 3–19

—, *Coping With Controversy* (Carlisle: Paternoster, 1996)

—, 'Infanticide: An ethical battlefield', *Science and Christian Belief* 10 (1998), 3–19

Kass, L.R., *Toward a More Natural Science: Biology and Human Affairs* (New York: Free, 1985)

—, *Life on the Line* (Grand Rapids, MI: Eerdmans, 1992)

Kilner, J.F., N.M. de S. Cameron and D.L. Schiedermayer (eds.), *Bioethics and the Future of Medicine: A Christian Appraisal* (Grand Rapids, MI: Eerdmans, 1995)

Kilner, J.F., R.D. Pentz and F.E. Young (eds.), *Genetic Ethics: Do the Ends Justify the Genes?* (Grand Rapids, MI: Eerdmans, 1997)

Kuhse, H., and P. Singer, *Should the Baby Live? The Problem of Handicapped Infants* (Oxford: Oxford University Press, 1985)

Lammers, S.E., and A. Verhey, *On Moral Medicine* (Grand Rapids, MI: Eerdmans, 1987)

Land, R.D., and L.A., Moore (eds.), *Life at Risk: The Crises in Medical Ethics* (Nashville, TN: Broadman and Holman, 1995)

Lee, T.F., *Gene Therapy: The Promise and Perils of the New Biology* (New York: Plenum, 1993)

McCarthy, B., *Fertility and Faith* (Leicester: IVP, 1997)

McCormick, R.A., *How Brave A New World?* (London: SCM, 1981)

Medina, J., *The Outer Limits of Life* (Nashville, TN: Nelson, 1991)

Meilaender, G., *Bioethics: A Primer for Christians* (Grand Rapids, MI: Eerdmans, 1996)

O'Donovan, O., *Begotten or Made?* (Oxford: Clarendon, 1984)

Orr, R.D., D.L. Schiedermayer and D.B. Biebel, *Life and Death Decisions* (Colorado Springs: Navpress, 1990)

Rachels, J., *The End of Life* (Oxford: Oxford University Press, 1988)

Ramsey, P., *The Patient as Person* (New Haven: Yale University Press, 1970)

—, *Ethics at the Edges of Life: Medical and Legal Intersections* (New Haven: Yale University Press, 1978)

Reichenbach, B.R., and V.E. Anderson, *On Behalf of God* (Grand Rapids, MI: Eerdmans, 1995)

Sittser, G.L., *A Grace Disguised: How the Soul Grows Through Loss* (Grand Rapids: Zondervan, 1997)

Smedes, L., *Mere Morality* (Tring: Lion, 1983)

—, *Choices* (San Francisco: Harper, 1991)

Thielicke, H., *The Doctor as Judge of Who Shall Live and Who Shall Die* (Philadelphia: Fortress, 1970)

Tooley, M., *Abortion and Infanticide* (Oxford: Clarendon, 1983)

Wennberg, R.N., *Life in the Balance* (Grand Rapids, MI: Eerdmans, 1985)

—, *Terminal Choices: Euthanasia, Suicide and the Right to Die* (Grand Rapids, MI: Eerdmans, 1989)

Wyatt, J., *Matters of Life and Death* (Leicester: IVP, 1998)

Index of Scripture References

Index of Names

Subject Index